DATE DUE

NOV 15 2021

PRINTED IN U.S.A.

THE
AMERICAN SPORTING COLLECTOR'S HANDBOOK

THE
AMERICAN
SPORTING
COLLECTOR'S
HANDBOOK

edited by
Allan J. Liu

Winchester Press

Copyright © 1976 by Winchester Press. All rights reserved.

Library of Congress Cataloging in Publication Data
Main entry under title:
The American sporting collector's handbook.
    Includes index.
     1. Hunting—Implements and appliances—Collectors and
collecting. 2. Fishing—Implements and appliances—
Collectors and collecting. I. Liu, Allan J.
Sk275.A45   688.7′6′075   76-16192
ISBN 0-87691-217-X

                Published by Winchester Press
                205 East 42nd Street
                New York, N.Y. 10017

Printed in the United States of America

CONTENTS

FOREWORD

Who would have thought twenty years ago, or even five years ago, that there would be such a demand not only for sporting art and literature but for all sorts of sporting paraphernalia? But one fact we must accept about modern civilization is that we don't make anything better, only cheaper and faster; yesterday's object of utility is today's prized example of craftsmanship.

In the last generation many of the craftsmen of sports have passed away: decoy carvers like Crowell and Verity, artists like Ripley and Weiler, rodmakers like Jim Payne, Pinky Gillum, and Everett Garrison. Fine American shotguns are almost completely a thing of the past. America's golden days of field sports have drawn to a close. What with population explosion, chemical pollution, damming of wild rivers, and filling of marshes, American sportsmen must be grateful for what remains.

Whatever the reasons, sporting collecting is growing by leaps and bounds. Many times, dealers have told me that their biggest problem is keeping an inventory. Yet there is still time to get in on the ground floor. Collectible sporting items are all over the countryside. Much can be gotten by doing your homework and by hard looking.

If there's any advice I can give the novice collector it's to collect what you like and buy the best you can afford. Be wary of bad condition and forgeries. Price ranges listed are for items in excellent condition. On consignment items, reputable dealers charge 33⅓ percent commission. If you wish to sell an item directly, most dealers will pay about 50 percent for an item in demand and downward as the demand decreases. Many times they will have poor items in their inventory for years. Don't begrudge the dealers their cut. They can save you a lot of shoe leather.

For man-to-man sales (dealers omitted), 75 percent of price listed is usually fair unless the item is a really "hot" one.

The sky's the limit on sporting collecting. Some prices lately have been $50,000 for a shotgun, $1,000 for a fly rod, $10,500 for a decoy. As the finer points of items become known and demand becomes greater, prices will naturally rise. Sporting collecting is a good hedge against inflation. The beauty of this collecting is that an item can be bought, utilized, and then sold for at least what you paid for it. If you've been discriminating in your buying, you'll probably walk away with a nice profit.

Happy collecting!
Allan J. Liu
March 1976

THE AMERICAN SPORTING COLLECTOR'S HANDBOOK

1

ORIGINAL ART

by Drew Holl

From the very beginning, a connection has existed between art and sport. Long before a written language was established, primitive man felt the desire to record his contests with the animals around him in crude cave drawings. Thousands of years later appeared medieval scenes of boar, stag, and, of course, unicorn hunts. The hunt with its ever growing fraternity spread into England from France. Stag hunting was probably the most popular, with its elaborate ceremony and pageantry. Certain rituals that developed during this time have been retained to this day.

In time, the wealthy of both Europe and England developed highly sophisticated forms of sport. Foxhunting became immensely popular, as did horse racing, shooting, and angling. Other sports gained in popularity—hawking, cockfighting, coursing, and, to a lesser degree, bearbaiting, otter spearing, and owling. All these activities generated various forms of art.

For the English country gentleman, racing and hunting remained the popular and fashionable pastimes through the eighteenth and nineteenth centuries. Sporting paintings of this time were in great demand and many fine artists developed a reputation that has lasted to the present.

While some artists earned their reputations and then livelihood from commissions to record famous horses and hunts, it is interesting to note that many shooting and angling paintings of this period were not the result of commissions, but were rather a pleasant record of personal experiences.

It is important for the collector to have some knowledge and background of some of the major English artists and the contributions they made to the sporting scene, although this chapter will deal primarily with American artists. Sporting art in America was slow in developing. It wasn't until the early 1800s that scenes depicting the hunter and his quarry began to appear, and these differed greatly from the sporting art that was so popular in England early during the same period. Early American sporting scenes were not graced with manicured gentlemen—rather by frontiersmen in the act of pursuing game for food.

American sporting art in most instances is a sound investment. In the late 1950s and early 1960s, paintings by Ogden Pleissner were offered for between $400 and $800. These same paintings today command prices of $6,000 to $15,000. Rungius paintings that sold for $2,000 to $3,000 in the late '50s have appreciated to $12,000 and $20,000. Remington and Russell paintings that were virtually given away at the turn of the century are today worth incredible sums.

Historically, paintings were almost always purchased because they pleased the buyer, who gave little, if any, thought to future values. Today, with the loss of faith in standard investment procedures, more and more people are turning to art as a hedge against inflation. But the owner still has the pleasure of enjoying his paintings over the years as they are appreciating in value.

Most of the artists discussed in this chapter saw their art appreciate in value during their lifetimes. Unfortunately, the greatest appreciation usually occurs after an artist's death. Collectors scramble to acquire what paintings are still available, and after they are gone, prices climb. It seems almost unfair that artists cannot participate in this renewed interest in their efforts.

HOW TO COLLECT

Art is a personal thing. No two people see the same thing in a painting. A man who owns a setter and primarily hunts woodcock and grouse can't really relate to a painting of a bull moose in a meadow; and, conversely, the big-game hunter would respond little to a portrait of a flushed woodcock. But sporting art fortunately offers a limitless range of subjects, styles, and price ranges; every collector can pursue his own interests.

Once the collector has decided what direction he's going in, one way to start a collection is to visit as many galleries as possible to see what's available. (A list of galleries appears later in this chapter.) Probably the best time to visit galleries is in June or July when they are putting their fall catalogs together. This is when you have first pick, as all the art to be reproduced in the catalogs has to be either physically present or represented in photographs. Of course almost every gallery keeps a "want list" and would be most happy to add your name and advise you when a particular artist's work becomes available.

Another way to start or add to a collection is through estate sales and auctions. Many a fine piece of art has been acquired this way, and often below present market value. Of course it is important to know what the present value is so you don't overbid.

With the current interest in garage sales, tag sales, etc., it is often possible to pick up interesting and even valuable pieces of art, and, occasionally, antique shops are sometimes the source of some fine old art. A word of caution, though: some unscrupulous "dealers" have been known to offer what seems to be a real find at a ridiculously low price. This could only mean two things—stolen art or possibly a copy. If the art is stolen, you run the risk of losing it at some future date. Most good art is insured, and insurance companies are very persistent in trying to recover stolen art of any value. If it's a copy, you will have purchased just that, a copy.

Any reliable source will guarantee the authenticity of any painting sold and will gladly refund your money if it is later proven not authentic. If you doubt your source, ask for a written description on the bill of sale for the item in question, with the written understanding that it may be returned within a reasonable time. The description should include the dimension, medium (oil, watercolor), and signature. Signature, for example, should read "signed by Frank Benson." The wording "signed Frank Benson" could mean just that—someone signed the name Frank Benson.

Forgeries and copies, unfortunately, exist in the realm of sporting art. There is a fine line of distinction between a forgery and a copy. A forgery is a deliberate attempt to duplicate the work of another with the intention of representing it as an original. A copy, on the other hand, is usually an innocent attempt to reproduce the subject and style of another with no thought of representing it as an original. Through the ages, it was common and accepted for artists to copy paintings they admired, and it's not surprising that this practice has been carried over to present times; occasionally a copy of a Frost or Remington appears.

CARE AND PROTECTION OF PAINTINGS

Just as important as having your acquisitions authenticated by reputable sources is protecting them once you own them. Paintings must be insured against possible damage or theft. An appraisal is in order, and photographs of each item should be submitted to your insurance company. The purpose of the photographs is twofold: to substantiate possession of the art, and to have a visual record in the event of a theft. Make two sets of photos, one for your insurance company and one for yourself. Appraisals are available through some galleries, and some experts who specialize in appraisals advertise in the yellow pages of the telephone directory.

Oil paintings and watercolors are subject to deterioration and should be properly cared for. Oil paintings in particular should receive special attention. Because of its very nature, canvas shrinks and stretches with atmospheric conditions; therefore, it is important never to subject canvases to rapid changes in temperature. Many a fine oil has been damaged sitting over a fireplace in a cold room; once a fire is lighted, the temperature rapidly climbs and the canvas stretches too quickly. If this is repeated often enough the painted surface can crack.

Watercolors, while not as sensitive as oils to rapid changes in temperature, are also affected adversely. Watercolors are usually behind glass, and a rapid change in temperature can cause the glass to sweat. This moisture on the surface will often mildew, leaving small unsightly brown stains on the painting. Watercolors are also subject to fading, so avoid placing them in direct sunlight. While extreme temperature fluctuations rarely exist in today's modern homes, they do often exist in vacation homes and, in particular, ones near water.

Oils should be periodically cleaned and revarnished. This is best left to a professional if they are particularly dirty, but in some cases an effective job can be done with mild soap and water applied with cotton. However, if there is a break in the canvas or the surface is cracked, under no circumstances attempt cleaning the painting yourself. Moisture under the surface of the painting can make it lift, causing it to discolor, or worse, fall off.

Restoration of paintings is an art in itself. A competent restorer can take a painting dark with age and rent with holes and bring it back to its former beauty. This type of quality work is often expensive, but certainly worth it. Good restoration work does not detract from the value of a painting, and it is safe to say that many fine old works of art have had some work done on them. Most galleries can recommend good restorers.

SPORTING ARTISTS

Most of the remainder of this chapter is an introduction to a few of the great names in sporting art. No such brief listing can pretend to be comprehensive, and Allan Liu (who contributed the information on contemporary artists) and I apologize if a favorite artist of yours is not included.

Please note that for each artist we have given a price range in which his paintings are currently being offered. There is a very wide range in some instances, because value is affected by size, condition, and quality of the work. Also, many artists worked in various mediums—pencil sketches, pen and ink, watercolor, oil. A small pencil sketch by Charles Schrevogel might bring only

$4,000 to $6,000, while his most famous oil, "The Silenced War Whoop," is valued at $275,000.

The artists are listed in alphabetical order.

Henry Alken, Sr. *(1785–1851)* was an artist with a delicate touch. He handled his subjects with meticulous care; every feature of each fox hunter and mount was always carefully recorded. His thorough knowledge of horses and the hunt enabled him to portray events that were often ignored by other artists of his time. His paintings are crisply detailed and fully animated, frequently including scenes of fallen riders and runaway horses. Range $8,000 to $50,000.

John Atherton *(1900–1952)* was a fishing artist. He was an expert fly-tier, the author of the book *The Fly & the Fish*, and a member of the Anglers Club of New York. His art factually and honestly depicts the American fishing scene. Range $1,000 to $5,000.

John James Audubon *(1785–1851)* emigrated to Philadelphia from Paris in 1803. He devoted his entire energies to the outdoors—fishing, hunting, and collecting specimens. Some of his subjects seem stiff and awkward, for he relied heavily on mounted specimens; but he developed a sureness of technique and skillfully depicted wildlife in natural settings. His Birds of America series earned him an unrivaled reputation. Audubon paintings are extremely rare; no range can be given, but $50,000 is a fairly typical price.

Frank Benson *(1862–1951)* drew his inspiration from his own shooting experiences. A prolific artist, he shared his many moments afield in drawings, watercolors, and oils. Benson's style is not that of stark realism, rather subtle portrayals, relying on the importance of composition and the interesting use of color. Range $2,000 to $15,000.

Albert Bierstadt *(1830–1902)*, German-born, developed an insatiable appetite for American wilderness and big game. He spent most of his life in the Rockies and Yosemite, and his canvases portray these areas in all their grandeur. Bierstadt paintings are characterized by a special use of color, imparting a moody feeling and giving the feeling of infinite depth. Yet his works have an unquestionable authenticity of detail, and are awesome and powerful. Range $25,000 to $100,000.

Richard Bishop *(1887–1975)* was one of America's most prolific artists, undoubtedly best known for his waterfowl paintings. An avid hunter and keen observer, he was extremely versatile and was at home with every medium—pencil sketches, pen and ink drawings, watercolors, and oils. His transformations of Edgar Queeny's photographs into line drawings from the book *Prairie Wings* have been the bible for many artists. He was one of the first winners of the Federal Duck Stamp design. His work ranges from $400 to $15,000.

George Brown paints with a softness that gives his subjects animation and movement. His oils were almost always game-bird portrayal—great flocks of geese or the twittering flush of a woodcock, all took on a special realism. Brown's work is difficult to obtain as his career was terminated by an unfortunate accident before he reached his full potential. Range $4,000 to $15,000.

Paul Brown *(1893–1958)* fell in love with horses at an early age, and they remained his favorite subject throughout his life. His specialty was horses in action—polo matches, hurdle races, flat races; almost anything to do with horses. He worked in various mediums—pen and ink, pencil sketches, pastels, watercolor, and oils—and was equally proficient in all. Range $200 to $4,000.

Charles L. Bull *(1874–1932)* is considered by many to be one of the greatest of animal artists. He was an accomplished taxidermist, working for many years for the National Museum in Washington, D.C. He was an undisputed expert on anatomy and his work reflects his thorough understanding of his subjects. Range $2,000 to $10,000.

George Catlin *(1796–1872)* was a lawyer turned portrait painter. Great interest in the West and especially its Indians led him to be known as the Dean of Indian Painters. Living with over forty tribes, he accurately recorded their culture with sketch pad and brush, creating an invaluable pictorial history of a complex society before the influence of the white man. His Indian portraits are especially appealing. Range $25,000 to $50,000.

Roland Clark *(1874–1957)* was a sportsman-artist and writer with few equals. Although mostly known for his etchings and dry points, his watercolors and oils are well executed and skillfully composed. His favorite theme was ducks, and in the foreword to his book *Pot Luck* he writes, "Doubtless youth sees with a glamorous eye, magnifying certain pictures and treasured memories of them for all the years to come. I believe I had that sort of eye. A hundred ducks were a thousand; the geese filled all the sky. There were forty quail in an average covey—once upon a time.

Oil painting of geese by Roland Clark. Clark worked in both oils and watercolor; his paintings have a certain softness and feeling that men who know the coldness of the blind appreciate.

To picture them on canvas and copperplate, to give them true resemblance of life has been my earnest endeavor for many, many years." He indeed accomplished what he intended. Range $1,000 to $18,000.

Guy Coheleach is well known as a painter of African wildlife, but his work runs the gamut of sports. Range to $25,000.

Montague Dawson painted oils of sea and ships that give the feeling of wind on your cheek. Range $6,000 to $70,000.

Nick Eggenhofer *(1897–   )* came to America from Bavaria as a young man, was strongly influenced by Remington and Russell, and devoted his full talents to Western art. His subject matter is spirited, and scenes of Western Americana predominate his efforts. Range $3,000 to $10,000.

John Fernely, Sr. *(1782–1860)* epitomized the spirit of fox hunting. His canvases are full of activity, with hounds and huntsmen going full tilt. He was very much a master of detail and reproduced all the blemishes and features of his subjects. He was extremely popular in his day and rather prolific. Range $2,000 to $40,000.

A. B. Frost *(1851–1928)* was the artist of rural America, and his paintings reflect all the subtleties of his time. His characters are unmistakably honest and, by the delicate use of color, combine to give his paintings a charm that few artists have achieved. Frost's subjects were generally hunting, fishing, and golf scenes. Range $3,000 to $18,000.

Philip R. Goodwin *(1882–1935)* was a student of Howard Pyle, and his work shows the strong influence of Pyle's discipline. His work is strong and bold, with northwoods scenes a favorite. He was an excellent portrayer of animal life. Range $1,000 to $8,000.

David Hagerbaumer is a watercolorist who specializes in wildfowl and upland game birds. Range $1,200 to $4,500.

John F. Herring, Sr. *(1795–1865)* was a prolific artist yet known for his careful attention to detail. For over a quarter-century, he painted almost all the famous race horses of his time. Herring's horses, somewhat exaggerated, often appear overly elongated; he subscribed to the theory that length of the back is directly related to the speed and stamina of the horse. Range $8,000 to $60,000.

James Hill *(1839–1922)*, a contemporary of A. F. Tait, was especially competent in his renderings of game birds. His work reveals Audubon's influence, but his paintings depict his subjects more convincingly as they are more lifelike. Range $1,500 to $8,000.

Winslow Homer *(1836–1910)* enjoyed early success as a Civil War battlefield artist and later turned his attention to Adirondack and Canadian woodland scenes. His paintings are an authentic documentation of that period, strong and well composed with effective use of tone and color. He was a prolific artist who captured the mood not only of the North Woods but of seascapes from New England to the Caribbean. Homer is an artist of permanent importance. Range $6,000 to $450,000.

Lynn Bogue Hunt *(1878–1960)* was a prolific artist yet maintained consistent high quality in his work. Early work as a taxidermist greatly contributed to his thorough anatomical knowledge, and almost all his works are of wildlife. Some of his finest works appeared in sporting magazines and as illustrations in books. Range $300 to $5,000.

Francis Lee Jaques *(1887–1969)* painted brilliant wildlife renderings that are truly representative of nature at its best. Jaques, a self-taught artist, spent twenty years as a staff artist for the American Museum of Natural History. Range $3,000 to $30,000.

J. D. Knap painted almost exclusively in watercolor and is best known for his sensitive renderings of waterfowl. He was a winner of the Federal Duck Stamp design in 1937. Range $200 to $1,500.

Robert Kuhn is a contemporary American artist whose works cover virtually everything sporting from upland gunning to African big game. His style is soft and pleasing. Range $4,500 to $10,000.

David Maass specializes in waterfowl and upland game birds. His renditions of ducks won him the Ducks Unlimited Artist of the Year award and the Federal Duck Stamp Design in 1974. Range $2,500 to $5,000.

Edwin Megargee painted oils of dogs and upland shooting. His dog portraits are some of the finest. Range $800 to $2,500.

"Pick Up Time at Barnegat Bay," watercolor by Milton C. Weiler

Gustav Muss-Arnolt *(1858–1927)* was an expert in depicting bird dogs in action. His art epitomized classic gun dogs, superb working animals staunchly holding point in flawless conformation. He was not too prolific an artist and his work is difficult to find. Range $3,000 to $12,000.

Edmund Osthaus, a German-born artist, is best known for his portraits of famous gun dogs. A field-trial devotee, he traveled throughout the country, capturing on canvas the best bird dogs of his time. Range $4,000 to $20,000.

Roger Tory Peterson is a contemporary bird painter. He works closely with the Audubon Society. He provides enough background to show habitat, and shows birds in great detail. Range $2,500 to $10,000.

Ogden M. Pleissner N.A; A.W.S; R.S.A. Without question, one of America's finest living artists, his contribution to the sporting scene is virtually unequalled. From Scottish highlands, salmon rivers of Canada, New England bird covers, to Southern waterfowl marshes, his paintings accurately record the elusive moments of the sportsman's world. Although an avid sportsman, Pleissner's sporting art is only a portion of his efforts. His landscapes and stilllife paintings are equally important. Range from $3,500 to $20,000.

Alexander Pope *(1849–1924)* was a master draftsman and is best known for his still-life paintings. A student of the *trompe l'oeil* school, he commanded superb technical dexterity; every detail is precisely depicted. His subjects usually contained the elements of a successful hunt—hat and coat, powder horn, rifle, and dead game. Range $5,000 to $30,000.

Maynard Reece, a many-time winner of the Federal Duck Stamp competition, paints fish and game in their natural habitat. Range $6,000 to $12,000.

Frederic Remington *(1861–1909)* was one of the finest artists this country has produced and his prodigious outpouring of art has enriched us with his picturesque portrayal of the old West. He had little formal art training, but his natural ability and the vigor and authenticity of his subject matter won him immediate recognition. Range $5,000 to $100,000.

A. Lassell Ripley *(1896–1969)* was extremely versatile in subject, style, and medium. He was an excellent portrait painter and a superb landscape and still-life artist, but undoubtedly some of his

finest work was generated by his love of the outdoors. A sportsman all his life, his hunters, dogs and quarry are very believable
and the viewer is easily drawn into the scene. Range $1,000 to
$15,000.

Carl Rungius *(1869–1959)* a German artist, migrated to America
in 1894. His fascination for big game so possessed him that he
turned all his energies to their pursuit with both gun and sketch
pad. For more than fifty years, he wandered throughout North
America, primarily in the Rockies, where his efforts produced
some of this country's finest examples of wildlife art. Range
$6,000 to $50,000.

Charles M. Russell *(1864–1926)* had a career similar in many
ways to Remington's. Both had little formal art training and both
spent their early years living in the West. Russell had a special
fascination with Indians and lived with them for a period of time.
Hence, his Indian paintings have an authenticity that is unrivaled. Today, his original works are eagerly sought by museums
and private collectors. Range $5,000 to $100,000.

Charles Schrevogel *(1861–1912)* shows the strong influence of
Remington and Russell's historical school of popular Western art.
His paintings are carefully composed, and he possessed an
immense technical facility. His love of the West and its inhabi-
tants is clearly reflected in all his art. Range $4,000 to $75,000.

William J. Schaldach, now in his eighties and living in Arizona,
paints watercolors of upland game and fish. His loose style has a
very "homey" feeling. Range $500 to $2,500.

David Shepherd is a contemporary oil painter whose specialty is
African big game. Having spent years studying them and their
habitat, he is able to capture their moods. His work ranges to
$25,000.

Eric Sloane *(1910–   )* is best known as an artist of rural America.
Throughout his career he has done some sporting work. Range
$1,200 to $20,000.

George Stubbs *(1724–1806)* was probably the first English artist
whose inspiration came directly from nature. His search for
realism was an obsession. At an early age he studied anatomy,
and became so proficient at it that he often lectured on the
subject. A self-driven perfectionist, he eagerly sought both live
and dead models for his animal studies. His popularity as an
animal artist earned him many commissions from the finest

judges of horses. Stubbs' work is considered by many to be the finest of his period. Many of his works have been published as engravings. Possibly the most interesting to sportsmen is the "Spanish Pointer," 1768. Stubbs' work is difficult to obtain, being much in demand. Range $12,000 to $200,000.

Arthur F. Tait *(1819–1905)* was an Englishman who journeyed to America in 1850, bringing with him a great artistic talent and an insatiable love for the outdoors. For more than thirty years, Tait hunted, fished, and camped in the Adirondacks, recording in detail the life of the sportsman. He was a superb draftsman and his paintings celebrate a robust outdoor life and the wildlife he shared it with. Range $3,000 to $20,000.

Milton C. Weiler was truly a sportsman's artist. His watercolors have a unique charm, loose and yet tight in style. His hunting and fishing scenes are very collectible. Since his death in 1974, his paintings have risen sharply in value. Range $3,000 to $5,500.

GALLERIES

Abercrombie & Fitch, New York

Ackermann, New York

Arts Unlimited, San Antonio

J. N. Bartfield, New York

The Crossroads of Sport, New York and Wellesley, Mass.

Dean's, Atlanta

Grand Central Art Galleries, New York

Kennedy Galleries, New York

Kerrs, Los Angeles

The Old Print Shop, New York

Petersen Galleries, Beverley Hills

Sporting Life, Washington

Sports Art, New Orleans

Sportsman's Edge, Ltd. New York

SELECTED BIBLIOGRAPHY

Allen, Douglas. *Frederic Remington's Own Outdoors*. Dial Press, 1964.

Biographical Sketches of American Artists, 4th edition. Michigan State Library, 1922.

Clark, Roland. *Pot Luck*. Countryman Press, 1945.

Elman, Robert. *The Great American Shooting Prints*. Knopf, 1972.

Frost, A. B. *A Book of Drawings*. P. F. Collier & Son, 1904.

Goodrich, Lloyd. *The Artist in America*. W. W. Norton & Co., 1967.

Nivel, Ralph. *Old English Sporting Prints and Their History*. The Studio, Limited, London, 1927.

Patterson, Jerry. *Antiques of Sport*. Crown, 1975.

Reed, Walter. *The Illustrators in America*. Reinhold, 1966.

Thomas, Joseph. *Hounds and Hunting Through the Ages*. Wendward House, 1933.

2

PRINTS AND ETCHINGS

by Allan J. Liu

Sporting prints are as much a part of the American scene as hot dogs and apple pie, and the history of their production in this country is almost as long as the history of the American field sports they depict. Yet as recently as five years ago, there was no demand for them among collectors; like many other items now considered antiques, they were taken for granted and were always available.

But times have changed. A few generations of spring house-cleanings have taken their toll; prints done in very large editions in the last century and even early in the present century to satisfy a popular demand for inexpensive sporting art were a glut on the market for decades, but now are being recognized as rarities. For example, the A. B. Frost 1895 Shooting Portfolio was done by Scribner's in an edition of 2,500—but today I would guess that no more than 25 intact portfolios in excellent condition exist.

Prints include woodcuts, etchings, and engravings. They can be either one color—usually black—or multicolored; colored prints can be further divided into those that are hand-colored and those that are printed in color. Prints come in all shapes and sizes—sometimes as calendars or advertisements. They may be unsigned or signed, unnumbered or numbered, unlimited or limited; some may even be remarqued, which means that the artist has added a small original sketch to the margin. All of these variables—and, of course, rarity and objective quality—affect the value of a print.

If you are starting a print collection, the best way to protect your investment is to choose a reputable dealer, one who will guarantee authenticity and condition, and tell him your interests. Follow your own taste, and buy the best you can afford—buy one fine print rather than three or four mediocre ones. Beware of the multitude of contemporary prints flooding the market today; these are fine if you are buying them simply because you like them, but how many of them will be in demand in half a century? Since the contemporary artist is still in business, if he has a successful edition he is apt to follow it up with another.

Take note of all the prints you come across as you go through dealers' stocks, and ask plenty of questions. Before long you will have acquired a working knowledge of print valuation— the significance of publisher, printing process, quality of paper, size of edition, and all the other finer points.

You can make a helter-skelter collection, just buying what- ever appeals to you, but it is more interesting and in the long run a wiser investment to build a collection in specific areas. You could collect the works of a single artist. You could specialize in Derrydale editions. You could collect etchings only, or woodcuts only, etc. You could restrict yourself to a certain period, or to a certain activity—freshwater fishing, foxhunting, or whatever activity you like.

CARING FOR YOUR COLLECTION

If a print is worth framing, it's worth framing right. According to Laurence F. Jonson, who runs The Art Shop and Gallery in Davenport, Iowa, the most destructive and avoidable abuse of paperborne art is caused by improper framing and improper

"Journey's End" by Roland Clark.

handling during framing. Framers must be selected with as much care as the prints themselves. Many framers do beautiful, creative work and are fine craftsmen, but through ignorance of proper material usage, are guilty of introducing destructive elements to the art works they should be protecting. The use of woodpulp boards, sulphite core mats, pressure-sensitive tapes, animal glues, contact papers, corrugated boards, and spray glues should be avoided as assiduously as trimming or lining art works or writing on their borders.

Questions to ask your framer include whether he uses museum standard procedures. These should include:

1. Mat and backing should be 100 percent cotton fiber museum board.

2. Print should be mounted with rag hinges or plastic flanges and vegetable glue.

3. If a colored mat is used, it should be undermatted with a rag board extended at least ¼ inch from the lip of the colored mat.

4. If a print is "floated," a fillet should be inserted between the glass and the print.

5. Hinging material should be weaker than the print support, so that if put under stress, the hinges will give first.

6. The print should always be attached to the backing board, not the window mat.

These are the major safeguards to insist upon. For further information, you might want to get hold of *A Guide to Collecting and Care of Original Prints*, by Carl Zigrosser and Christa Gaehde, Crown Publishers, Inc., New York, and *How to Care for Works of Art on Paper*, by Francis W. Dolloff and Roy L. Perkinson, Boston Museum of Fine Arts. And when you hang a framed print, make sure it will not be exposed to high humidity, sunlight, or fluorescent light, all of which will deteriorate the print in one way or another.

Prints can be framed in special ways. William Cushner, of Gallery 19 in New York City, makes constructions with prints. He considers trout and salmon flies to be art forms in their own right, and he very cleverly mounts them around angling prints; an example is shown on the jacket of this book. Such constructions are bound by the imagination alone—at the moment I'm looking for a carved trout so that I can get Cushner to put it in a shadowbox construction rising to a fly.

If you don't frame all your prints, you should store them flat in a dry place. Serious collectors use blueprint cabinets such as are found in architects' and engineers' offices; the wide shallow drawers are ideal.

CURRENT VALUES OF SPORTING PRINTS

The following list of values is up to date at the time of writing, but with inflation unchecked, they are apt to be out of date rapidly. Relative values should stay about the same, except in the case of recently released editions. All values are given for a print in excellent condition, with full margins and no stains, or foxing, or folds.

Current prices listed in italic type indicate the publisher's original price and apply to prints that are still available from the publisher or those that have not been unavailable long enough for a price to have become established. Those prices that are omitted are unavailable. An asterisk next to the number of copies means that the edition was numbered and signed by the artist. ☛

	Year of issue	Publisher	Edition size	Current value
ROBERT ABBETT				
Down Wind	1973	Crossroads & R. Abbett	500*	-
Luke	1973	Sportsman's Edge	500*	$50
Gray Water, Black Lab	1974	Crossroads	500*	55
Windfall		Sportsman's Edge	550*	55
Ringneck and Setter	1975	Greenwich Workshop	1,000*	65
Bobwhites and Pointer			1,000*	65
First Season			1,000*	65
HARRY C. ADAMSON				
Winging In—Pintails	1971	Wild Wings	450*	$100–350
Wild Bounty—Black Ducks	1972	Wild Wings	450*	100–400
Whispering Wings—Pintails	1973	Wild Wings	600*	50
Oxbow Sorlery—Mallards	1973	Wild Wings	480*	50
Autumn's Echelon—Canada Geese	1973	Wild Wings	480*	50
Winter Quarters—Widgeon	1974	Wild Wings	580*	50
Arctic Citadel—Dall Sheep	1974	Wild Wings	580*	50
Greenhead Exodus—Mallards	1974	Wild Wings	580*	50

JOHN J. AUDUBON

Birds of America   1827–38   Havell

(Volumes upon volumes have been done on the man and his works, and deservedly so. This edition is the collectible one. The last price I've heard of was about $250,000 at auction for the complete portfolio. The Havell Edition is an elephant folio containing 435 hand-colored prints.)

FRANK W. BENSON

etchings $200–400

EDWARD J. BIERLY

African Queen   1969   Abercrombie & Fitch   750*   -

	Year of issue	Publisher	Edition size	Current value
Lions at Wankie	1969	Abercrombie & Fitch	500*	-
Emperor Geese	1972	Sportsman's Edge	500*	$50
Giant Pandas	1972	Sportsman's Edge	500*	50
The Survivor	1974	Russell F. Fink	250*	60

RICHARD BISHOP
etchings

signed $50–150
unsigned $20–50

(A prime mover in Ducks Unlimited. Market for his etchings not high since many of his editions are unlimited.)

HERB BOOTH

Mill Pond Mallards	1971	Crossroads	450*	$37.50
Winter Haven Ruffed Grouse	1971	Crossroads	450*	37.50
The Three Wise Men	1974	Crossroads	600*	50
The Home Place	1974	Crossroads	600*	50

RALPH L. BOYER

Fathers of American Sport	(set of 6) 1931	Derrydale	250*	$250
After a Big One	1936	Derrydale	200*	300
An Anxious Moment	1937	Derrydale	250*	300
etchings				200

REX BRASHER
prints

$75–200

PAUL BROWN

American Polo Scenes	(set of 4) 1930	Derrydale	175*	$3,500
The Meadowbrook Cup	1931	Derrydale	250*	150
Hoick! Hoick! Hoick!	1937	Derrydale	250*	250
Pressing Him	1937	Derrydale	250*	250
Music Ahead	1941	Derrydale	250*	250
Kennel Bound	1941	Derrydale	250*	250

(One of America's top equestrian artists.)

DR. EDGAR BURKE

Canada Geese	1941	Derrydale	250*	$225
The Vanguard		Frank J. Lowe	250*	110–165

GEORGE CATLIN
signed prints

$400

ROLAND CLARK

The Alarm	1937	Derrydale	250*	$1,200
Down Wind	1937	Derrydale	250*	450
Sanctuary	1938	Derrydale	250*	450
The Scout	1938	Derrydale	250*	450
Winter Marsh	1939	Derrydale	250*	750
Dawn	1939	Derrydale	250*	350
A Straggler	1940	Derrydale	250*	600
Calm Weather	1940	Derrydale	250*	750
Taking Off	1941	Derrydale	250*	750
Dropping In	1941	Derrydale	250*	550
Mallards Rising	1942	Derrydale	250*	1,200
Pintails Coming In	1942	Frank J. Lowe	250*	600–1,000

	Year of issue	Publisher	Edition size	Current value
Open Water	1943	Frank J. Lowe	250*	350–650
Fairhaven	1943	Frank J. Lowe	250*	800–1,200
The Rendezvous	1944	Frank J. Lowe	250*	200–500
The Raider	1944	Frank J. Lowe	250*	250–400
Seclusion	1945	Frank J. Lowe	250*	150–250
Visitors	1945	Frank J. Lowe	250*	300–600
Tranquillity	1946	Frank J. Lowe	250*	150–250
Journey's End	1946	Frank J. Lowe	250*	800–1,200
etchings				200–400

(Noted for his waterfowl, Clark painted birds the way a hunter sees them. "The Alarm," a single black duck, is the best of this species I've seen.)

GUY COHELEACH

Jungle Jaguar	1973	Regency House	5,000*	$115
Clouded Leopard	1973			90
Charging Elephant	1974			100

ARTHUR COOK

Backwaters—Duck		Art Cook	600*	$35
The Travelers Rests—Arctic Tern	1974	Wild Wings	450*	50
After the Storm—Pheasants	1975	Art Cook	350*	50

"The Trout Stream," one of the Currier & Ives hand-colored stone lithographs.

	Year of issue	Publisher	Edition size	Current value
JOHN P. COWAN				
Off Base		Merideth Long		-
Dawn Flight		Merideth Long	600*	-
Early Limits		Merideth Long	600*	-
Night Feeders		Merideth Long	600*	-
Hot Tank		Merideth Long	750*	-
Too Soon		Merideth Long	600*	-
Gettin' Well		Merideth Long	600*	$40
Deep Run		Merideth Long	600*	40
Two Down		Merideth Long	600*	50
New Gun	1974	Merideth Long	600*	50
Mallards High	1974	Merideth Long	600*	50
CURRIER & IVES	(c. 1850–1895)			
Small Folio				$125–400
Medium Folio				800–1,200
Large Folio				1,000–6,000

(A good sporting art collection must have a Currier or two in it. For the angler, two of the most famous are Tait's "Trout Fishing, an Anxious Moment" and Palmer's "The Trout Stream." Any collector in this area should have the reference book *Currier and Ives Sporting Prints* by Peters.)

	Year of issue	Publisher	Edition size	Current value
MONTAGUE DAWSON				
Rolling Home	1925	Frost & Reed	250	$750–1,500
Racing Clippers	1926	Frost & Reed	250	750–1,500
Searching the Seas		Frost & Reed		-
Lord Nelson's Flagship "Victory"	1926	Frost & Reed	250	750–1,500
Flying Cloud	1926	Frost & Reed	250	750–1,500
The Golden Hind	1927	Frost & Reed	325	750–1,500
Boundless Ocean	1928	Frost & Reed	250	750–1,500
Homeward Bound	1928	Frost & Reed	250	750–1,500
Southerly Wind—The Waimate	1928	Frost & Reed	250	750–1,500
Happy Days	1929	Frost & Reed	250	750–1,500
Chasing the Smuggler	1930	Frost & Reed	250	750–1,500
Picking Up the Pilot		Frost & Reed		-
The Cutty Sark	1930	Frost & Reed	250	750–1,500
Twilight Shadows	1931	Frost & Reed	275	750–1,500
Mist of Morning	1932	Frost & Reed	250	750–1,500
A Winning Tack	1933	Frost & Reed	250	1,200–1,500
Sails of Evening	1934	Frost & Reed	250	750–1,500
Neck and Neck	1935	Frost & Reed	250	1,200–1,500
A Following Wind	1936	Frost & Reed	250	750–1,500
White Clipper	1937	Frost & Reed	250	750–1,500
Wind and Sun	1937	Frost & Reed	250	750–1,500
The Silvered Way	1938	Frost & Reed	250	750–1,500
Narvk Fjord (The Altmark)	1940	Frost & Reed	No Proofs	-
A Stretch to Seaward	1940	Frost & Reed	250	750–1,500
The Run Home	1941	Frost & Reed	No Information Available	-
The North America—Far Horizon	1941	Frost & Reed	250	750–1,500
"Caught"-The Doomed Bismark	1941	Frost & Reed	No Proofs	-

	Year of issue	Publisher	Edition size	Current value
Breaking Out the Royals	1943	Frost & Reed	No Information Available	-
Fine Weather and a Far Wind	1946	Frost & Reed	100	1,800–2,100
Evening Gold—The Red Jacket	1947	Frost & Reed	250	750–1,500
The Homecoming	1947	Frost & Reed	150	750–1,500
Racing Wings	1950	Frost & Reed	150	750–1,500
Ocean Racers	1954	Frost & Reed	200	1,200–1,600
Royal Racers	1954	Frost & Reed	200	1,200–1,600
Eight Bells—Belaying the Anchor	1955	Frost & Reed	200	2,500–3,000
Days of Adventure	1957	Frost & Reed	200	1,500–2,000
The Golden West	1958	Frost & Reed	200	1,200–1,500
Summer Breezes	1961	Frost & Reed	250	1,000–1,250
The Thermopylae Leaving Foochow	1962	Frost & Reed	250	1,500–2,000
Racing Home—The Cutty Sark	1963	Frost & Reed	300	4,000–6,000
Ariel and Taeping	1964	Frost & Reed	500 24″×30″	1,000–1,500
		Frost & Reed	Unknown 29″×36″	2,000–2,750
U.S.S. Constellation	1966	Frost & Reed	200	500–1,000
The Java and Constitution	1966	Frost & Reed	500	1,200–1,700
Horn Abeam	1967	Frost & Reed	150	3,500–4,500
Up Channel—The Lahloo	1968	Frost & Reed	500	750–1,200
The Tall Ship	1969	Frost & Reed	1,000	750–1,000
The Rising Wind	1969	Frost & Reed	500	800–1,100
The Gallant Mayflower	1970	Frost & Reed	500	500–1,000
Crescent Moon	1970	Frost & Reed	500	750–1,000
Pieces of Eight	1971	Frost & Reed	500	750–1,000
Smoke of Battle	1972	Frost & Reed	500	750–1,200
In Full Sail	1972	Frost & Reed	500	600–1,000
Night Mist	1973	Frost & Reed	500	600–1,000
Pagoda Anchorage	1973	Frost & Reed	500	600–1,000
Battle of Trafalgar	1973	Frost & Reed	750	1,500

(An English artist. His love of wind and sea and sailing ships lives in his work.)

J.&T. DOUGHTY
hand-colored prints $50–100
(First American colored sporting prints. The book *Cabinet of Natural History and American Rural Sports Illustrated* came in three volumes. Many of these books have been cut up, so prints are available.)

RICHARD ELLIS
Sperm Whale	1975	Sportsman's Edge	450*	$150
Tiger Shark	1975	Sportsman's Edge	450*	150

CHURCHILL ETTINGER
Worn Rock Pool				$100
etchings				50–200

JAMES P. FISHER
Pintail	1974	Sportsman's Edge	450*	$45
Woodduck	1974	Sportsman's Edge	450*	45
Black Labrador	1974	Sportsman's Edge	450*	55
Yellow Labrador	1974	Sportsman's Edge	450*	55

LOUIS FRISINO
Golden Retriever with Mallard			550*	-

	Year of issue	Publisher	Edition size	Current value
Labrador Retriever with Pintail			550*	-
Labrador Retriever with Mallard			500*	-
Labrador Retriever with Canvasback			550*	-
Chesapeake Retriever with Goose			550*	-

ARTHUR B. FROST

	Year of issue	Publisher	Edition size	Current value
Scribner's Shooting Portfolio (set of 12 complete)	1895	Scribner's	2,500	$8,500
Autumn Grouse				250–450
Autumn Woodcock				250–450
Quail—A Dead Stand				250–450
Quail—A Covey Rise				250–450
Rabbit Shooting				250–450
Summer Woodcock				250–450
Duck Shooting from a Blind				250–450
Duck Shooting from a Battery				250–450
Rail Shooting				250–450
Prairie Chickens				250–450
English Snipe				250–450
Bay Snipe				250–450
A Day's Shooting (set of 6 complete)	1903	Scribner's		3,250
Ordered Off				350–600
Gun Shy				350–600
Good Luck				350–600
Bad Luck				350–600
Smoking Him Out				350–600
We've Got Him				350–600
Chance Shot While Setting Out Decoys	1933	Derrydale	200	800–1,200
October Woodcock Shooting	1933	Derrydale	200	1,500
Coming Ashore	1934	Derrydale	200	1,200
Grouse Shooting in the Rhododendrons	1934	Derrydale	200	800

(Anything with Frost's name on it is worth something, and he's the only artist listed here whose unsigned prints are highly collectible and worth a tidy sum of money. Henry M. Reed's *The A. B. Frost Book*, Tuttle, 1967, is a must for the Frost collector.)

JOHN FROST

	Year of issue	Publisher	Edition size	Current value
Maryland Marsh	1936	Derrydale	150*	$275

ARTHUR FULLER

	Year of issue	Publisher	Edition size	Current value
colored prints				$25–100

GORDON GRANT

	Year of issue	Publisher	Edition size	Current value
Off Soundings	1941	Derrydale	250*	$150
The Weather Mark	1941	Derrydale	250*	150

OWEN GROMME

	Year of issue	Publisher	Edition size	Current value
Wintering Quail	1971	Wild Wings	450*	$100–250
Brittany on Point	1971	Wild Wings	450*	75–175
Back to Cover—Pheasant	1971	Wild Wings	450*	-
Late Season—Canvasback	1972	Wild Wings	450*	50

	Year of issue	Publisher	Edition size	Current value
Sunlit Glade—Ruffed Grouse	1972	Wild Wings	450*	75–150
Wintering Grosbeaks	1973	Wild Wings	600*	50
Blue Jay	1973	Wild Wings	800*	40
Startled Grouse—Golden Retriever	1973	Wild Wings	480*	60
Over the Triangle—Pintails	1973	Wild Wings	480*	60
Island Lake Loon	1973	Wild Wings	580*	60
Expectation	1973	Wild Wings	580*	60
Sacred Cranes over Hokkaido	1974	Wild Wings	600*	60
English Setter	1974	Wild Wings	580*	60
Pileated Woodpecker	1974	Wild Wings	580*	50
Tamarack Lake—Canada Geese	1974	Wild Wings	580*	60
California Quail	1974	Wild Wings	580*	60
Hemlock Hideaway	1974	Wild Wings	580*	60
Whistling Swans	1974	Wild Wings	580*	60
Dropping In—Mourning Doves	1974	Wild Wings	580*	60
Edge of the Field—Pointer	1974	Wild Wings	580*	60
The Rascal's Revenge—Owl	1974	Wild Wings	580*	60
Winter Afternoon—Pheasants	1975	Wild Wings	580*	60
Scurrying Greenwings	1975	Wild Wings	580*	60

"Silver Riffles" by W. Goadby Lawrence.

	Year of issue	Publisher	Edition size	Current value
JOHN GROTH				$50–250
etchings				75–100
prints				
DAVID HAGERBAUMER				
Oct. Evening—Pintails	1963	Frost & Reed & Sportsman Gallery	400*	$600–1,000
Placid Marsh—Black Duck	1964	Frost & Reed & Sportsman Gallery	400*	500–800
Woodcut Covey—Quail	1965	Frost & Reed & Sportsman Gallery	400*	500–750
Foggy Morning—Mallards	1965	Frost & Reed & Sportsman Gallery	400*	400–700
Portfolio of 4 Prints	1967	Frost & Reed & Crossroads of Sport	400*	200–450
Green Wing Flurry	1969	Venture Prints & D. Hagerbaumer	600*	150–275
Autumn Ruffs—Grouse	1969	Venture Prints & D. Hagerbaumer	600*	150–300
The Narrows—Woodduck	1971	D. Hagerbaumer	450*	150–250
Double Rise—Woodduck	1971	D. Hagerbaumer	450*	150–250
The Shanty	1972	D. Hagerbaumer	450*	-
Thru the Pines—Mourning Doves	1972	D. Hagerbaumer	450*	100–300
Hill Country Gobblers	1972	D. Hagerbaumer	450*	100–300
Gathering Storm—Pintails	1972	D. Hagerbaumer	450*	75–150
Over the Ridge—Pheasants	1973	D. Hagerbaumer	450*	125–300
Minus Tide—Cans	1973	D. Hagerbaumer	450*	-
Timber Potholes	1973	D. Hagerbaumer	350*	100–200
Hog Ranch Point	1974	D. Hagerbaumer	350*	-
Sink Box Gunning	1974	D. Hagerbaumer	350*	-
Twin Island Marsh	1974	D. Hagerbaumer	450*	-
The Old Duck Camp	1974	D. Hagerbaumer	450*	-

A fine contemporary artist, his "Over the Ridge—Pheasants" is one of the best pheasant prints around.)

	Year of issue	Publisher	Edition size	Current value
GERARD HARDENBERG				
prints not signed				$50–150
ELDRIDGE HARDIE				
Set of 4 Trout (with flies)				$150
Brown Trout & Light Cahills	1973	E. Hardie	450*	50
Brook Trout	1974	E. Hardie	450*	50
WINSLOW HOMER				
Canoe in the Rapids (unsigned)				-
Leaping Trout		Anglers Club		$100–250

(Despite his renown, he did not sign his prints, which explains the low prices.)

	Year of issue	Publisher	Edition size	Current value
LYNN BOGUE HUNT				
series of sporting birds done for du Pont, unsigned				$200
etchings				100–250

	Year of issue	Publisher	Edition size	Current value
D. W. HUNTINGTON				
prints, not signed				$100
EDWARD KING				
Saratoga Racing (set of 4)	1928	Derrydale	80*	$800
The Aiken Drag	1929	Derrydale	80*	100
Hunt Race (set of 4)	1929	Derrydale		-
American Hunting Scenes (set of 4)	1929–30	Derrydale	250*	1,000
Belmont Terminal Lithographs (set of 2)	1929	Derrydale		100
American Shooting Scenes—Quail Shooting	1929	Derrydale		300
Hunting Lithographs (set of 2)	1929	Derrydale	250*	450
Woodcock Shooting—In the Birches	1930	Derrydale	350*	100
Quail Shooting—The Briar Patch	1930	Derrydale	350*	100
Diana Goes Hunting (set of 4)	1930	Derrydale	250*	300
Rochester	1932	Derrydale	250*	100
A Glorious Burst	1932	Derrydale	250*	250
S. A. KILBOURNE				
Fish Portfolio	1876			$35–200 each
MARGUERITE KIRMSE				
The Fox	1931	Derrydale	250*	$600
The Hounds	1933	Derrydale	250*	600
etchings				75–200
HANS KLIEGER				
signed, limited prints				$50–200
J. D. KNAP				
Daybreak		Frank J. Lowe		$100–225
The Inlet		Frank J. Lowe		100–225
Reflections		Frank J. Lowe		100–225
All Clear		Frank J. Lowe		100–225
LES KOUBA				
signed, limited prints				$25–75
BOB KUHN				
The Soft Touch	1973	Art Unltd., Inc.	1,500	$80
Jaguar and Egret	1974	Emerson Hall	100*	60
Sunshine and Shadow	1975	Tryon Gallery, Ltd.	500	70
W. GOADBY LAWRENCE				
Rising Mists	1946	Frank J. Lowe	300*	$150–350
Silver Riffles	1946	Frank J. Lowe	300*	400–700

(Although his speciality is big-game fishing, "Silver Riffles" is one of the nicest trout scenes around.)

	Year of issue	Publisher	Edition size	Current value
LEE LEBLANC				
Ruffed Grouse				$45
Bobwhite Quail				45
Arkansas Mallards			400*	-
Honkers at Horkon			400*	45
A Noble Pair—Wild Turkey	1974		580*	60
A Stately Pair—Mallards	1974		580*	60
DAVID LOCKHART				
Dixie Idyl			50*	-
Covey Point Quail			480*	$60
MICHAEL LYNE				
Away			500*	$90
VIP			500*	90
Hurdle Race			500*	90
Point to Point Impression				150
The Grand National—Canal Turn				100
DAVID MAASS				
Canvasback	1966	Crossroads	50 remarqued	$500–1,100
			400 signed	500–1,000
Grouse	1966	Crossroads	50 remarqued	300–700
			400 signed	300–600
Coming In, Canada Geese	1969	Crossroads		150–350
Mallards	1971	Venture		75–150
Quail	1971	Venture		75–150
Misty Morning, Woodcock	1972	Wild Wings	450*	400–900
Back Bay Mallards	1973	Wild Wings	600*	80–150
Breaking Weather—Canada Geese	1973	Wild Wings	580*	100–200
Misty Morning Grouse	1973	Wild Wings	580*	275–600
Breaking In, Bluebills	1973	Wild Wings	450*	150–275
Among the Pines, Quail	1973	Wild Wings	600*	80–165
Misty Morning Wood Duck	1974	Wild Wings	580*	125–250
The River Flats, Pintails	1974	Wild Wings	580*	70
On the Move, Canvasback	1974	Wild Wings	580*	-
Ridge Line, Ruffed Grouse	1974	Wild Wings	580*	70
Autumn Birch, Woodcock	1974	Wild Wings	580*	70
Misty Morning, Mallard	1975	Wild Wings	580*	85
Dusk in the Bay, Canada Geese	1975	Wild Wings	600*	50
Misty Morning, Quail	1975	Wild Wings	580*	85
DU—Artist of the Year Print: The King of Ducks—Canvasback	1974	Ducks Unlimited	600*	275–800
Grouse in Snow			40 remarqued	500–800
			signed	125–300
Canvasback				-
Greenwing Teal			40 remarqued	225–500
Canada Geese				-
ALDERSON MAGEE				
Coachman's Conquest—Brook Trout	1975	Sportsman's Edge	450*	$45

	Year of issue	Publisher	Edition size	Current value
HENRY MCDANIELS				
Fishing the Dry on the Upper Conn.	1973	Anglers Club	400*	$150–225
An Unnamed Pool	1974	Crossroads	325*	-
EDWIN MEGARGEE				
Pheasant Shooting	1930	Derrydale		$300
Woodcock Shooting	1931	Derrydale	250*	300
Grouse Shooting	1931	Derrydale	250*	300
American Cock Fighting Scenes (set of 4)	1932	Derrydale	250*	1,200
Closing In	1939	Derrydale	250*	125
Golden Retriever in Action	1972	West Surf		15–25
GARY NEEL				
October Flight	1974	Crossroads	375*	$50

"Grouse in Snow" by David Maass. Note the remarque in the lower-left corner.

	Year of issue	Publisher	Edition size	Current value
EDMUND OSTHAUS				
dog prints			unsigned	$20–50
ROBERT F. PATTERSON				
The America and Defenders of the	1935	Gosden Head	260*	$6,000
ROGER TORY PETERSON				
Great Horned Owl	1974	Mill Pond	750*	$250–600
Bald Eagle	1974	Mill Pond	950*	200–450
Ruffed Grouse	1975	Mill Pond	950*	200–450
(Primarily an artist in the style of Audubon.)				
OGDEN M. PLEISSNER				
Atlantic Salmon Fishing	1939			$800
Downs Gulch		Anglers Club	300*	750
Casting for Salmon	1949	Sportsman's Gallery & Bookshelf		300–600
Beaverkill Bridge	1953	Anglers Club	221*	500–1,000
Leaping Sea Trout	1957	Frost & Reed		350–700
The Bridge Pool	1957	Frost & Reed		200–600
West Duncan, Clove Valley		Clove Valley Club		450
Grande River, Upper Malbraie	1959	Frost & Reed		500–800
Driven Grouse, Glancie Beat	1959	Frost & Reed		400–800
October Snow	1959	Anglers Club	350*	400–900
Blue Boat on the Saint Anne				500–1,000
Raising Salmon	1961	Sportsman's Gallery & Bookshelf		300–850
Lye Brook Pool		American Museum of Flyfishing	400*	150–400
June Trout Fishing	1967	Theodore Gordon Flyfishers	350*	150–450
Grouse Shooting				300–700
Trout Fishing				150–450
Quail Hunters	1973	Crossroads	425*	
Hillside Orchard, Grouse Shooting	1975	Crossroads	275*	

(A member of the National Academy, his "Beaverkill Bridge" and "Blue Boat" are musts for any angling art collection.)

	Year of issue	Publisher	Edition size	Current value
ALEXANDER POPE				
Upland game birds and waterfowl	1878			$75–200
GORDON POWER				
signed prints				$50–125
MAYNARD REECE				
Mallards	1964	Maynard Reece	250*	$75–250
Bobwhites	1964	Maynard Reece	250*	75–250
Mallards—Pitching In	1969	Maynard Reece	500*	100–200
Edge of the Hedge Row—Bobwhites	1970	Maynard Reece	1,000*	100–225

	Year of issue	Publisher	Edition size	Current value
Against the Wind—Canvasback	1972	Maynard Reece	550*	100–250
Marshlander Mallards	1973	Ducks Unlimited	550*	250–600
Pheasant Country	1973	Maynard Reece	600*	-
Feeding Time—Canada Geese	1973	Maynard Reece	550*	-
Wood Ducks	1973	Mill Pond	550*	-
Late Afternoon—Mallards	1973	Mill Pond	450*	150
Quail Cover	1974	Mill Pond	750*	150
Snow Geese—Blue Geese	1974	Mill Pond	750*	150
Winging South—Canada Geese	1974	Mill Pond	750*	150
Courtship Flight—Pintails	1974	Mill Pond	950*	75
Snowy Creek—Mallards	1974	Mill Pond	950*	75
Mallards—Dropping In	1974	Mill Pond	950*	-
Solitude—Whitetail Deer	1974	Mill Pond	950*	85
A Burst of Color—Ringneck Pheasant	1974	Mill Pond	950*	-
Early Arrivals—Mallards	1974	Mill Pond	950*	50
The Sandbar—Canada Geese	1974	Mill Pond	950*	50
The Passing Storm—Canvasbacks	1974	Mill Pond	950*	50
Flooded Oaks—Mallards	1974	Mill Pond	850*	150
Afternoon Shadows—Bobwhites	1975	Mill Pond	950*	100
Hazy Day—Bobwhites	1975	Mill Pond	950*	150

JOYCE HAGERBAUMER REED

Backwater Teal	1974		450*	$50
Wintering Doves	1975		450*	60

FREDERIC REMINGTON

prints			signed	$2,500
prints			unsigned	75–150

CHET RENESON

Snow Squall	1972	Chet Reneson	400	$40
Opening Day	1973	Chet Reneson	400	50
West Wind	1974	Chet Reneson	400	50

LOUIS RHEAD

prints			signed	$50–125

A. LASSELL RIPLEY

Gunning in America	1947	Field & Stream		$50–275
Grouse Cover	1952	Frost & Reed		800–1,200
Pheasants in the Corn Field	1952	Frost & Reed		800–1,200
Covey by the Cabin	1957	Frost & Reed		800–1,200
The Turkey Blind	1957	Sportsman's Gallery and Bookshelf, Frost & Reed		300–750
Mallards Coming In	1963	Frost & Reed		150–350
Woodcock Cover	1963	Frost & Reed		250–675
End of the Grouse Season	1966	Frost & Reed		250–550
A Turkey Drive	1966	Frost & Reed		200–450
etchings			signed	150–250

(Sporting art at its best showing scenes with gun in hand.)

	Year of issue	Publisher	Edition size	Current value
PERCIVAL ROSSEAU				
prints			signed	$200–400
prints			unsigned	50
CARL RUNGIUS				
etchings				$150
(North American big game is his subject.)				
JOHN N. RUTHVEN				
Canvasbacks			1,000*	$200
Cinnamon Teal			1,000*	-
Ruddy Ducks			1,000*	200
WILLIAM J. SCHALDACH				
American Game Birds—Woodcock	1931	Derrydale	250*	750
Brook Trout		David Ashley		$15
Eastern Brook Trout	1974	Theodore Gordon Flyfishers	300*	100–150
etchings			signed	100–350
(His etchings of upland-game hunting are especially important.)				
OLAF SELZER				
prints			signed	$50–200
DAVID SHEPHERD				
Wise Old Elephant			unsigned, unlimited	$95
Elephant at Amboseli			unsigned, unlimited	240
African Children			unsigned, limited	700
African Children			signed, limited (1,800)	2,200
Baby Kudu		Solomon & Whitehead	unsigned, limited	400
Baby Kudu		Solomon & Whitehead	signed, limited (1,800)	2,200
Old George Under His Favorite Baobab Tree			unsigned, limited	650
Old George Under His Favorite Baobab Tree			signed, limited (1,800*)	2,200
Lion Majesty		Solomon & Whitehead	500*	1,900
Elephant and the Ant Hill			850*	650
Tiger Fire			850*	2,400
The Big Five	1974	Solomon & Whitehead	850*	1,500
Elephant Heaven	1975	Solomon & Whitehead	850*	210
DONALD SHOFFSTALL				
The Single—Black Duck	1972	Princeton Printing	750*	$15
Clearing Skies—Brant	1972	Princeton Printing	750*	25
Autumn—Ruffed Grouse	1972	Princeton Printing	750*	30

	Year of issue	Publisher	Edition size	Current value
The Winter Blind	1972	Princeton Printing	750*	30
Drifting Down—Canada Geese	1972	Princeton Printing	750*	40
Mates—Canada Geese	1974	DeVries Bros., Inc.	550*	50
Winter Moon—Canada Geese	1975	Barton Cotton	1,100*	15
etchings			signed	-

JOHN STOBART

South Street—N.Y. 1874	1967	Kennedy Galleries	250	$200
South Street—N.Y. 1880	1975	Maritime Heritage Press	950	200

JOHN W. TAYLOR

prints			signed	$50–85

WILLIAM REDD TAYLOR

Cautious Descent, Black Ducks	1974	Wild Wings	580*	

"Atlantic Salmon Fishing on the Matapedia" by Milton C. Weiler.

	Year of issue	Publisher	Edition size	Current value
LARRY TOSCHIK				
The Mallard Hole				-
The Beet Field				-
DOUGLAS VAN HOWD				
Kenya's Ahmed				-
Kilimanjaro				-
Big Tom				-
Moment of Truth				-
High Vantage Point				-
Bob White Flushed				-
Passing Parade				-
Indian Summer				-
Peace On Earth				-
EDWARD S. VOSS				
The Hartford Fox	1943	Edward S. Voss	400*	$125
FRANKLIN B. VOSS				
Foxhunting in America—Over the Open	1939	Derrydale	250*	$750
Foxhunting in America—On a Fresh Line	1939	Derrydale	250*	750
Foxhunting in America—Working It Out	1941	Derrydale	250*	750
Tally Ho		Frank J. Lowe		-
ARTHUR WEAVER				
Play on 12th Green, Augusta			250*	$250
View of 18th Green, Pebble Beach	1974	Robert J. Perham	750*	300
Cypress Point		Robert J. Perham	750*	50
WALTER WEBER				
Snow Geese	1974	Russell F. Fink	550*	$60
MILTON C. WEILER				
Classic Shorebird Series	1969	Winchester Press	1,000	$10–20
Classic Decoy Series	1969	Winchester Press	1,000	15–25
Pick Up Time—Barnegat Bay	1970	Winchester Press		100–150
Atlantic Salmon Fishing on the Matapedia	1972	M. C. Weiler		125–200
Plate from *Upstream and Down*	1973	Derrydale	60*	200
Upper Twin Pool—Henryville	1973	Henryville Conservation Club	125*	375
Virgin Water	1973	American League of Anglers	500*	-

(Fishing collectors should have "Henryville" and "Matapedia." Classic Decoy Series already a classic—and those prints signed by Weiler bring $25 more.)

LEVEN WEST

etchings				$40–175

DEALERS IN SPORTING PRINTS AND OTHER ART

Irving Steinhardt
Abercrombie & Fitch Co.
Madison Ave. & 45th St.
New York, N.Y. 10017

Drew Holl
The Crossroads of Sport
5 East 47th St.
New York, N.Y. 10017

William Webster
Wild Wings, Inc.
Lake City, Minn. 55041

Ernest Hickok
382 Springfield Ave.
Summit, N.J. 07901

Sportsman's Edge, Ltd.
136 East 74th St.
New York, N.Y. 10021

Chrisman Wildlife Art &
Framing Shop
Star Route
Dexter, Mo. 63841

Lee Talcott
The Orvis Co., Inc.
Manchester, Vt. 05254

Harold Whitman
The Bedford Sportsman
Bedford Hills, N.Y. 10507

The 1807 House
R.D. 4
Farmingdale, N.J. 07727

Robert C. Reed
Reed Galleries
Independence, Ore. 97351

Jene C. Gilmore
Petersen Galleries
9433 Wilshire Blvd.
Beverly Hills, Calif. 90212

3

⌒≈⌒

WILDFOWL
DECOYS

by George Ross Starr, Jr., M.D.

T hat year the rains did not come at all. The crops failed and
the lakes fell to half their normal depth. It was as if the
Great Spirit had deserted them entirely. As all the tribe
commented and wailed about these conditions, he gradually
became aware that despite the decreased water areas of their
lakes, the ducks were still making their annual migration to the
south according to the ancient rule of the seasons' change. Ducks
would solve the food problem of the tribe, but it had never been
possible in all the years of the tribe's history to profit from this
great heaven-sent invasion, because the ducks always stayed far
enough from shore to be out of range even of the most powerful archers. Then he remembered!

He was just ten years old when one day he ambled away from
the encampment toward one of the ponds the tribe customarily
camped near on their own migrational path from north to south.
There were the ducks. His approach was quiet in the manner he
had been taught, so that he saw a sight he had never seen before.
Sure, most of the ducks were concentrated in the middle of the
pond, but why was it that in the little bays and guzzles two or
three ducks quietly eating invariably drew another two or three
into their feeding area? No one could approach any of these small
concentrations of ducks in guzzles, but could there be another
way of getting to these little aggregations near shore which might
possibly put them within range of the arrow? Slowly light dawned.
Do the ducks in little coves have to be real? Then the final
awakening to the situation. No!

Ahah, then! If we can create something that closely resem-
bles a floating duck, would that not draw the wild ones into range?

It worked.

And thus the duck decoy was brought into existence by the
American Indians of the Southwest. Believe me, it did work—

and it has never ceased to work—because no duck has ever solved the mystery of the decoy.

When the white men arrived in this country, it did not take them long to realize the value of the artificial ducks that the Indians had invented. However, it was soon apparent that the Indians had not created any word as a name for their invention. The English were familiar only with the decoy as it was used at home—a contraction from the Dutch *ende cooy* or duck cage— and so the fake bird became known as a decoy. The combination of decoys and the musket enabled the settler to get all the ducks he needed during the spring and fall migrations. Along about 1830 a market developed for wild ducks, and this in turn gave birth to the market gunner, who from then until about 1920 made a career of supplying ducks for sale. It was a great period for the development of the decoy as a working tool and simultaneously a sad time because of the numbers of wildfowl killed and the species that were completely obliterated.

Joel Barber said that the decoy was the only utilitarian floating sculpture (as opposed to purely decorative sculpture) ever produced. It was not until the market-gunning era ended that there was any appreciation outside that very restricted fraternity for the aesthetics of their working tools. And so the great hobby of decoy collecting was born. The real father of decoy collecting was Joel Barber, who became interested in them about 1920 from the purely aesthetic angle—he never fired a gun at a living bird. In 1934 he published *Wild Fowl Decoys*, which was the story of his experiences in collecting these artifacts and the great impression that decoys made on him and his life. By 1949, when I started to collect for the same aesthetic reasons—decoys at that time had no real monetary value—Bill Mackey was the only other serious collector aside from Joel that I could find. As time went by, other people came along with the desire to collect, but with no standards of good, bad, or indifferent on which to judge what they had or what they should attempt to acquire. Then Hal Sorenson began publication of the "Decoy Collectors Guide," which was the first concrete step on the road to establishing good criteria for decoy collecting. Collecting groups were formed in various parts of the country, and programs of meetings, contests, and shows began to develop. Books by various people followed, each of which became another ashlar in the wall of our knowledge. We have now about arrived at the point where most of the decoy makers who can truly be identified have been named, and the relative values of their products are gradually falling into a semblance of order. While an unknown amount of buying, selling, and trading goes on among collectors, the final evaluation in dollars is more and more determined by the annual decoy auc-

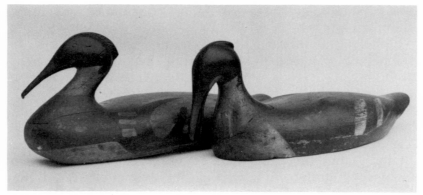

Pair of mergansers by unknown Maine maker.

tions held by Richard Bourne in Hyannis, Mass. From the prices obtained at these sales a very definite pattern is emerging. Collectors are gradually declaring which birds and which makers they like by their bids. But enough for now of the history and background of decoy collecting per se.

Generally, decoys consist of full-size replicas of actual species of ducks that are hunted as game in some or all parts of the country. Joel Barber held out for about thirty-four species. The most usual ones are: mallard, black duck, bluebill, redhead, canvasback, widgeon, pintail, goldeneye, merganser, goose, brant, scoter, and eider.

The second category that must be considered is that of shorebirds. This group comprises those wading birds that live on the edges of salt marshes and ponds and in order of size include: sicklebill curlew, willet, Hudsonian curlew, yellowlegs, black-breasted plover, golden plover, dowitcher, ruddy turnstone, and a whole bunch of little plover and shorebirds handily grouped in New England under the name "peeps."

Because of the vagaries in the social life of the bird kingdom, some species have very definite likes and dislikes with respect to with whom they will associate. Seagulls have a deep inherent dislike for black ducks and are usually delighted to attack them on any or no provocation. Thus a black duck coming into a rig with a lone seagull set to one side figures that détente has really arrived and this is the place to set down. The hunter profits. From this phenomenon comes the term "confidence decoy." Because the swan pulls up plants by the roots and eats only small bits before diving for more, the lazy widgeon follows the swan, happily eating the leftovers. Thus a swan decoy ahead of the widgeon decoy brings in more than would widgeons alone.

Actual duck decoys are primarily of two types—handmade

or factory. Until the Civil War era, all duck decoys were hand-made, but with the advent of the duplicating lathe some men went into the production of decoys on a commercial basis. No one has yet written a treatise on the production of commercial decoys, but until someone does, three makers will be outstanding: Mason, Stevens, and Dodge. Mason factory decoys have become the most important of all because of the large numbers produced and the extremely high quality that was maintained through all the years of many design changes.

Why are any decoys collectible? Because they represent the efforts over many lifetimes to produce a replica of a living water-fowl. Some men came very close and some missed by a mile. The glorious thing about any decoy is that it is the best that any man could fashion toward this ultimate goal. Decoys have become recognized as an outstanding American folk art form and are represented in many museums around the country.

The identification of decoys as to when, where, and by whom they were made presents many problems and always will, since it was the exception for a maker to sign and date his work. A brand on a decoy had best be assumed to be that of the owner until definitely proven otherwise. It is interesting that once a man began to carve, certain individual characteristics—such as how he outlined a bill or shaped the tail—became constant in all his work despite periodic design changes, and became for all practi-cal purposes his personal signature. Although Elmer Crowell did not have his famous oval brand made until 1915, there is no difficulty in identifying his work before that date. There have been enough pictures reproduced to enable a collector to identify the work of the documented makers. Decoys were designed to function best under the gunning conditions that prevailed where they were used. The small round-bottom hollow Jersey decoys would not be worth much in the deepwater conditions in New England, any more than the generally heavy and oversize decoys of Maine would be anything more than a nuisance to the hunters along the Illinois River. Knowing these area characteristics can be a big help as a starting point in identification. It is also a great help to know where the various species of ducks occur along the various flyways—especially on the Atlantic Flyway, where some birds appear in certain areas and not at all or very rarely in others. So don't expect to find canvasbacks in Maine or eiders on the Susquehanna Flats. Despite all the published guidelines to identi-fication, there is really only one way to become at all adept at it—by visiting and inspecting collections of documented decoys. Once you have held a Joe Lincoln old-squaw and stroked it with your hands and examined it carefully, you will never confuse it with the work of any other maker. This applies equally well to the birds of Elmer Crowell, Shang Wheeler, Ben Holmes, Harry Shourdes, and a slew of other known makers.

Starting a collection is nowhere near as difficult as it may seem. We recently had some visitors from Paris who spent a month in our town and were exposed to decoys—or *canards du bois*, as they prefer to call them—and became as beguiled by them as any of the rest of us. Before returning home one of them wanted to get a decoy as a souvenir of his visit. My son brought down three moderately priced decoys for him to choose from. It did not work exactly according to plan, because while Claude decided on the bluebill by Frank Schmidt of Michigan, his wife, Françoise, would not relinquish the old, worn, and patined black duck by an unknown maker from Barnegat Bay. I have no doubt that once these decoys have been displayed in their apartment in Neuilly they will be on the prowl for more on their next visit here.

I still feel that the basic requirement in collecting is to acquire a few decoys regardless of their age or condition. Study them, identify them, and learn what you can from them about

Mason curlews like this one have brought as much as $3,400 at auction.

the whole business of collecting in general and decoy collecting in particular. As you learn more, evaluate, then retain or discard on the basis of the knowledge you have gained. At a recent auction, which was undoubtedly influenced by the national economic situation at the moment, very collectible birds were selling at from $5 to $20. Any young collector with the guts to spend $500 would have ended up with a nucleus of twenty decoys—and a braver one who risked $1,000 could have had twenty really fine decoys. You have to be there when it happens.

Any new collector should become connected with a local group which conducts "buy, sell, and trade" sessions. Among the best of these are the meetings at Davenport, Chicago, Detroit, Babylon, Salisbury, and the outstanding session each November in Easton. State names were purposely left out because even as a neophyte, you should know. These groups are usually indoors, but in many instances the main display is in station wagons and cars in the parking area. Prices are usually put on most birds with what may be known of origin and maker, but much of the fun

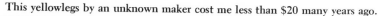

This yellowlegs by an unknown maker cost me less than $20 many years ago.

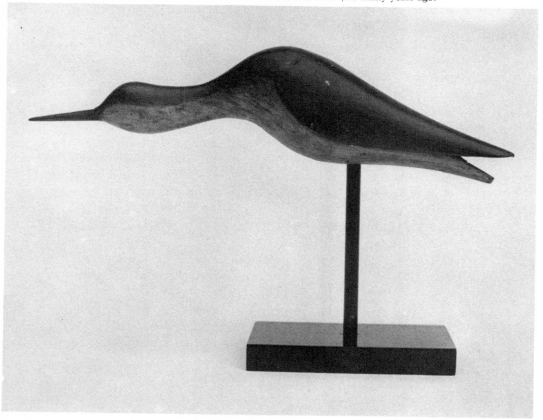

comes from dickering on the price. Most decoy people love to dicker or swap. Flea markets have become another good source of decoys and it pays to follow them closely, and here again a dicker can often be made because the seller is no more sure of the true value than you are. If you are willing to pay the legitimate markup, good antique dealers are one of the best sources of good decoys. Usually, in any given area one dealer becomes known as the decoy man and other dealers who are less sure of price scales will commonly sell to him. Because of their overhead, there is usually no dickering. On the other hand, what they sell is generally fairly priced and a good dealer is willing to back up his merchandise if any question arises later. Decoys are not always traded on an open market, but at private sales. Established collectors from time to time are given word of a particularly fine decoy which is owned by someone who finds he would like to convert it to cash with the least amount of overhead cost. Auctions cost the consignor 20% and up, plus any sales tax which may apply. For a much lower percentage an individual can act as a private agent, and by knowing which collectors specialize in certain species of birds, can get the buyer and seller together and arrange a deal. This procedure is not for the novice, but is a means used for distributing the finer and more expensive birds to those who can afford them and will really appreciate them.

Selling decoys is quite obviously the obverse side of the coin from the above account of buying. I find myself at this particular point in very much of a bind, because in twenty-six years of collecting I have never sold a decoy. In the course of time some have been given away and some traded, but never have I sold a decoy I have collected. It would not be a good idea to give this advice to new collectors, because with the changing times this policy is no longer valid. New collectors are sincerely advised to upgrade their collections by either selling or buying. If you have, say, a challenge grade in not too good condition and you see another of the same in much better condition, buy it. Later you can sell or trade your first one—but you have by then made a definite step in the right direction.

Appraising decoy values in a monetary sense can be very difficult, and opinions may vary widely on the value of any given decoy. In the field of stamp collecting we have a very accurate idea of how many stamps of each issue were printed and approximately how many may still be in existence so that the law of supply and demand can readily be applied to determining the current market price of any stamp. Decoy collecting has not been organized long enough for these conditions to be applicable. Pricing is gradually being stabilized by auctions and private sales, but it will be a long time before anything like the Scott stamp

A good average shorebird decoy, this blackbreast plover has a replacement bill.

A Mason black duck, now worth about $50.

catalog will be written for decoy circles. Not too long ago a unique situation arose. One man had a certain species of duck by a recognized maker that was the only one that had ever come to light. Through a series of accidental happenings it was found that another man who was not a collector had one and had never thought to mention it, since he honestly had no idea of its rarity. It was sold privately to another collector at a price that had to be purely arbitrary, since such a duck had never appeared on the open market. Someday, after enough trading, values on decoys will become truly stabilized.

One law will always dominate valuation in the field of decoys, as it does in all other collecting fields, and it may be expressed in one word: condition. The term "mint" describes the pristine condition in which a decoy first comes from the hands of the maker. However, since decoys are working tools, if they have been used at all they are bound to show some signs of it even though they may be slight. Since necks, bills, and tails are the most friable parts of decoys, they must be inspected for injury and any repairs made must be evaluated and will have some effect on overall value. The biggest problem to the real collector is paint. Entire original paint is preferred even if it shows signs of wear from use. Careful repainting of worn areas usually does not have any drastic effect on price, but a complete repaint job does. A new term has come into use describing the condition of older decoys that have seen years of hard usage and were repainted

A hooded merganser drake by Samuel Jester of Chincoteague, now worth about $100.

every year or two over the same patterns. The term is "in use repainted" and applies, for instance, to the old battery decoys of the Susquehanna Flats with sixty years or so of hard work behind them. To strip and repaint those birds like new would deprive them of most of their charm. Their chipped layers of paint and shot holes are their Purple Hearts—and no one should deprive them of these. Shot holes in decoys are always mentioned when a bird comes up for auction. To me they do not detract from the value of the decoy, but simply mean that the gunner was over-eager and would not wait for the birds to clear the decoys before firing. Others say they were purposely shot on the water to keep the breast meat free of shot—probably just another of them downeast Maine stories.

Normally a decoy has nothing sticking up very high in the way of tail or primary feathers that might be damaged in lugging the decoys to and from the hunting grounds. However, over the last few years, more realistic styles have been espoused by the contemporary carvers. It was soon realized that they were much too detailed and finely carved to really qualify as working decoys. As a result, at the more recent shows these finer birds have been judged under the class of Decorative Floating Decoys. This means that while they may be delicately carved, their floatability and action in the water must be judged on the same basis as regular "workin' stool." As yet it is impossible to set any values on this type of carving, because all have been disposed of at private sale. It is sufficient to say that the prize money alone at the Ward Foundation show in Salisbury, Md., amounts to $2,000 for the winning pair.

Shorebirds present a tremendous problem from the appraisal angle, since they seem to be advancing in value even faster than duck decoys. Because they were almost all produced along the Atlantic Coast and yet as new collectors are coming into existence all over the country, the supply of good old shorebirds is being exhausted while at the same time the demand for them is increasing. At this juncture we must interpose a discussion of aesthetics or the ability to see true beauty in decoys. Most decoys while perfectly serviceable do not arouse any feelings of being beautiful. Other decoys were made by men who unknowingly were true artists, like the pair of American mergansers on page 38 by an unknown maker in the Monhegan Island–Penobscot Bay area of Maine. In the purest sense, decoys are symbols, not replicas, and they should suggest, not define, the characteristics of birds in the water. In the simplicity of carving and plumage pattern and the utter grace of line, this pair represents the very best in decoy design. Other men in this area tried to copy this man's work, but even a cursory glance will show that they missed the essential spirit of these birds. No true value can be put on these birds since none have been sold on the open market.

Because of just plain scarcity almost any half-decent old shorebird can be considered to be worth around $200. Most shorebirds have a great share of beauty, but some are pure clunkers and should be recognized as such. The Mason curlew shown on page 40 will give one illustration as to how shorebirds have increased in price. Two of these were in the Bourne auction in July, 1973, and brought $1,600 each; in July, 1974, a single one brought $2,300; and in October, 1974, two others brought $3,400 each. Other "name" shorebirds have done well over the years, if maybe not quite so spectacularly. Admittedly, 1975 has shown some softening of the market about in line with national monetary conditions. Shorebirds by unknown makers very often get a big play due to the aesthetics of the bird itself. The yellowlegs on page 41 was purchased by me in 1957 from a Mr. Eldridge in Chatham, Mass., for under $20. I have always liked him and now I know that I'm not the only one. At a recent auction a small plover by this same man and in the same position went through some spirited bidding to bring $1,700. The only way to get a good idea of shorebird values is to check the price and condition of every one you see for sale in any shop and to really study the Bourne auction catalogs since 1968, when the whole thing really got off the ground.

An example of a good average shorebird is the blackbreast plover on page 43 by an unknown maker of Cape Cod. His paint is original and only slightly worn. The shot holes do not detract, but the bill is a replacement—maybe the old one was shot off.

Duck decoys happily enjoy a more stable market than shorebirds, and it is possible to place fairly accurate values on a majority of those which come up for sale. Two actual price lists are published at intervals which can be a great help to new collectors, since they list decoys actually for sale. "A Compendium of Antique and Contemporary Decoys" is published by Bob Denny of the Wildlife Shop of Conway, N.H. Charles Murphy of The Sneak Box of Concord, Mass., sends out price lists at irregular intervals. Both are worth close study.

Several birds are illustrated in various ranges with notes as to their origin and condition to explain the valuations. On page 44 is a Detroit-grade black duck by the Mason Decoy Factory, which went out of business about 1920, and has a current value of around $50. It is in generally good condition with the paint almost intact but worn enough to show the grain underneath, plus a shrinkage crack the length of his back. The eyes are tacks—this grade came with painted, tack, or glass eyes. All the putty is missing from the joint between the head and the body. It is a representative Mason decoy, but neither really fine nor rare. The

A redhead drake by Benjamin Schmidt of Centerline, Mich., now worth about $200.

A goldeneye drake by a Yarmouth maker, now worth between $400 and $500.

hooded merganser drake on page 45 was made by Samuel "Doug" Jester of Chincoteague, and was new when I bought it from him for a pittance about 1953, but now has a value of $100. The carving shows tool marks and the painting pattern is of the simplest, but it is an effective decoy. There have been many decoy makers in Chincoteague over the years, and Jester's work is quite typical of most of them in degree of refinement, and yet they seem to have an increasing appeal to collectors, which perhaps explains the present prices.

Although I am primarily an East Coast collector, it is a real pleasure to introduce the decoy picked to represent the $200 class. On page 47 is a redhead drake by Benjamin Schmidt (1884–1968) of Centerline, Mich. Ben was a market gunner by trade, so his decoys had to be good if he was to make a living. The good rugged lines and effectiveness of these decoys have made them increasingly desirable to collectors—five years ago they brought only a quarter of this price.

Probably around 1880 to 1890 an unknown carver in Yarmouth, Mass., created the goldeneye drake shown above, which has a value of from $400 to $500. His lines are fine and graceful and show that distinct bit of individuality that distinguishes a fine decoy from a run-of-the-mill job. The wings are carved and the tips are raised. The neck is part of the body and has been scooped out to receive the head. The age cracks, shot holes, and many repaints can't detract from his overall fineness.

Geese and swan decoys are very collectible, but because of

their size present some storage problems and as a result may bring less money than might seem indicated. An exceptional Lincoln or Cobb Island goose can bring $500 or more, while the average runs $50 to $100. Because of the relative scarcity of good swan decoys, they run higher, and any swan is a good buy if it is in good condition. An excellent swan decoy is worth from $2,000 to $3,000.

Happily, decoys blend nicely into any decor from Colonial to contemporary. Since collections tend to be very small in their early stages, places can easily be found, but soon the obvious places become full and some solution must be found. I can recall rooms with beautiful built-in bookcases which had one decoy on the top shelf of each section—only to return on a later visit to find all the books gone and the shelves full of decoys. Many collectors have fixed over attics, cellar play rooms, and even garages lined on all walls with enough shelves to accommodate good-size collections. This concentration makes it very nice for the visitor to examine the collection quietly without disturbing the entire household. Some people have built special rooms into their homes to house collections, and some of these are outstanding.

Despite the increase in housebreaking in recent years, decoy collections do not seem to have too high a priority. A television or a silver tea set is much easier to dispose of at a profit than some old wooden duck. So far we collectors have been lucky, but it may not always be so. Good locks and a nasty dog are the best bets at the moment. In the case of the more valuable birds, a good photographic record in the form of 8×10 glossy prints of the best quality can identify just about any decoy should the occasion arise. Personally, I am always pleased with publication of photos of the better birds in my collection on the premise that the more people who can recognize them the harder it would be to sell any illegally and the more apt they are to be recognized and reported if offered for sale. The collectors I know would not want a bird acquired in such a manner. All collections should be insured. Some companies will permit any bird under $100 to be listed at the regular homeowner's rate, while decoys above that limit must be listed individually under a fine-arts policy.

I would never attempt to predict in which direction the stock market may go at any time, but there is only one direction the decoy market can possibly go—up. It is reasonable to assume that a good majority of the old decoys in barns, lofts, and fish sheds have come to light, thanks to diligent work on the part of an army of collectors. At the same time the number of collectors is on the increase, so the supply is inevitably running short of the demand—first on the more expensive decoys and then spreading down through all values. This also applies to the work of the better contemporary makers who cannot possibly keep up quality production to equal the demands made upon them. ➥

SELECTED BIBLIOGRAPHY

For the enlightenment of those readers who might wish to delve further into the world of decoys, I am happy to say that there is a modest, but growing, number of books on the subject.

Foremost among my own favorites, of course, is *Wild Fowl Decoys* by Joel Barber, now available as a $3.50 Dover paperback. This wonderful book represents years of research and remains the basic source. *Decoys at Shelburne Museum* by David S. Webster and William Kehoe (Washington, D.C.: Hobby House, 1961) depicts many decoys from four good collections and is used a great deal for identification. *American Bird Decoys* by William J. Mackey, Jr. (New York: Dutton, 1965) is an excellent survey of the whole decoy field. *The Art of the Decoy* by Adele Earnest (New York: Potter, 1970) considers decoys from the aesthetic and artistic standpoint rather than the practical.

Duck Shooting Along the Atlantic Tidewater, edited by Eugene V. Connett (New York: Morrow, 1947), is a series of reminiscences of hunting and decoys all along the coast. *Decoys and Decoy Carvers of Illinois* by P. W. Parmalee and F. D. Loomis (Northern Illinois University Press, 1969) is a scholarly and well-illustrated treatise on the decoy makers of a particular area. *The Ward Brothers* by Byron Cheever (Heber City, Utah: North American Decoys, 1971) shows the changing styles of Lem and Steve Ward over more than fifty years of decoy carving. *Chesapeake Bay Decoys*, edited by R. H. Richardson (Cambridge, Md.: Crow Haven Publishers, 1973), uses examples from eight collections to give a very complete and well-rounded picture of all the various types of decoys used in the Bay. *The Atlantic Flyway* by Robert Elman (New York: Winchester Press, 1972) is the story of this great highway of the air from the historical, ecological, and hunting viewpoints.

Game Bird Carving by Bruce Burk (New York: Winchester Press, 1972) is a definitive text on ornamental carving and painting, but the carving instructions should benefit all decoy makers. *The Outlaw Gunner* by Dr. Harry Walsh (Cambridge, Md.: Tidewater, 1971) tells the fascinating story of those market gunners who operated on the very edge of the law and shows all the equipment they used.

And last but not least is my own *Decoys of the Atlantic Flyway* (New York: Winchester Press, 1974).

4

~&~

FEDERAL DUCK STAMP PRINTS

by Jene C. Gilmore

Federal Migratory Waterfowl Stamp Prints were initiated in 1936 by Ralph Terrell, Dr. Samuel Milbank, and Richard E. Bishop. This was of the 1936–37 stamp of Canada geese by Bishop. At that time Terrell was head of the Book and Art Department of Abercrombie & Fitch in New York City. Later that year, Ding Darling and Frank Benson, who had designed earlier duck stamps, were both asked to do prints of their stamps. Darling complied immediately, Benson the following year.

The series has long since become a collector's item. One print is issued each year, and the current market value of a complete set is $55,000. The prints are usually limited in numbers and editions. It is extremely difficult to identify different editions, because they are not marked; an expert must determine. The first edition is always worth at least $200 more than subsequent editions, except in the case of the 1939–40 print by Lynn Bogue Hunt, which had a first edition of 100, second edition of 25, and 15 replicas. The replicas are actually original pencil drawings, and thus are more valuable than either the first or the second edition.

The rarest of the prints is the 1935–36 canvasback by Frank Benson. Only 70 were made, and thus there can never be more than 70 complete sets. The second rarest is the 1945–46 print by Gromme. It was done in an edition of 250, but since Gromme is the Honorary State Artist of Wisconsin, every dairy farmer in the state seems to have bought a print, and it has become extremely hard to find.

Anyone beginning a collection should start with the current ones; the right time to buy a print is when it is issued, since you pay the original selling price. A next step might be to try to find all of the colored series, which began with the 1970–71 Ross' goose by Edward Bierly. Then go after the earlier prints.

1940 federal duck stamp design by Jaques, shown matted with the stamp. Photo: Sportsman's Edge, Ltd.

Collectors can buy, sell, and obtain appraisals at any of the following dealers, all of whom make a specialty of duck-stamp prints:

Petersen Galleries, Beverly Hills, Calif.
The Sportsman's Edge, Ltd., New York City
Abercrombie & Fitch, New York City
The Crossroads of Sport, New York City
Wild Wings, Lake City, Minn.
Russell Fink, Lorton, Va.

The best way to display the prints is framed with the stamp, using rag mat board and, generally, a ⅜-inch black molding.

Whether or not the artist signs the stamp is a matter of personal taste. Many people prefer that the artist sign the stamp; others prefer the signature to appear only on the print. The stamp is usually worth more signed when the artist dies.

Duck-stamp prints should be insured for their replacement value. ✒

VALUES OF FEDERAL DUCK STAMP PRINTS

All Prices Are Retail and Are Based on
1st Editions, Framed With Stamp

Year	Subject	Artist	Current value
1934–35	Mallards	Darling	$1,750
1935–36	Canvasbacks	Benson	5,000
1936–37	Canada Geese	Bishop	
		early edition	500
		later edition	150
1937–38	Broadbill	Knap	1,600
1938–39	Pintails	Clark	1,750
1939–40	Greenwing Teal	Hunt	
		1st & 2nd edition	3,750
		replica (ed. 15)	3,000
1940–41	Black Ducks	Jaques	
		1st & 2nd edition	2,000
		3rd edition	1,250
1941–42	Ruddy Ducks	Kalmbach	
		reversed	1,250
		regular	350
1942–43	Widgeon	Ripley	500
		signature, Mrs. Ripley	125
1943–44	Wood Ducks	Bohl	

Year	Subject	Artist	Current value
		1st edition	750
		2nd edition	300
1944–45	White Fronted Geese	Weber	
		reversed	1,500
		1st edition	1,500
		2nd edition	300
1945–46	Shovellers	Gromme	4,500
1946–47	Red Heads	Hines	1,400
1947–48	Snow Geese	Murray	1,000
1948–49	Buffleheads	Reece	
		1st edition	750
		2nd edition	350
		3rd edition	150
1949–50	Golden Eyes	Preuss	1,500
1950–51	Trumpeter Swans	Weber	750
1951–52	Gadwall	Reece	
		1st edition	750
		2nd edition	125
1952–53	Harlequins	Dick	900
1953–54	Blue Wing Teal	Seagears	900
1954–55	Ring Neck Ducks	Sandstrom	1,000
1955–56	Blue Geese	Stearns	
		1st edition, 1st print	750
		1st edition, 2nd print	700
		2nd edition	250
1956–57	Mergansers	Bierly	
		1st edition	750
		2nd edition	250
1957–58	Eider Ducks	Abbott	
		1st edition	1,250
		2nd edition	100
1958–59	Canada Geese	Kouba	
		1st edition	750
		2nd edition	450
1959–60	Labrador King Buck	Reece	
		1st edition	750
		2nd edition	350
		3rd edition	125
1960–61	Redhead Family	Ruthven	
		1st edition	500
		2nd edition	250
1961–62	Mallard Family	Morris	650
1962–63	Pintails	Morris	650
1963–64	Brant	Bierly	
		1st edition	600
		2nd edition	250

Year	Subject	Artist	Current value
1964–65	Nene Geese	Stearns	
		1st edition	700
		2nd edition	300
1965–66	Canvasbacks	Jenkins	
		1st edition	400
		2nd edition	200
1966–67	Whistling Swans	Stearns	
		1st edition	900
		2nd edition	500
1967–68	Old Squaws	Kouba	600
1968–69	Hooded Merganser	Pritchard	
		#200 and below	500
		#201 and above	350
1969–70	Scooters	Reece	
		#200 and below	600
		#201 and above	300
		remarqued	800
1970–71	Ross' Geese	Bierly	
		#300 and below	700
		#301 and above	500

Printer's proof of 1971–72 federal duck stamp design by Maynard Reece.

Year	Subject	Artist	Current value
1971–72	Cinnamon Teal	Reece	
		#250 and below	1,200
		#251 and above	1,100
1972–73	Emperor Geese	Cook	
		#200 and below	750
		#201 and above	700
1973–74	Stellers Eider	LeBlanc	
		1st edition	700
1974–75	Wood Ducks	Maass	
		1st edition	300
1975–76	Decoy	Fisher	
		1st edition	350
1976–77	Canada Geese	Magee	100

5

$\sim\!\!\sim$

STATE DUCK STAMP PRINTS

By Alfred F. King, III

State duck stamp prints are one of the newest areas of collecting for the sportsman today; if you are interested, now is the time to get in on the ground floor. Since 1971 there have been five states that have issued duck stamps for which there are prints: California, Iowa, Maryland, Massachusetts, and Illinois. As time goes on, chances are that more states will do the same; and as in the case of the Federal Duck Stamp proceeds, virtually all the revenues go toward the purchase of wetlands.

The following is a breakdown of the prints by state, with information regarding their selection. Values are for the print alone, without stamp or frame.

CALIFORNIA

California has had a state duck stamp since 1971. The state hired Paul B. Johnson to do the stamps every year. At first the prints were not made to correspond to the yearly duck stamp by Mr. Johnson, but in 1974 he published one print which contained the first four years (there are 150 of these). This edition is referred to as part of the executive series and was followed by a print in 1975 with the image size corresponding to the image size of the

Year	Artist	Edition size	Original value	Current value
1971–4	Paul B. Johnson exec. series ⎫			
1975	Paul B. Johnson ⎭	150	$125	$925
1971	Paul B. Johnson	500	60	75
1972	Paul B. Johnson	12	-	375
1973	Paul B. Johnson	500	50	75
1974	Paul B. Johnson	500	50	75
1975	Paul B. Johnson	500	50	75

individual years of the large print covering all four years. Following the executive series it was felt that the first year could not be cut from the plate of the first four years and still be considered a mint-condition print, so separate editions of each year were printed. These have a smaller image area than the executive series and are limited to 500.

IOWA

Iowa's first duck stamp design was done for the 1972 calendar year by Maynard Reece, five time Federal Duck Stamp Design Winner. Subsequently there has been a contest for the design, and this is limited to state residents.

Year	Artist	Edition size	Original value	Current* value
1972	Maynard Reece	500	$60	$970
1973	Thomas Murphy	500	60	80
1974	J. F. Landenberger	500	60	80
1975	Mark Reece	900	60	60
1976	Nick Klepinger	560	60	60

MARYLAND

Maryland's first duck stamp was done for the 1974–75 hunting season. The first year John W. Taylor did the design by appointment. Since then the design has been awarded in a competition restricted to Maryland residents.

Year	Artist	Edition size	Original value	Current value
1974–75	John W. Taylor	500	$60	$170
1975–76	Stanley Stearns	650	70	70

MASSACHUSETTS

Massachusetts started its duck stamp design with the calendar year of 1974. This design is restricted to a Massachusetts decoy and it is open to nonresidents. The first design was done without a contest, and was Milton C. Weiler's Wood Duck decoy carved by Joseph Lincoln. Unfortunately Milton Weiler died before he could publish a signed duck-stamp print. However, the same original was reproduced in the Classic Decoy Series published by Winchester Press, 1969. Milton Weiler signed a few of these plates, and some people regard this as the first signed duck stamp print. Technically and ethically speaking, however, the first signed duck stamp print was done by Tom Hennessey.

Year	Artist	Edition size	Original value	Current value
1975	Tom Hennessey	500	$60	$70
1976	William P. Tyner	500	60	60

ILLINOIS

Illinois' first duck stamp was done for this year's season, 1975–76, by Robert F. Eschenfeldt, who was commissioned for the design. In future years they plan to have a competition for the winning design. This contest will be limited to state residents.

Year	Artist	Edition	Original value	Current value
1975–76	Robert F. Eschenfeldt	500	$70	$115

For the collector, I cannot recommend collecting the print of every state every year, though to the purist this will be important and will result in a fantastic collection. My suggestion,

This is the first Maryland state duck stamp, 1974–5, by John W. Taylor. Photo: Sportsman's Edge, Ltd.

First Illinois state duck stamp, 1975–6, by Robert F. Eschenfeldt. Photo: Sportsman's Edge, Ltd.

however, is that the initial (first) state duck stamp print of each state is the one to collect. The first of any series is very often the one that carries the greatest premium, and many collectors are late in collecting it. It gets harder to obtain and thus more valuable. I feel strongly that in time, the complete set of initial state duck stamp prints will be as unique and historically important as the federal duck stamp print collection. ➤

Following is a list of the dealers most capable of handling your requirements for the state duck stamp prints:

The Art Shop & Galleries
Attn.: Larry Jonson
PO Box 3774 (4th & Main)
Davenport, Iowa 52808

Russell A. Fink
PO Box 250 (9843 Gunston Rd.)
Lorton, Va. 22079

Petersen Galleries
Attn.: Jene C. Gilmore
9433 Wilshire Blvd.
Beverly Hills, Calif. 90212

Sportsman's Edge, Ltd
Attn.: Alfred F. King III
136 East 74th St.
New York, N.Y. 10021

6

FEDERAL DUCK STAMPS AND POSTAGE STAMPS

by Leo Scarlet

Postage stamps were first issued in 1840 and from the very beginning there was a keen interest in collecting them. The very nature of their use and the extensive variety of different colors and designs captivated an audience that extends to every country in the world and to all walks of life. During the past thirty years there has developed a rapid upsurge of interest in collecting stamps based upon special themes. This is known as "topical" collecting. Collections are formed concentrating solely upon single topics, such as religion, medicine, guns, sports, the Olympics, etc. There is an organization of philatelists, the American Topical Association, which carefully lists all the various stamps issued throughout the world, and breaks up all these issues into the various topics.

A collection of stamps specializing only in sports can be a fascinating project. Most countries issue stamps commemorating major sports events, or sports of the country. In the United States, many collect duck-hunting stamps, which are not postage stamps but are issued as a license fee for duck hunting by the U.S. Conservation Department. They were first issued in 1934 and are issued yearly, with a different design each year. All designs used are paintings or drawings by well-known artists. Forming a complete collection of duck stamps can be quite a challenge.

Many duck stamps were printed in colors, and all are beautiful. Any hunter would immediately appreciate the beauty and recognize the type of duck. Among the famous artists that painted the originals are J. N. Darling, Frank Benson, Roland Clark, Maynard Reece, Edward J. Bierly, and Stanley Stearns. The scarcest stamp is the 1935 issue (canvasback ducks) painted by Frank Benson. A decent unused single stamp will fetch $150, and a used (signed by hunter) example is worth $35.

Less than ten years ago, one could obtain a complete set of

duck stamps for about $100. Today, you would be lucky to find a complete set for less than $900. Some collectors of duck stamps make up a fascinating collection of stamps on the original license. Most states have hunting stamps for individual game and fish. There are many hundreds, and obviously the only way to pursue the collection of these is to work out a reciprocal arrangement with hunters in other states, or seek out a dealer for assistance.

Covers (envelopes) advertising arms companies. The upper one was printed by Winchester for one of its dealers, Hunnewell in Maine. Photo: Matthew Vinciguerra.

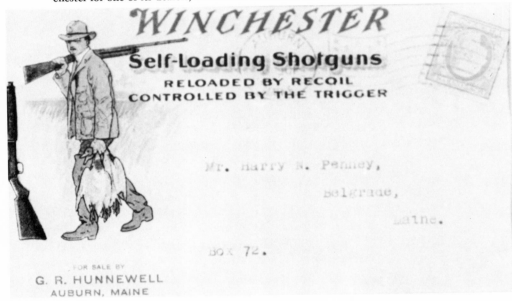

A serious factor enters the pricing of stamps. This is the factor of condition. A stamp that is torn, creased, or discolored will fetch less than one in pristine, fresh condition. Unfortunately, there is no easy path to learning these variations. It is simply something you learn from experience. Any stamp dealer will be happy to help in this area.

Another aspect of collecting is the collecting of covers (envelopes), which picture the various topics. Late-nineteenth-century and early-twentieth-century businesses often used envelopes with designs, some in color, and many are intricate and interesting. Among the most difficult to locate these days are covers advertising different guns and ammunition. A collection of such covers is fascination itself. These can be obtained for moderate prices. Selling prices range from $20 to $50 depending upon scarcity.

The identification of stamps is really a simple matter with the use of the Scott Standard Postage Stamp Catalog. It is an annual and lists every stamp issued by every country in the world, even making a brave attempt to price each stamp. Catalog values should serve only as a relative guide, since prices in the open market are too volatile. Strangely, values of stamps seem to move only upwards. This is truer today than ever before, because so many people are turning to stamps an as investment or as a hedge against inflation. Some stamps are quite rare. One stamp actually sold for $280,000 at a public auction! Fortunately, one can form an interesting collection with a modest expenditure of money.

Stamps can be purchased from several thousand stamp dealers located throughout the country. The American Stamp Dealers Association will be glad to supply the names of dealer members nearest you. See the proper pages in your telephone directory. Stamp dealers advertise regularly in local newspapers and in several national weekly stamp magazines. Public auctions and regular exhibitions are held at regular intervals. Visit one of these. You will find it worthwhile. You will find most stamp dealers to be helpful and cooperative. They know you need help, and it is to their advantage to win you as a customer. ➤

REFERENCE SOURCES FOR STAMPS

American Stamp Dealers Association, 595 Madison Ave., New York, N.Y. 10022. (Lists all stamp dealers in U.S. and other parts of the world.)

American Topical Association, Mr. Jerome Husak, Exec. Secretary, 3306 N. 50th St., Milwaukee, Wis. 53216. (Period lists of stamps broken down by topic.)

Scott Standard Postage Stamp Catalog, Scott Publishing Co., 530 Fifth Avenue, New York, N.Y. 10036. (Lists all stamps issued in the world since 1840.)

Minkus Stamp Catalog, Minkus Publications, 116 W. 32nd St., New York, N.Y. 10001. (Similar to Scott's. Sold by Gimbel's chain in over 40 department stores.)

Stamps Magazine, 153 Waverly Place, New York, N.Y. 10014.

Linns Weekly Stamp News, P.O. Box 29, Sidney, Ohio 45365.

Western Stamp Collector, P.O. Box 10, Albany, Ore. 97321.

Meekels Magazine, P.O. Box 1660, Portland, Me. 04104.

United States Postage Stamps, United States Postal Service, U.S. Government Printing Office, Washington, D.C. 20402.

United States Stamps & Stories, United States Postal Service. Published by Scott Publishing Company, New York, N.Y.

Duck Stamp Data, United States Department of the Interior, Fish and Wildlife Service, U.S. Government Printing Office, Washington, D.C. 20402.

Stamp list catalog sold at major post offices.

CURRENT VALUES OF DUCK STAMPS

Scott #	Year of issue	Denomination and color	Value unused	Value used
RW 1	1934	$1 blue	$ 55.00	$22.00
RW 2	1935	$1 rose lake	150.00	34.85
RW 3	1936	$1 brown black	49.50	19.95
RW 4	1937	$1 light green	27.50	8.50
RW 5	1938	$1 light violet	38.50	8.50
RW 6	1939	$1 chocolate	28.75	7.50
RW 7	1940	$1 sepia	29.95	5.85
RW 8	1941	$1 brown carmine	29.95	6.50
RW 9	1942	$1 violet brown	29.95	6.50
RW 10	1943	$1 deep rose	21.50	6.50
RW 11	1944	$1 red orange	18.50	5.50
RW 12	1945	$1 black	12.75	3.75
RW 13	1946	$1 red brown	12.75	3.00
RW 14	1947	$1 black	12.75	3.00
RW 15	1948	$1 bright blue	15.50	3.00
RW 16	1949	$2 bright green	15.50	3.00
RW 17	1950	$2 violet	15.50	3.00
RW 18	1951	$2 gray black	15.50	3.00
RW 19	1952	$2 dp. ultramarine	15.50	3.00
RW 20	1953	$2 dark rose brown	15.00	3.00

RW 21	1954	$2 black	$ 15.00	$ 3.00
RW 22	1955	$2 dark blue	15.00	2.80
RW 23	1956	$2 black	15.00	2.80
RW 24	1957	$2 emerald	15.00	2.80
RW 25	1958	$2 black	15.00	2.80
RW 26	1959	$3 bl. ochre black	32.00	2.80
RW 27	1960	$3 red brn. bl. bist.	32.00	2.80
RW 28	1961	$3 blue, bistre br.	32.00	2.80
RW 29	1962	$3 blue, brown, black	50.00	2.50
RW 30	1963	$3 blk, blue, yel, grn.	55.00	2.80
RW 31	1964	$3 blue, blk, bistre	55.00	2.80
RW 32	1965	$3 green, blk, brown	30.00	2.80
RW 33	1966	$3 blue, green, black	55.00	2.80
RW 34	1967	$3 multicolored	50.00	2.80
RW 35	1968	$3 green, blk, brown	25.00	2.80
RW 36	1969	$3 multicolored	25.00	2.80
RW 37	1970	$3 multicolored	22.00	2.80
RW 38	1971	$3 multicolored	20.00	2.80
RW 39	1972	$5 multicolored	12.50	2.95
RW 40	1973	$5 multicolored	9.50	2.95
RW 41	1974	$5 multicolored	7.95	-
RW 42	1975	$5 multicolored	7.95	-

7

SPORTING FIREARMS

by Norm Flayderman

There have been few fields in the past twenty years that have grown more rapidly in both devotees and values than the collecting of firearms. The mere numbers of books written and published in the field are in themselves indicative of its rapid and popular growth.

It is best for our purposes to define "sporting guns" in the broadest possible sense: all firearms designed for hunting and target-shooting purposes. Obviously many firearms originally intended solely for utilitarian purposes—for example, to put meat in the pot for the frontiersman, settler, or pioneer—could hardly be called sporting guns if the term is defined narrowly. But we will define it broadly; if you do get involved in collecting, you are free to decide for yourself just what constitutes a sporting arm.

TYPES OF COLLECTIONS

Sporting firearms encompass the entire period of arms-making from its very beginnings in the fourteenth century to the present day. Commencing with the increased popularity and manufacture of firearms in the sixteenth century, sporting guns have always been made in a multitude of grades and qualities to satisfy the fancies as well as the pocketbooks of a variety of sportsmen— from those of little means and taste to those possessing great wealth and refined aesthetic judgment (which is not to say that money and taste always go hand in hand).

Considering the countless paths down which one may go in collecting sporting arms, you would do well to select a specific field and confine yourself to that area, at least until you've learned the basics of collecting. If you are already a hunter, you might start by collecting those guns most closely allied to your own particular hunting interest; for example, bird or wildfowl guns, small-game rifles, or big-game rifles. You could collect everything of this type you find, or concentrate further in a particular historical period.

However, to me, one of the most interesting types of collections is the general one that shows sporting arms from their earliest matchlock types right down to modern-day arms, including at least one of every different ignition system—wheellock, flintlock, miquelet, percussion, and breech-loading-cartridge styles. For the neophyte collector it is a way of acquiring a broad understanding of antique arms and their major changes over five

For the low budget and neophyte collectors, muzzle-loading percussion-lock half-stock fowling pieces offer a very wide range of material to collect. Shotguns of these types would have been found in almost every country home in Europe and America. Top: Inexpensively made Belgian 12-gauge percussion fowling piece. A type widely exported throughout the world during the mid-nineteenth century and later eras. Easily available on the current market. Retail selling prices $35 to $70. Middle: English percussion 12-gauge fowling piece, circa 1850–1870, showing excellent workmanship, typical of British gunmakers. Back-action-style engraved lock with London maker's name. Retail value $85 to $150. Bottom: American-made by the famed Whitney Arms Company, percussion 12-gauge fowling piece, circa 1866 to 1880. Very likely the least expensive Whitney-made arm of its day as well as on the collector's market. Retail value $75 to $150.

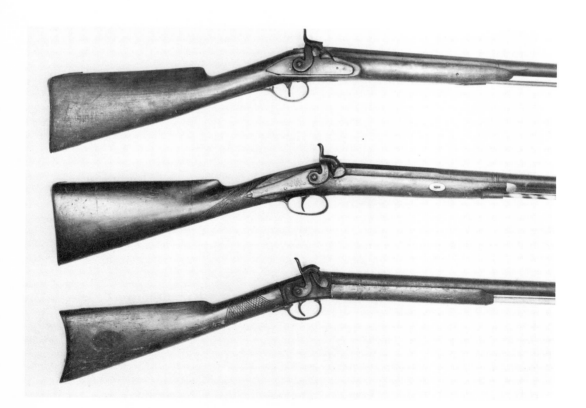

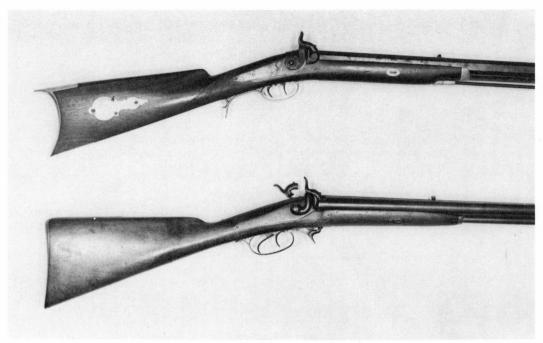

Top: American half-stock muzzle-loading percussion sporting rifle. Classic example of the type made throughout America in the 1840s to 1870s. This is representative of the simpler, more common type with full octagon rifle barrel, double set triggers, and small simple patchbox, and either unmarked as to maker or bearing names of lesser-known gunsmiths. Value at retail $175 to $300. Prices vary considerably depending upon both exterior and bore condition. Bottom: Three-barrel American rifle-shotgun. This specimen is a 14-gauge double-barrel muzzle-loading percussion shotgun over a .38-caliber muzzle-loading rifle and has three exterior hammers. Depending upon quality and maker, and of course condition, prices on similar pieces vary from $250 to $750. This particular example, in normal worn condition but bearing the California maker's marking, is worth $500. In this particular instance the Western maker adds to its desirability.

centuries, and he will find that the items he collects are of wide general interest to others also.

It is worth digressing for just a moment on this last point of "wide general interest." One of the greatest satisfactions in collecting is being able to communicate your enthusiasm for the items you have gathered to completely unknowledgeable, even uninterested, noncollectors, and seeing them show a genuine interest. If you have an esoteric collection—and firearms collections can be very esoteric; the placement of a screw or a variation in a maker's mark may affect value by many hundreds of dollars—you will find it very difficult to share your enthusiasm with a casual visitor to your gun room. Your collection will be of interest only to another dyed-in-the-wool advanced collector or student. But general collections that show a progression of arms through a long era of history lend themselves quite beautifully to an interesting, attractive display that is easily understood by the non-gun person. You will be amazed how easy it is to give an interesting tour through your collection if you keep it of this more general, broad scope. The more highly specialized and detailed your collection becomes, the less interesting it is to the public at large.

I do not mean to disparage highly specialized collectors and ones interested in technical variations, for such pursuits also offer much and have added greatly to the field of gun collecting. It can be easily seen, though, that the more you become involved in detail and fine points, the more you lose your audience. Thus, depending on your own needs and gregariousness, it is worth keeping in mind how much and with whom you would like to share your collecting.

Surprisingly, of the hundreds of books written on the subject of firearms and gun collecting, and the tens of thousands of arms collections there are in the world, there are relatively few that could be considered as devoting themselves solely to "sporting" or "hunting" guns as their major theme. The same is true of the many fine museum collections throughout the world. Although hunting and sporting arms are prominently shown in every arms museum, and are by no means relegated to second place in importance, there are less than a handful of museums (one is the wonderful Musée de la Chasse of Paris) whose primary emphasis is the integral evolution of hunting and hunting weapons. Such arms are certainly actively sought and collected, but regrettably they are generally disassociated from their original hunting/sporting intent, with major emphasis and stress placed on either craftsmanship and artistry, technical features and variations of manufacture, or representation of a type used during a specific era of history. This observation is not intended to reflect detrimentally on the arms or on collecting itself, but merely again points out the fact that collecting often forces the collected items into a context other than that for which they were originally designed.

Thus if you collect sporting arms and show them as closely paralleling the history of sporting and hunting itself, you will be in relatively untrodden territory. Instead of merely collecting firearms and firearms history, you will have the opportunity to broaden your knowledge and share your interest in sporting and hunting history as well. The two, after all, go hand in hand.

Two major categories, each offering limitless possibilities, are muzzle-loading arms and breech-loading arms. Each of these categories is easily subdivided into smoothbore (single or double barrel) fowling pieces or shotguns; smallbore rifles or large-bore rifles for the whole gamut of game animals; and target rifles. Considerable challenges are offered in each of these fields and a vast wealth of information on each specific type is readily avail-

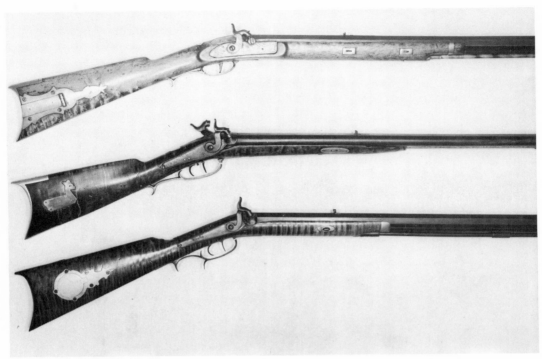

A wide range of half-stock American Kentucky or plains-type rifles of the mid-nineteenth century era are available. Prices vary greatly depending on exterior appearance, maker, and condition. Top: Half-stock Kentucky rifle, beautifully grained birdseye and curly maple stock, all brass-mounted with fancy large patchbox. Retail value $400 to $600. Middle: Side-by-side double-barrel muzzle-loading percussion plains-type Western rifle, circa 1850s. Has a rarity value as a double rifle, and St. Louis dealer's markings on it indicate its actual use on the Western frontier. Retail value $450 to $750. Bottom: Fine percussion half-stock sporting rifle with elegantly grained tiger-stripe maple half stock, finely made fittings, and the markings of a famed maker, S. Odell of Natchez, Mississippi, who was known to have sold many arms to emigrants heading west to Arkansas, Texas, and Santa Fe. In this case, quality and historic significance combine to establish a retail value of $1200.

able for reference. These major categories may be further narrowed by collecting more specialized types, each of which parallels an era or distinct hunting style. A notable example is the American Kentucky rifle. Certainly one of the best-known hunting and sporting arms, it covers the broad spectrum of American history from Colonial times through the mid-nineteenth century, undergoing numerous style changes as it adapted itself to different hunting, sporting, and target-shooting purposes. Other notable areas for specialization are breech-loading sporting rifles of the American West, covering the second half of the nineteenth century; lever-action sporting rifles; flintlock fowling pieces; single-shot varmint rifles; and big-game double rifles. This last group

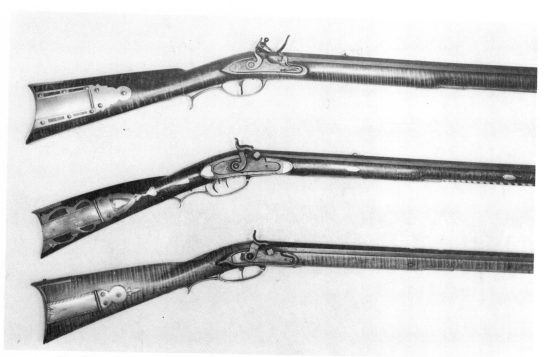

Top: Pennsylvania-Kentucky-style full-stock flintlock rifle displaying some of the classic features of that most eagerly sought after type, undoubtedly qualifying as one of the most handsome of all American guns. The most often encountered and desirable features of these are their fancy brass fittings with large brass patchboxes and stocks of closely tiger-striped, curly maple. Quite rare in original flintlock condition; when so found, prices will begin at $1,750 with the sky the limit for the very fine early ones. Prices vary greatly depending upon maker, condition, embellishments, and incised or relief carving. Middle: Pennsylvania-Kentucky-style rifle converted to percussion. Although lessening in importance in this past decade, the matter of originality of ignition system (that is, flintlock or percussion) does decidedly play a role in influencing market value. This particular specimen, because of its well-known maker and numerous fancy inlays, as well as very large pierced-design patchbox, is valued at $1,250. However, this style is often encountered in the collector's market priced from $500 to $2000 with the values very much established by the outward appearance and condition of the piece, as well as the rarity of the maker. Bottom: New England piece, but fashioned directly after the more famed Pennsylvania-Kentucky rifle. This piece shown in percussion conversion displays the classic style of patchbox found invariably on New England rifles. A few other features about its brass furniture also clearly indicate its New England manufacture. Most often found full-stocked in walnut or cherry. They normally retail in percussion at $450 to $750, and in flintlock at $1,250 or more. This particular specimen, quite unusually stocked in very handsomely striped curly maple, commands a premium price.

holds a great deal of fascination for the collector; the guns themselves almost always display the very finest of quality and craftsmanship and exude the aura of romance and excitement associated with African and Asian hunting. A category that is relatively untapped and that certainly offers a very wide potential for future growth is the field of Damascus double-barrel breech-loading shotguns designed for black-powder use.

In each of these fields it is possible to collect an extremely wide range of items; vast differences in style, quality, and appearance exist. Many of these differences are not merely manufacturing variations, but were deliberate adaptations to different hunting methods, and the collector will find it of genuine interest to form a collection paralleling them.

BECOMING A COLLECTOR

Guns are costly, to be sure; the sky is really the limit with some specimens. Recent years have seen ever-higher records set for certain types of fine arms, with many reaching the six-figure

American-made Scheutzen-style offhand target rifles were often made in the mid-nineteenth century by German immigrant gunsmiths. Both of these pieces exemplify some of the best of American quality arms used in the many "Scheutzenfests" popular throughout the country before the turn of the century. Top: New Jersey offhand target rifle displaying the best of quality and workmanship, made by J. Widmer of Newark, weighing 11 pounds with exceptional chiseled and engraved fittings, all silvered finish, and in fine condition. Its retail value is $1,250. Bottom: St. Louis Scheutzen-type rifle by Charles Schaerff. This piece also displays classic lines often found in German rifles of the same era; being valued both for its St. Louis maker's name and its superb condition, it recently listed at $1,150. Other specimens similar to both these pieces may be found in the $400 to $750 range depending upon quality and condition.

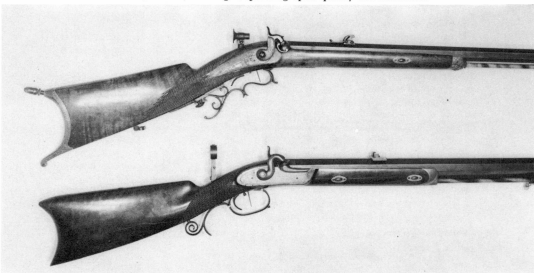

category. As a generalization, it would be fair to say that all gun prices, antique and modern, have risen sharply over the past decade. But the astronomical figures quoted for the rarest guns should in no way frighten you off; they are the exception and not the rule. There are tens of thousands of guns still available, well within the reach of the average pocketbook. To be sure, in collecting there is expense involved, and at the risk of triteness I cannot help but quote an expression that concisely sums the matter up: "Rich or poor, it's good to have money!" Your taste and your pocketbook will undoubtedly determine the category that you choose to start collecting. If you become proficient at it, and keep your eyes and ears open, you might even be able to turn a profit by buying guns that are not of interest to you personally, selling them at a profit, and turning the profits into your own particular field of specialization. Quite a few important collections have started just that way. Knowledge of guns and collecting are the most valuable assets you can acquire; money is secondary.

Myriad are the reasons why people become collectors. Each has its own validity and virtues. If, however, you are contemplating collecting purely on an investment basis, my best advice would be to quit now while you are ahead! If you have read one of those articles in the *Wall Street Journal* or some other publication that reports the skyrocketing prices in antique arms and the big money that has been made or could be made on them, and you are lured into speculative collecting, you might be in for a rude awakening. It is true that many collectors have turned very handsome profits on their antique arms, especially those who have been in the field for several years. A small handful of speculators in recent years have also made killings on a few choice pieces (and a few not so savory characters have made killings on spurious specimens). But speculation failures are rarely found newsworthy. There have been many. It is just not possible to buy antique guns, or for that matter antique furniture, coins, art, or anything collectible, without being armed with some knowledge and a good deal of patience. Few who come into collecting on a purely speculative basis stay long. The very essence of collecting is the acquisition of knowledge, and that takes time. The key requisite for collecting must be a sincere interest in the items themselves, and the ultimate remuneration you should expect is the enjoyment you have had from your collecting activities. Obviously, your money should be well spent; an investment in anything of value should be carefully considered. In the field of firearms, prudent investments have brought very rich returns, and indications are clear that gun values will continue to increase—but go into this field only if you are prepared to open your mind as well as your pocketbook.

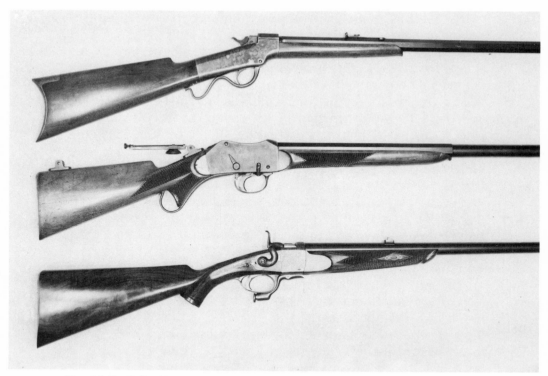

Top: Marlin-Ballard breech-loading "Model #2" single-shot rifle made in a great variety of calibers, barrel lengths, and stock styles. This particular specimen can be found anywhere from $100 to over $500 (if in brand-new condition). The Marlin-Ballard range is so vast, entire collections could be formed around them; the most deluxe specimens with long-range barrels and sights bring well upward of $1,500. Middle: American Peabody-Martini single-shot long-range target rifle made by the Providence Tool Company. One of the more eagerly sought of American single-shots developed for the famed Creedmore shooting of the 1870s–1890s. This piece, in new condition, catalogs at $2,250. There are various sporting, short, and mid-range models of this as well. Price proportionately less. Condition is highly important and affects value of these pieces. Bottom: Exemplifying the very fine guns of almost every British maker, this breech-loading (falling-block) single-shot .450-caliber sporting rifle is the type that can be found in many grades and styles, sporting to long-range target lengths. Prices range from $750 to $1,450 depending very much on condition and embellishments. Prices are considerably lower on guns showing heavy wear.

All right, you are ready to start. Where do you begin? My very best advice is to buy a few books and read them well. This is, by the way, the least often taken advice! It just takes too much time, and with your money burning a hole in your pocket you cannot visualize a book hanging on two gun hooks on your wall.

Go slow. Pick up a few basic primers on arms collecting. Any reasonably sized library is bound to have a number of them on its shelves, as will any larger bookseller. There are a few dealers specializing in gun books who issue catalogs of them, and if you happen to visit a gun show, undoubtedly there will be dealers there with a large selection of books on collecting. Just for openers, a good choice would be *The Collecting of Guns*, edited by James Serven, which gives a great introduction to the field. A few others you will find worthy of reviewing are *The Age of Firearms*, by Robert Held; *The National Rifle Association's Gun Collectors' Guide*; *Gun Collector's Digest*, edited by Joseph Schroeder; and *Guns and Collecting*, by Bailey, Hogg, Boothroyd, and Wilkinson. Although numerous titles are available on specialized sporting arms, there are but a handful available on the field in general, and they are well worth reading: *Hunting and Shooting from Earliest Times to the Present Day*, by Michael Brander; *Sporting Guns*, by Richard Akehurst; *Hunting Weapons* and *Royal Sporting Guns at Windsor*, by Howard L. Blackmore. After thoroughly digesting these primers, you will have acquired at least a basic knowledge of what the field of sporting weapons encompasses and are prepared to get your feet wet . . . maybe.

Next on your agenda should be visits to museums that specialize in or have good collections of firearms (and there are a number of them throughout the country); a visit to a gun collector's home; a visit to a gun show that might be in your area or nearby. These need not occur in that order. New horizons will undoubtedly open for you, especially when you visit your first gun show and see perhaps several hundred tables with thousands of guns for sale; you will suddenly realize that a new world is just waiting for you. Assuming that you are a cautious individual and that your money is still reposing at the bottom of your pocket, your next step should be to subscribe to a few of the arms periodicals that are regularly issued. I cannot overemphasize the importance of belonging to the National Rifle Association and receiving their very fine publication *The American Rifleman*. Two pure collectors' magazines are *The Gun Report* and *Arms Gazette*, both of which are oriented primarily toward antique arms. There are also a host of other periodicals covering the field of modern weapons. The importance of these magazines to you as a neophyte is not only their wealth of informative arms articles, but the hundreds of advertisements of dealers and collectors all over the country who either offer their catalogs or items for sale. One of the best mediums of exchange in the arms business, especially for antique weapons, is mail order. Of equal importance in these periodicals are the advertisements and listings for all the regularly scheduled gun shows throughout the country. Just about every weekend of the year there are from two to five different shows held somewhere in America; there is every likelihood that some will be close enough for you to attend.

Well, just possibly you are now ready to buy something. If you've been lucky, you have found a mentor in collecting whose

At the very top of the list and capturing the imagination (and the pocketbook) of both the hunter and collector are fine-quality double rifles, most notably those of the finer British makers. Prices are very heavily influenced by calibers. Those designed for smokeless modern loads and for which ammunition is still available most often fetch the top prices and are in greatest demand. The earlier outside-hammer black-powder models generally fetch from $450 to $2,000. Prices very much depend upon notoriety or the maker and condition. Later specimens such as the two British pieces shown will have values influenced by caliber, condition, and maker. British pieces will fetch higher prices than those of other European countries. Top: Westley Richards double rifle, .300 H&H magnum with original scope. Value $3,500. Middle: Manton, London, double rifle, .470, value $3,500 to $4,000. Bottom: Extremely rare double rifle, .45-70 made by Colt Firearms Company. Although they never achieved great popularity in this country, there were some double rifles made during the black-powder era by lesser-known makers. Their values vary anywhere from $250 to $750. This particular piece, by virtue of its being manufactured by Colt, one of the top collecting lines in American antique firearms, and of the fact that but 30 of them or so were made and only a handful known, will fetch, depending upon condition and the collector's market, $6,000 to $15,000.

opinion you feel you can value (and who is not trying to sell you his guns!), and in making a selection at a show or in a dealer's shop you can get one outside impartial opinion. This will do much to get you started on the right foot. If you are on your own, then you have to use your own discernment, good common sense, and judgment of human nature. A check of the reputation of the party selling it is certainly worth making. Remember, guarantees, whether in writing or not, are only as good as the party giving them.

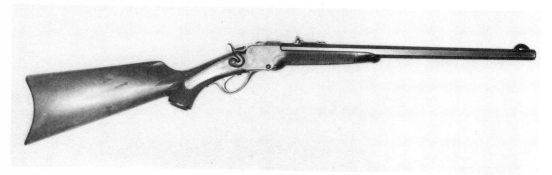

The ultimate in an American rarity, an elegant .40 carbine made by the most famed of American frontier gunsmiths, Frank W. Freund, in his "Wyoming Armory" at Cheyenne, Wyoming Territory, circa 1870. Known as his Wyoming Saddle Gun, having a Sharps-type (but completely Freund-made) miniature falling-block action and other features for which Freund was noted, the gun was made in extremely limited quantity with a total of but seven or eight at most believed to be the total manufacture. The few known existing specimens fetch from $5,000 to $10,000 depending upon condition and historic association.

HOW MUCH IS IT WORTH?

Arriving at a price is one of the most perplexing situations that the new collector encounters. It does take a little bit of experience to understand how it is done—the complexities of it and very often the inequities as well. Basically, the most important factors in determining value are demand, rarity, and condition—in that order. After nosing around a few gun shows and reading dealers' catalogs, you will get the hang of how things are valued and understand why an item that may have been manufactured in very large quantities can often bring five or ten times the price of a far rarer item of which but a handful were made—a classic, pure example of demand setting the price.

Another rule of thumb and advice that you will hear innumerable times, and that is worth repeating here, is to confine yourself as closely as possible to quality and condition. It is far better to have one good piece than a dozen "dogs." This is one of the toughest points to get across to new collectors, especially if they have the packrat syndrome. Human nature being what it is, the new collector most often commits all the sins he has been warned to avoid. Those bargains are just so damned hard to pass by in the beginning!

A final rule of thumb on bargains is worth bearing in mind if you are new at the game and are attending an auction. Under no circumstances ever bid at any gun auction (or any other for that matter) unless you have closely examined the item at the exhibition preceding the auction. Further, if you are a novice at it and

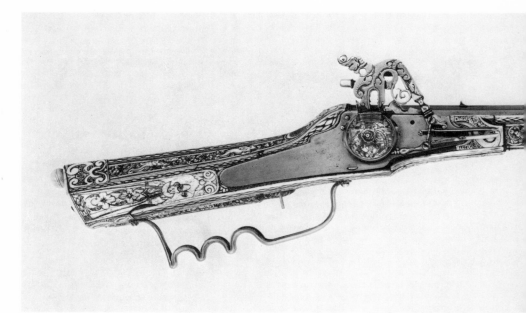

Sixteenth century German wheellock sporting gun. This particular specimen has a part-octagon, part-round smoothbore barrel. A majority of these wheellocks have rifled barrels. Stock inlaid from butt to muzzle with thousands of pieces of ivory and bone in decorative floral and scroll patterns with larger plaques bearing engraved hunting designs. Among the most desirable and certainly handsome of all ancient sporting weapons, these elegantly embellished pieces were made for men of wealth in their day. Great care should be exercised in their purchase as a number of specimens on the market today were made in the nineteenth century for purely decorative purposes; the buyer should be well informed before investing in these pieces. Prices vary greatly depending upon importance of maker, quality of workmanship, and condition. Specimens with only the smallest amount of inlay and decorative work start at about $1,750. Heavily embellished specimens similar to this will start at about $5,000 with no limit for the best. Prices have reached well into the six-figure range in recent years. Photo courtesy of Winchester Gun Museum.

have no idea of values, you have no business bidding at that auction anyway. Be patient and wait until you know more. There will be more guns and more auctions in the future. When you stand toe to toe and slug it out with other bidders—and that is what auctions are all about—you should at the very least know what you are doing.

This seems a good place to insert the classic "Caveat Emptor." It has been the case in just about every field of collecting that as prices have risen, so have the numbers of nefarious individuals who are attracted to that particular field. Fortunately, good guys by far outnumber the bad guys; but forewarned is forearmed. A wonderful and certainly practical book that is most heartily recommended is *How Do You Know It Is Old?*, by

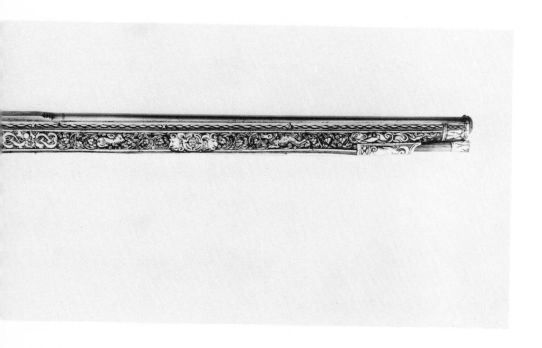

Harold L. Peterson. Just recently issued, it covers a wide range of antique collecting with considerable material on antique arms.

SELLING ITEMS FROM YOUR COLLECTION

As your accumulating activities progress and your collection grows, you will undoubtedly find yourself with pieces that no longer hold an interest for you. A number of methods of selling them are available, depending on the time and effort you wish to spend. You may find that the "book" or advertised price on a specific piece is not always what you can get. In some cases there just might not be any takers at any price. It might very well be that just at this point you get one of your most painful lessons in the fine art of gun trading! But if you have bought wisely, you may well find that a dealer will pay you as high a price as any collector in your area. His own specialized market and access to a national market allows him to know exactly where to place that gun quickly, and in such cases he is willing to pay a premium price for it. He also is usually willing to pay cash immediately for the item; in many private sales you may have to accept trade items in lieu of money.

Should you not realize the price you want through a dealer, you have three other options available. They all take a little time and extra effort, but it might be well spent. The easiest is to take space at a regularly scheduled gun show and display your piece as

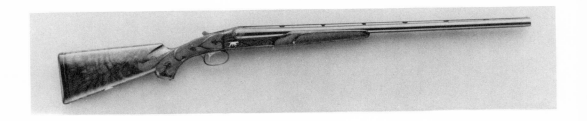

Among the best-known shotguns made by Winchester are the different varieties of the Model 21. The 21 was first announced in the May 8, 1930, price list in Standard Grade with either double or single trigger. A note, however, continued that only Standard-Grade, double-trigger 12-gauge guns were available immediately, with other styles to be delivered as of April 1, 1931. The original price was $59.50. Current prices—for custom-made guns only—begin with $3,500 for the Custom Grade, go to $5,000 for the Pigeon Model, and up to $7,500 for the Grand American. Although made in all gauges, the 410-bore and 28-gauge guns are the rarest and command the highest prices. Moreover, 20's bring better prices than 12's, which are in turn more desirable than 16's. Top: Model 21 Pigeon Model. Bottom: Model 21 Grand American Model.

attractively as possible. You stand a good chance of selling it or trading it, provided, of course, that you have placed a realistic price on it. A second means is by way of auction. There could be both hazard and expense involved, and you should be well aware in advance of the rules of the game. If the auctioneer runs an "open" or "no reserve" auction in which every item must be sold to the high bidder and it happens to be one of those bad days, your piece could be sold for much less than its cost, and on top of that, you have to pay the auctioneer's commission. Should the

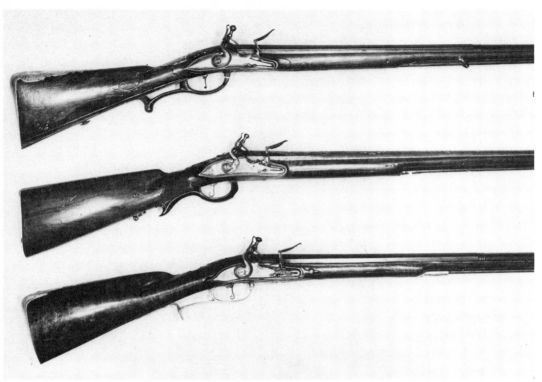

European flintlock fowling pieces of the eighteenth century come in a wide range of values. Top: Austrian full-stock flintlock fowling piece, circa 1750, by noted Austrian maker Marcus Zelmer, Vienna. Displaying the finest in the gunsmith's art, this particular specimen is unusual in being solid-silver-mounted (normally they are found only in brass) and in almost unfired condition as well as bearing the arms of royalty. Its current market value is $3,500 to $4,000. Pieces of lesser quality and distinction, although still displaying fine workmanship, may be found in the $700 to $1,500 range. Middle: Another Austrian full-stock flintlock fowling piece of the mid-eighteenth century, with all-wood trigger guard. It displays the finest talents of an accomplished gunsmith, and in superb almost unfired condition this particular specimen recently sold for $2,500. Pieces of a similar nature although a bit less elegant in quality can still be found in the $500 to $1,000 range. Bottom: Eighteenth-century French gentlemen's flintlock full-stock fowling piece. Displays all the features of the very early eighteenth-century and with exquisitely grained burled wood stock as well as heavy gilt-finished chiseled-brass embellishments. This piece, by Claude Niquet, is valued at $3,500. Its price is determined by its superior quality and its exceptional condition as well as its very handsome embellishments. Similar pieces of this same era more simply fashioned (yet of good quality) showing normal wear and use, and with fittings less elegant, are more often encountered and usually sell in the $600 to $1,200 range.

auction allow you to place a reserve figure on the piece—that is, a price under which they will not sell it—you at least have the opportunity to protect it from being undersold, but usually a commission must still be paid to the auctioneer. This latter method has its strong detractors as well as supporters; probably the key to successful utilization of it is the quality of the other material in the sale and the reputation of the auction house.

The last option, which entails the most time but certainly will reach the widest possible audience, is to advertise your arm in one of the gun-collecting publications. These are widely circulated throughout the United States and abroad, and you certainly stand the very best chance of finding the ultimate specialized collector most actively seeking that particular model. In mail order, however, you must remember there is a considerable time lapse between the placement of your advertisement and its appearance in print—usually a minimum of two months. You must be prepared to service and answer all inquiries, and you must further be prepared after shipping the gun to take it back for full refund (within a reasonable amount of time, of course) if the buyer, after seeing it, does not find it up to his specifications. Not a few well-known dealers in business today started off that way, dabbling in part-time mail order.

There are legal complications in buying and selling firearms of all types, and most especially through the mail. You would do well to familiarize yourself with the Federal Firearms Act of 1968, which regulates interstate trade in firearms. Be certain to familiarize yourself with your own state and local firearms ordinances— they can vary greatly from place to place. Generally speaking, anything made before 1898 is free of regulations under the Federal Firearms Act, but this in itself does not cancel any existing state or local laws that might be in effect in your own area. Read the laws themselves (they are readily available), and then check the finer points with your own local gun clubs.

PROTECTING YOUR COLLECTION

Since the world is filled with scoundrels, rogues, knaves, and scalawags, not to mention thieves, prowlers, and the light-fingered, you would do well to safeguard your valuable collection. The hazard of fire, of course, is ever-present. Quite a few articles have been written on the subject of insurance, and it is well covered in Jim Serven's *The Collecting of Guns* as well as in some of the National Rifle Association publications. Generally speaking, if you have accumulated a good collection, you should not merely have it listed under your home-owners policy, but should have it specially covered under insurance policies known as "fine-arts floaters." Any good insurance agent will be familiar with these policies. A number of attractive plans are offered by some of the larger collecting organizations. The key feature of the fine-arts policy is that each and every item in your collection is itemized and valued and kept on record with the insurance company and agent. When there is a loss, settlements are usually quicker and are usually for the amount on your schedule. Of course, it is necessary to update these schedules as prices rise or as you dispose of or add pieces. Coverage is usually the very broadest and rates the most advantageous.

Appraisals are often important in establishing value. Such valuations are necessary not only for insurance, but for estate and tax plans, gift and damage claims, and other purposes. The validity of appraisals depends on the credentials and background of the appraiser. It is easy to get anybody with the slightest knowledge of guns to write you an evaluation on your pieces or to pull figures out of the air for them; all it takes is a typewriter and some paper. However, remember that those figures are subject to review by quite a few parties who may accept them or reject them. Credibility is the key word here. There are major appraisers' associations throughout the United States, and they will be pleased to give lists of appraisers whose specialty is firearms. A number of the well-known dealers in the field are also quite well qualified and make it a part of their usual business routine to perform such appraisals. Appraisals are best performed by someone who is professionally involved in the field of firearms and whose specialty includes the exact type of firearms you wish to have evaluated. Fees are usually moderate; they are computed according to the quantity and values of the items appraised. ◄

REPRESENTATIVE PRICES OF RIFLES

Maker and model	Current value
Browning	
.22 Auto Grade I	$ 80–110
.22 Auto Grade II	125–150
.22 Auto Grade III	250–350
bolt-action, Safari Grade	300–325
Marlin	
lever-action Models 92, 93, 95	150–400
pump-action Models 18, 20, 25, 27, 29, 38	110–140
lever-action Model 39	175–210
bolt-action Model 100	20–30
Mauser bolt-action rifles	300–500

Maker and model	Current value
Mossberg bolt-action, slide-action, auto	25–65
Remington	
slide-action Models 12, 121, 141	75–175
bolt-action Models 720, 721, 722, 760	125–160
Sako bolt-action rifles	200–300
Savage Model 99 lever-action rifles	100–300
Weatherby bolt-action rifles	175–400
Winchester	
lever-action Model 53,	225–400
lever-action Model 86,	250–750
lever-action Model 94	90–175
lever-action Model 95	225–550
slide-action Model 62	125–200
auto Model 63	150–250
bolt-action Model 70, pre-'64	225–500
bolt-action Model 70, post-'64	125–150
bolt-action Model 43	150–200

REPRESENTATIVE PRICES OF SHOTGUNS

Maker and model	Current value
Baker Batavia	$ 200–350
Beretta Golden Snipe O/U	450
Browning	
Auto-5	200–300
Superposed, Standard Grade	600–700
Superposed, Pigeon Grade	1,000–1,200
Superposed, Diana Grade	1,200–1,400
Superposed, Midas Grade	1,500–2,450
A. H. Fox	
Sterlingworth Grade	200–400
A Grade	400–600
Model B	125–225
H&R single-barrel shotguns	25–35
High Standard pumps and autos	90–145
Hunter Arms double-barreled	200–500
Ithaca	
Field Grade double-barreled	200–325
4E Grade double-barreled	700–800
trap gun, single-barreled, Victory Grade	400–600
pump gun Model 37	75–250

Maker and model	Current value
Iver Johnson double-barreled	150–400
Lefever Nitro Special double-barreled	150–250
Marlin Model 90 O/U	200–350
Mossberg bolt-action	25–50
Parker	
Trojan double-barreled	250–750
VHE double-barreled	800–1,000
DHE double-barreled	1,000–1,700
SC Grade single-barreled trap	900–1,500
SB Grade single-barreled trap	1,600–1,800
Remington	
standard pumps	100–250
auto models	100–250
Model 32 O/U	500–900
Richland S/S and O/U	150–250
L.C. Smith Field Grade double-barreled	175–400
Winchester	
Model 97 pump gun	150–175
Model 12 pump gun, Standard Grade	250–400
Model 42 pump gun, Standard Grade	250–350
Model 21 double-barreled	800–7,500

8

CARTRIDGES, SHOTSHELLS, AND ACCESSORIES

by Charles R. Suydam

The firearms collections of Louis XIV of France and Henry VIII of England may have been the first to achieve high fame, but since their day, the collecting of "guns," even if not of royal quality, has grown rapidly and widely. Few gun collections, however, delve into the whole field of shooting; most contain only the gun itself, and are not concerned with the powder, bullets, bullet molds, and later the cartridges without which the gun is but an unwieldy club.

Perhaps to fill that void, there have risen specialty collections of these related items—which frequently and properly contain none of the guns to which they are related. Most developed, organized, and widespread of these is the collecting of cartridges. Powder flasks and powder horns, singly or together, are another field of specialty, followed at considerable distance by the collecting of bullet molds, loading tools, and other accoutrements relating to shooting.

CARTRIDGES AND SHOTSHELLS

"Cartridge" is a term that describes the union of the components of the firearm that make it shoot: bullet, powder, ignition device (primer), and the metallic case that contains them. In addition, those united components used before the development of the modern metallic are called cartridges: ball and powder in a paper container, from the seventeenth century to about 1865; and the separate-primed foil, skin, paper, or metallic cartridges of the developmental period, 1850–70. While "cartridge" may also describe the same components for the smoothbore shotgun, the approved term for this ammunition is "shotshell"—leaving "cartridge" for rifle and handgun ammunition. Thus cartridge collecting may include wooden or metal "cartouches" of the seventeenth century, paper-wrapped charges from the middle of the eighteenth century through the American Civil War, a wide variety of experimental types of the period 1850–70, paper and metallic shotshells, and the metallic cartridges of war and sport since then. As with firearms, history and the development of the machine age are contained in these small objects.

Cartridges are nearly as ubiquitous as postage stamps and matchbox covers—and as safe, as far as that goes; there is *no* inherent "gunpowder" danger in amassing a collection of sporting rifle, pistol, or shotgun ammunition. Collections vary with the interests and opportunities of the collector. They may be general—as the name implies, a sampling of all types—or specialized: shotshells, "buffalo guns," pinfire, military (both modern and old), auto pistol, and so on. Some collect only one type of cartridge: 9mm Luger, perhaps the most widely made of all centerfire cartridges, or .30-06 USG (one collector has over 1,800 specimens, all different), or .22 rimfire (another collector has nearly 1,500 different *full* boxes).

Shotshells fall into two major categories: metallic shells from the period of the introduction of the breechloader to roughly 1900, and the paper (recently, plastic) shells that essentially replaced the metallic shell (because of lower cost) sometime between 1890 and 1900.

Metallic shells are found in all gauges from 2 to .410 and even in the little .22 rimfire. They are primarily of brass, although early iron cases are known, and there were experiments after World War II in aluminum. Manufacturers' headstamps, case-length variations, and some nickel-plated cases, as well as the experimentals, provide a basis for differentiation in the collection. As in other fields, prices for individual specimens vary from 50 cents to $100 or more.

Paper shells have a long history: the Houiller pinfire cartridge of 1846 and the Pottet centerfire of 1855 both used metallic head and paper case. These and other early experimentals developed into the familiar and typical paper-cased shotshell. They were made in sizes from 1-gauge (for saluting cannon, and perhaps for punt guns) to the tiny 5.5mm rimfire. After World War II, plastic replaced the paper tube as case material because of greater strength and moisture resistance. Shotshell collecting seems centered in the Mississippi River Valley, where a great abundance of small game made shotguns the natural firearm accessory of farm and village home. Prices range from $200–$300 for a rare Peters candy-striped case to 25 cents or less for a common fired case.

Cartridge collectors are well organized: the International Cartridge Collectors Association (USA) has nearly 500 members worldwide, and the European Cartridge Collector's Club is nearly as large. There are a number of state and local collector's groups

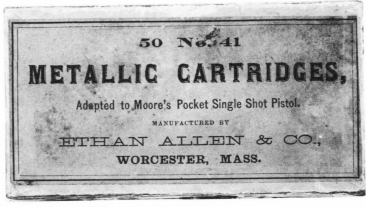

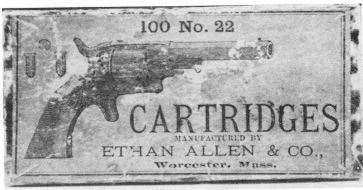

in the United States. The Cartridge Collectors Association meeting held each spring near Chicago has as many as 500 participants and brings collectors from Canada and Europe as well as the United States to its meeting. The state and local groups mentioned above have monthly or quarterly meetings, to which others are invited. Nor is information lacking to assist the cartridge collector: the ICCA and the ECCC put out monthly bulletins, and the ICCA also publishes an annual yearbook. Frank Wheeler, the dean of American cartridge collectors, recently celebrated the twentieth anniversary of his important cartridge column in *The Gun Report* magazine. Nor are book references lacking: the December 1970 ICCA annual was devoted to reference materials: it contained a 14-page annotated bibliography of over 150 sources having material of interest and aid to cartridge collectors. Since then other references have been published. Dealers—there *are* specialists who deal only in collector's cartridges—offer catalogs which have both descriptive material and price ranges.

One of the chief appeals of the cartridge is its relatively low cost in relation to other arms-field collectibles: a large collection can still be formed for less than 50 cents per specimen, and an

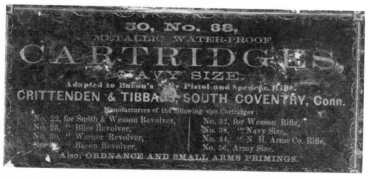

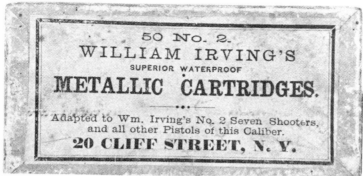

Boxes of cartridges from the early days of their manufacture are rare today and offer one of the more attractive variations of cartridge collecting. Here are rare boxes by Ethan Allen (opposite), and Crittenden & Tibbals and William Irving (above), all made before 1873.

enormous one for less than $1 per specimen. *The Gun Report* magazine publishes a cartridge price list alternately with a gun-price list, in which over 1,600 variations are listed; prices range from 10 cents to $300. A comparison of these lists from their inception in 1965 through the present time will show that cartridges, like other historical items, have been a good financial investment: as interest in cartridge collecting has grown, so has their value.

Another desirable feature of cartridge collecting is that they require relatively little storage space. While display and storage methods vary with the desires of the collector, ranging from shoe boxes to elaborate wall displays, most collectors build or acquire cabinets with shallow drawers having a corrugated bottom, in which the specimens rest securely, yet can be examined and studied easily. Simple sliding bars or a finished wooden panel can conceal the collection. Cartridges are easy to collect, have intrinsic and historic interest, are popular, and have the advantage of requiring relatively little space.

POWDER HORNS AND POWDER FLASKS

From the earliest days of the gun, the admonition "Keep your powder dry" has been of greatest importance, and how to do so

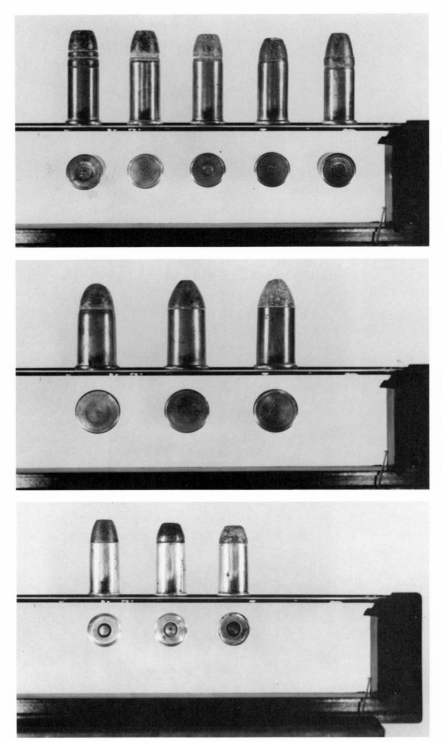

The use of a prismatic reflector makes it possible to record cartridge profiles and headstamps at the same time. Shown are variations of the .44 Henry rimfire (top), the .50 Remington pistol rimfire (center), and unusual variations of the .44 Webley centerfire (bottom) made in the United States.

has been one of the great problems. Containers of leather, wood, lead and other metals, bone, and horn were all used. By the time guns got to the New World, the commonplace cowhorn had become the most universal powder container. From the elaborate and beautiful map horns of the East Coast and Canada to the factory-made horns for the Kentucky rifle to the buffalo horns at the end of the muzzle-loading era, the powder horn accompanied the westward-moving American. There were large horns for military supply, long, winding horns to fit under the arm, small flattened horns to hold fine priming powder (and salt, which must also be kept dry), even crude, unfinished horns that carried grease for the wheels of the Conestoga wagons; the horn was as much a part of the westward movement as it was of the bovine on which it originally grew. Kentucky rifles were possibly the first and most famous of American firearms, hence among the first to be romanticized, studied, and collected, and with them the powder horns that fed them.

Horn is not only waterproof; it is soft and easily marked with a knife or pointed object, and, scraped and polished, it offers an ideal surface upon which an owner may record the important events of his life. Powder horns from the Colonial period through the Civil War are a prime historical record of their time, and are eagerly sought after by persons who may have little other interest in anything to do with firearms. Major museums have collections and exhibitions of horns. One of the major references to fine horns is *American Engraved Powder Horns*, by Stephen V. Grancsay, Curator Emeritus, Department of Arms and Armor, Metropolitan Museum of Art. It is based on horns in the collection of the Metropolitan.

But these early and elaborate—and expensive—horns are not the only ones of interest. One collection includes a small priming horn, crudely engraved with a deer and a bobcat, and with the name David Tripp in two places; a Pennsylvania commercial horn (that is, a horn made in a factory between 1830 and 1860 for sale by gunsmiths and suppliers) with an engraved cabin, trees, and Indian teepee, and marked "John Williams Horn 1835"; and a plain smooth buffalo horn with wooden end plug held in place by wooden pegs. These and many more are typical of those still to be found in antique stores and gun shows across the nation, and at reasonably low prices. But beware of fakes or newly made horns: these are generally easy to spot by color and a "fresh" look, as compared to the dry look of the genuinely old horns.

There is nothing more traditionally American than a Kentucky rifle and its powder horn hanging on the front of a fireplace; lacking the fireplace and the rifle, a couple of old horns can instill the same nostalgia.

Items associated with a percussion "Kentucky" rifle: knife and sheath, rare leather cap holder, box of early English percussion caps, cap horn (or salt or flintlock priming horn), powder measures made from cartridge cases, bullet mold and balls from it. Photo courtesy *Arms Gazette Magazine*.

Powder flasks, metallic rather than horn, were also used early in the history of firearms, but were uncommon until the development of precision metal stamping in about 1830. Then matching sides could be soldered together, and a spring closure attached to the top and carrying rings to the sides—and we have a lightweight, durable, and inexpensive device that can protect powder as well as a horn, and be used with greater convenience. From about 1830 to the end of the muzzle-loading period, flasks of copper, brass, zinc, tin, iron, and silver were made in a dazzling array of sizes, shapes, and styles. While probably the best were made in England and France, the United States was not far behind, and all industrialized nations made them. The *magnum opus* on the subject is Ray Riling's 495-page, quarto-sized work succinctly named *The Powder Flask Book*. While not needed to actually start a collection of flasks, it becomes required reading when the collector becomes a student of them. Sales catalogs of collections—still good reference materials—were produced by F. Theodore Dexter of Topeka, Kansas, in 1947 and by Jackson Arms of Dallas, Texas, about 1962, and may still be found in specialty bookstores.

The value of powder flasks seems to be inversely proportional to their size: the smallest ones, to accompany cased sets of pistols and revolvers, are most desirable, and so are U.S. military ones. Fancy rifle-sized ones are next in value, while the large ones for shotguns, carrying a half-pound or more, are generally less expensive. Again, the buyer is cautioned to beware of fakes—or reproductions—offered as originals. Perhaps without intending to deceive, many of the old flask patterns have been made from original dies and by the original British makers in recent years, to accommodate the growing interest in muzzle-loading shooting. Others have been made in the old patterns, but from new dies. Most can be readily identified by finish or greater weight. As in

Indian trade beads and an engraved powder horn on a bearskin hunting pouch. The horn is a factory horn, engraved by the owner and dated 1836. Beads are late but authentic, as is the pouch.

all collecting, it is a good idea to study many specimens carefully before investing in them, and to get a written guarantee from the seller if a high price is involved.

Somewhat related to powder horns and powder flasks are powder cans—the metallic cans in which powder was supplied to both the shooter of muzzle-loading arms and the reloader of metallic cartridges and paper shells after about 1870. Before that time, black powder was sold in 50-, 25-, and 12½-pound kegs or casks, from which it was distributed by storekeeper, gunsmith, or the leader of a wagon train.

With the coming of the tin can shortly before the Civil War, it became possible to supply powder in 2½-, 1-, or ½-pound cans directly from the powder mills. Painted or printed paper labels on these cans—plus the challenge of finding the rare early ones— makes them an attractive item to accompany a collection of guns, or, as has been the case in several instances, as a collection for the wife of an avid gun collector, so that she may participate in part, at least, in his hobby. Many of the early powders were given fanciful names: Pointer, Pheasant, Grouse, Waidmanns heil, etc., and had appropriate figures on their labels, which add to their rarity and interest today. As in other accessory fields, specimens vary in price from a few dollars to several hundred for a specimen that is early, rare, and in good condition.

BULLET MOLDS, LOADING TOOLS, AND OTHER ACCESSORIES

Even as it was necessary to have a container for the powder of a muzzle-loading gun, so it was necessary to have a mold to make bullets for that gun. "Bullet" means, literally, a small ball, and from the first firearms of the fourteenth century to the middle of the nineteenth, bullet and ball were synonymous. The bore size of smoothbore guns is that of the number of balls per pound of lead: 12 bore = 12 balls to the pound, which have a diameter of about .72 inch. Part of the art of the Kentucky rifle maker was his ability to make a mold of the proper size so that a cloth- or buckskin-wrapped ("patched") ball from it would fit the rifling of the gun he had made. With the development of the science of ballistics between 1830 and 1850, bullets became elongated, cylindro-conoidal in shape, with grooves of varying pattern around the cylindrical part and, frequently, a hollow base that allowed propellant gases to expand that base into the rifling. With the coming of the breech-loading gun and metallic cartridges there came also the realization that a reloadable cartridge was more economical than one that couldn't be reloaded, and so tools were developed to enable the shooter to reload, at home or in the field. Parallel to the development of reloading cartridges for rifle and pistol was that of the metal-based, paper-bodied cartridge ("shell") for smoothbore guns that could also be reloaded.

Both bullet molds and reloading tools offer a collecting field: molds for early round balls, both military and civilian; molds for the early lead bullets of cartridge rifles and pistols in their wide variety of sizes and shapes. Some of the latter were proprietary—"For Sharps rifles" or "For Smith & Wesson .44 American" and made by or for the firms named. Others were made by firms specializing in such items. Reloading tools followed the same paths: special tools by and for Winchester rifles, or Marlin, Remington, Colt, etc., plus those made by such specialty houses as the Bridgeport Gun Implement Company or the Ideal Manufacturing Company. Shotguns had their own accessories: wooden boxes, opening on both sides, for priming and loading; wad cutters, wad funnels, shot drippers or dispensers for powder, bore scrubbers, cleaning rods, shell extractors, and many others. Military gun tools and instruments are another popular area of collecting.

A few collectors have assembled comprehensive groups of this material, but in general it has been neglected and still offers an opportunity for both inexpensive collecting and extensive research. Reference material is primarily found in original and reproduced catalogs, but there are a few monographs, such as *Early Loading Tools and Bullet Molds*, by R. H. Chamberlain, and a few shorter articles included in general arms reference works such as *Gun Digest*, *Guns & Ammo Annual*, and others of that kind.

Military accoutrements—primarily bayonets, but other items as well—offer another collecting interest in the arms field. Civil War material has been well studied and brings relatively

Engraved horns: a small priming horn, c. 1840, with crude deer and the name David Tripp, resting against a calling horn of c. 1835–40, masterfully engraved with Diana and her stag, and a fox hunting scene. Photo by Scott Beinfeld.

high prices, but militaria from the two world wars is still available in quantity and at "war surplus" prices, and offers both a collecting and a studying challenge. Quite a bit of material has been printed on bayonets, but slings, belts, holsters, uniform buttons and insignia, and similar items are relatively untouched and unknown.

To the collector with limited means or limited space, cartridges, powder horns and flasks, loading tools and accessories, and military accouterments offer a challenging field for acquisition and study. ✐

SELECTED BIBLIOGRAPHY

As mentioned in the text, the ICCA listed over 150 sources of information on collectors' cartridges in their 1970 yearbook; anyone making a collection of cartridges should write to A. D. Amesbury, 4065 Montecito Ave, Tucson, Ariz. 85711 to inquire about membership and the availability of back issues of the yearbook. In addition, Frank Wheeler, R.R. 1, Box 30, Osborne, Kan. 67473, publishes a list of cartridge-related books in print, and should be contacted for latest materials available. *The Gun Report*, Box 111, Aledo, Ill. 61231, has the best monthly feature on cartridges in print, and the only current-value list published. In addition, the following books will be of value to the collector.

Amesbury, A. D. *Let's Start a Cartridge Collection*. Printed by the author, 4065 Montecito Ave., Tucson, Ariz. 85711 Introductory monograph.

Barnes, F. C. *Cartridges of the World*. Digest Books, Inc., 1965. A wide-ranging survey of the cartridge field.

Datig, F. A. *Cartridges for Collectors*, Vols. I, II, III. Borden, 1965 et seq. Drawings and data on a wide variety of cartridges.

Erlmeier, H. A., and Brandt, J. K. *Manual of Pistol and Revolver Cartridges*. J. E. Erlmeier Verlag, Wiesbaden, Germany, 1967. Excellent reference with English and German text, good photos.

Lewis, Col. B. R. *Small Arms & Ammunition in the U.S. Service 1776–1865*. Smithsonian Institution, 1956 and reprints. The basic reference on Civil War and pre-Civil War military ammunition.

Logan, H. C. *Cartridges*. Standard Publications, 1948 and reprints. A basic and introductory work of great value.

Steward, Frank. *Shotgun Shells*. B&P Associates, St. Louis Mo., 1969. The only reference on shotshells.

Suydam, C. R. *The American Cartridge*. Borden, 1974 (reprint). The basic reference on rimfires.

White, H. P., and Munhall, B. D. *Cartridge Headstamp Guide*. White Laboratories, 1963 and reprints. A wide review of headstamps, sporting and military.

OTHER FIELDS

Chamberlain, R. H. *Early Loading Tools and Bullet Molds*. Published by the author, Porterville, Cal., 1970. A good but brief introduction to the field.

Gavin, Wm. G. *Accoutrement Plates, North & South, 1861–65*. Riling & Lentz, Philadelphia, 1963. Excellent study of this material.

Grancsay, S. V. *American Engraved Powder Horns*. Ray Riling Arms Books, Inc., 1965. Descriptive list of horns in the collection of the Metropolitan Museum of Art, New York City.

Riling, Ray. *The Powder Flask Book*. Bonanza Books Reprint, 1953. The basic and complete reference on this material.

9

MODERN HANDMADE KNIVES

by Sid Latham

With the renaissance in blademaking now taking place in our country, craftsmen are turning out knives that have not been equaled at any time in history. Today's masters of the benchmade knife are using steels that were unknown to their predecessors a decade ago. These blades are the result of metallurgical research and experimentation, much of it by the craftsmen themselves. Progress has accelerated to the point where improvements evolve in months rather than years. Just six years ago there were fewer than a dozen full-time knifemakers in the country; now there are more than 200.

The turning point in the history of knifemaking began in 1969 when men like Bob Loveless, Dan Dennehy, Lloyd Hale, Bob Dozier, Ted Dowell, Bill Moran, and a small group of other fine craftsmen suddenly received recognition by the sporting press. Their names became household words, at least among sportsmen, and orders suddenly began to cram their mailboxes. The knives were excellent, many crafted of steels that held an edge better than any knife used before, and the workmanship was superb. What had started as an adjunct to the sporting scene soon became a province of the collector as well.

The skill of modern cutlers in bringing together raw materials into a thing of beauty enters into the realm of art. Rod "Caribou" Chappel says, "When a man buys a handmade knife he is also buying something of the immortality of the maker." That there are degrees of immortality, or skill, enters the picture, but, in essence, any man working as an artist, regardless of the medium, is creating his vision of beauty.

Naturally the collector frequently becomes confused by the plethora of knives offered; where to begin, or what to collect, can often become overwhelming problems. Some men collect every-

97

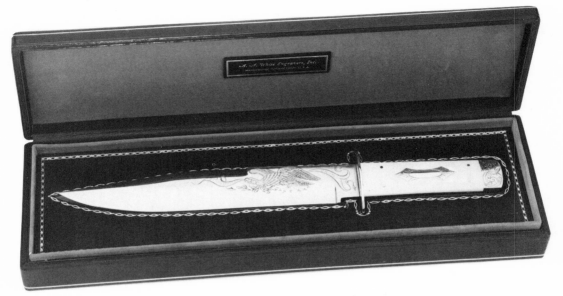

A finely engraved Bowie by A. A. White. This is typical of an expensive collector's knife. It is 14K-gold-mounted with ivory grips and is beautifully engraved. The value is about $1,250.

thing in sight, while others, perhaps more selective, gain some experience before defining their interest. There are, for example, fighting knives, boot knives, Bowies, Arkansas Toothpicks, hunters, skinners, caping knives, fishing knives, replicas of ancient weapons, folders, knives for skin divers—and George Herron even makes a knife for shucking oysters. So it's easily seen there are enough sizes, shapes, and categories for the most ardent collector. Some specialize in the knives of one maker, but with the variation of style, model, blade length, handle material, and examples of all those extras for dressing up a knife it might take a lifetime to gather from a prolific maker like Bo Randall, Jr.

What should the collector seek in a knife? Superb craftsmanship should be the one prime requisite for the acquisition of any benchmade knife. If it's from one of the better-known current makers, fine, but the work of many old-timers, some of whom have passed on in recent years, shouldn't be ignored. Unfortunately, many of these oldsters didn't have the skills or tools of today's craftsmen, but their work is a valuable addition to any collection.

In spite of Bo Randall's popularity—and he is often regarded as the dean of modern American knifemakers—the father of the custom knife was Bill Scagel, who passed away at the age of ninety some fifteen years ago. Scagel began making knives in the mid-1920s and had some pretty revolutionary ideas even in those days. Scagel felt the Bowie style, a large cumbersome knife used by sportsmen of the era, was impractical, and he was right. Scagel came up with the idea of special knives for special needs: skinning, dressing game, and filleting fish. He developed many excellent blades that were practically extensions of the user's fingers. They were graceful, small, and light, and were so popular that sportsmen practically beat a path to his cabin in the Michigan woods. While many regard Bill Scagel as the greatest knifemaker who ever lived, it might be more truthful to record that he was probably the best craftsman of his time. Scagel was an eccentric; he was a recluse who made his own tools, sanding discs, buffing wheels, and the other implements of the craft. He lived with a couple of dogs for company and ran everything off an old gas engine. Scagel knives were not only excellent for their time, but are a scarce item today. Collectors have recently paid as high as $400 for a knife that originally sold for between $20 and $50. Although Scagel lived a long life, and made knives for almost forty years, few of his knives remain today. Bo Randall has a good collection, and a Southern collector has another dozen, but what happened to the vast output is indeed a mystery to collectors. A genuine Scagel is easily identifiable by looking at the blade. A small, curved dagger was his hallmark, stamped on the blade. Frequently he would add his name on the ricasso, but some well-known collectors have his knives and the name isn't always present. The handles are another clue, since most were made of leather washers topped off with a piece of horn or crown stag. Even in those early days Scagel had an eye for the unusual and would occasionally finish off a knife with an anaconda rib or hippo tooth for the handle.

The late Harry Morseth was another pioneer who belongs in the early group of American knifemakers. Although his work was probably finer than that of any of his contemporaries, his knives never reached the values of the old Scagels. The Morseth knives were originally made in Washington state. In those days they sold for around $35 and were bargains. Unfortunately, Morseth tried to maintain that price, even with constantly rising costs, and the company slowly moved toward financial disaster.

His grandson, Steve Morseth, took over, and while he proved to be an excellent craftsman he wasn't able to salvage the company. A. G. Russell, a knife entrepreneur from Springdale, Ark., came along and purchased the failing outfit, moved it to Springdale, and set about to revive the famed Morseth name. The original knives were crafted of an unusual steel and they are made the same way today. It had a Rockwell rating of 63-64 and was a high-carbon Norwegian product laminated between two pieces of ductile iron. Russell explains how to tell an original Morseth. "Hold the knife in the right hand and the name will appear on the right side of the blade. Brusletto, the name of the steel, will be seen on the left side of the blade. Those knives with

A selection of knife types from master craftsman Lloyd Hale. The large Bowie is engraved by Henry Frank with fancy filework on the guard by Hale. The double-edged dagger at right has an ivory grip with buffalo-horn scabbard finished with sterling silver. The hunting knife (left of the Bowie) has an ivory handle, and both boot knives are also finished with ivory. The value of these superb specimens is around $2,000.

the name on the right only were made by Steve Morseth, and the later models, made in Arkansas, have the name on the left." The present production has maintained modest prices, around $50 to $65, with Harry Morseth's early models bringing about $100 to $125 on the collector's market.

The remaining member of the trio, Rudy Ruana of Bonner, Mont., is still pounding steel at the age of seventy and turning out honest knives for the prices he charges. While Ruana's knives never reached the perfection of some other early makers, there is no denying his are among the biggest bargains around and belong in any collection of early modern knives. Ruana forges his knives (he is a fine blacksmith) and practically fills an order by return mail. Even with today's rising prices he still charges between $15 and $20 for a hunting knife and around $70 for a Bowie. Ruana gives excellent value.

Among the modern makers many are excellent craftsmen and there is a long wait for their knives: seven years for a fine Damascus blade from Bill Moran and a couple of years for an intricately engraved folder from Henry Frank. Incidentally, while a fine folder from Frank might set you back over $400, with full engraving and ivory covers (sides), the cost could jump to $750 as soon as you took possession. So it's easy to see fine quality will boost the value of a knife.

The collector should keep an eye out for the maker's marks on the blade. When Bill Moran began making knives he lived in Lime Kiln, Md., and when he moved to Frederick, in the same state, he refused to change his mark so the value wouldn't increase—but it did anyway. On the other hand, Bob Loveless' original shop in Lawndale, Calif., saw the production of many fine knives and were so marked. With the acquisition of a new partner, Loveless moved to nearby Riverside and the mark was changed to read Loveless & Johnson. With young Steve Johnson's injury in an accident a few years ago Bob was left without a partner and soon changed the mark to read "R. W. Loveless, Riverside, Calif.," with a small nude etched under his name. Each change, and each mark, affects the value of a knife, and the Loveless & Johnson models will probably be the highest risers in value due to their limited production. Even early knives from good makers grow in value. When Bob Loveless first got into the business he sold knives to New York's Abercrombie & Fitch under the Delaware Maid mark. Although these first efforts were crude compared to today's perfection, they have taken a considerable jump in value. One knife dealer recently offered a couple for around $450, which is probably a 900 percent increase.

There is little doubt that fine knives will grow in value, but for the newcomer it's safer and more fun to collect for the pleasure knives will bring. Even a noted collector like Phil Lobred of Anchorage, Alaska—certainly out of the mainstream of collecting—has his frustrations. For the past four years Phil has journeyed to Kansas City for the Knifemakers' Guild show, feeling it's one of the few ways he can add knives to his collection. "I want absolute perfection," Phil says, "and I hate waiting years for a knife." His lament is shared by many collectors who become frustrated trying to obtain knives through the mail from the makers. Visiting these knife shows is a good idea, since many new craftsmen display their wares for the first time. A few years ago, Corbet Sigman traveled to Kansas City from Red House, W.Va. (he has since moved to Liberty, W.Va.) and displayed some of the most beautiful knives any newcomer has ever shown. A former chemical technician, Sigman had quickly learned the skills of knifemaking, and the grind of the blade, bevels, and polish were superb. At that 1972 show he had knives that could have been purchased for about $75. Now, with the public's acceptance of his work, his prices have almost doubled. Many collectors who were fortunate (or wise) enough to get an early Sigman knife have frequently been offered double or triple the purchase price.

The same thing happened with a couple of other fairly new makers. Billy Mace Imel and Buster Warenski both shot to the top after their first knife show. Imel, a tool and die maker from Indiana, sold everything he displayed, and even though many thought his prices were high, that didn't deter the public.

Buster Warenski, a quiet cowpoke from Richfield, Utah, is already famed for the spectacular quality of his work. His forte is making replicas of old Bowies, push daggers, and reproductions of early work. His sterling-silver sheaths, and carved ivory grips, many inlaid with silver and gold thread and fancy escutcheons, aren't cheap—$300 to $500—but they will enhance the collection of any serious, and wealthy, collector.

At the 1974 Knifemakers' Guild show, held in Kansas City, one investor was buying fine knives with an eye toward the future. Admitting he knew little about knives (his expertise was in porcelain and antique paperweights), he still felt he couldn't make a mistake with knives from the better makers. Whose knives did he select? Imel, Moran, Warenski, Frank, Hale, and Sigman. In spite of his being a novice, the connoisseur's eye had taken him to the top group of craftsmen.

But there are also top knifemakers who with great talent haven't yet received their share of fame—men like Don Zaccagnino, John Smith, Bob Dozier, and Dan Dennehy. Dennehy provides a good example with a recently completed Bowie. The ivory handle is inlaid with turquoise, the blade fully etched by Shaw-Leibowitz, and the guard and pommel engraved by Angel Garcia

Santa Ana of Yuma, Ariz. The knife is now owned by Craig Fox Huber, a former lawman, who paid a handsome price for the privilege of adding it to his fine collection.

Artful decoration by fine engravers like Ralph Alpen, Winston Churchill, Lynton McKenzie, Alvin White, and Walter Kolouch will add value to any knife. But the novice collector should beware of poor engraving, even on expensive knives. It won't enhance the value and may even reduce it.

Acid etching is one of the more popular techniques used on blades because it may be done before or after heat treatment, and the hardness of the steel doesn't affect the work done. Sherrill Shaw and Leonard Leibowitz are two skilled artists who have brought this ancient skill to a high degree of perfection. They have developed a way of brazing gold, silver, or copper onto the blade to get striking new effects. A new method of miniature paintings on ivory handles, fully protected by space-age epoxy and lacquers, makes an unusual and highly decorative display piece. The Shaw-Leibowitz work is in great demand by knifemakers, and the knife owner may add scenes of historical significance or have a favorite picture reproduced in the most minute detail.

From left to right: Bill Moran's handsome Damascus dagger, selling for $125 per inch; fighting knife from Rod "Caribou" Chappel with acid-etched blade by Shaw-Leibowitz; Ted Dowell Bowie with engraving by Henry Frank; and a small boot knife by Buster Warenski with carved ivory grip and sterling silver sheath inlaid with ivory rose. These knives are fine examples of the knifemaker's art brought to a high degree of perfection. These four would cost better than $3,000.

On the opposite side of the coin, however, are the exceptionally high prices recently asked for some ornately decorated knives. Even a $500 job done by a top artist shouldn't command $300 when it's executed on a $75 knife. There are many who feel such ridiculous prices will drive enthusiasts away. Even knowledgeable collectors are frequently shocked at the asking price of a knife, particularly from unskilled makers. But value has a way of seeking its own level and the less talented eager beavers soon fall along the wayside.

Apart from those unusual or finely decorated knives, there are some blades that aren't available at any price—at least during the lifetime of the present owner. One such knife is the large brass-backed Bowie that Bob Loveless made for himself back in 1957. It has almost a half pound of engraved sterling silver on the hilt and pommel. Bob intended to keep the knife, but weakened in 1959 and sold it for $450. Since that time it has been resold many times at ever higher prices and the present owner, who paid $1,100 and requests anonymity, has refused offers of $2,500. What makes it so valuable? Any Loveless knife will fetch a high price, but one marked "R. W. Loveless—his knife" is bound to command a high figure. It is also believed to be the first Loveless knife to incorporate a sub-hilt as part of its design.

As we said earlier, fine craftsmanship is one criterion for judging a knife. Another is unusual design. A few years ago, Ted Dowell conceived the idea of a knife with an integral hilt, and it was a lovely piece of work. The natural progression, of course,

Dan Dennehy's famous Bowie with blade etched by Shaw-Leibowitz, guard and butt engraved by Angel Garcia Santa Ana, and ivory handle inlaid with turquoise by Dennehy. The knife is now owned by Craig Fox Huber and is not for sale. The value is estimated to be near $1,000.

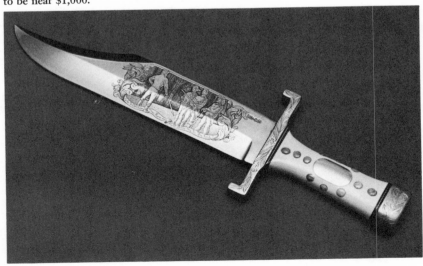

was a later model with integral hilt and butt cap. This knife is one of Dowell's most popular and expensive models. It will cost $250 to add one to your collection. Both hilt and pommel are machined from a 2½-pound block of steel. When the knife is completed, it weighs about 6 ounces. Since Dowell can produce only about ten a month and the work is pretty intricate, it can be easily understood why the wait is long and the price high.

Bargains are rare, and how to judge a knife is just as important as what to buy. There are some guidelines, and these include a thorough inspection of the knife. Turn it over and see if bevels meet on both sides of the blade. Is the solder work clean, without pinholes or excess material? Does the blade have an evenly ground edge, and is the polish excellent, without grind marks showing? All these are important points when judging any knife. In spite of poor work, a rare knife—a Scagel, for example—should be regarded as a find, and the flaws should be balanced against the collector's desire to add the knife to his collection.

Just being around knives (and knifemakers and collectors) will give anyone an opportunity to absorb knowledge, and there will come an instinct for quality work. Reading about knives will give an excellent education about the varied aspects of steels, handle materials, and the makers themselves.

Knife collecting is still in its infancy, so—in addition to the fun of owning fine blades—there's the hope that if the collector buys wisely and well, his collection will grow tremendously in value.

A new collector's item that has proved popular is the folding knife. Folders, or pocketknives if you prefer, have turned many makers exclusively to this new field. Jess Horn, when his replica of the Remington Bullet knife became popular, gave up sheath knives to concentrate on the more intricately crafted folder. Some of Horn's recent innovations are knives designed by Bob Loveless and crafted by Horn. Another superb craftsman is Ron Lake. While Lake makes fine sheath knives, the folder he introduced at the Houston show in 1971 won him the greatest praise. The innovation was a lock-release tab that extended the length of the top and didn't interfere with the smoothly flowing lines of the knife. Also innovative were the inlet sides of brass, inlaid with exotic woods or ivory. The early models could have been purchased for only $75. Now the price has jumped to $185.

Probably the most prized folders of all are those of Henry Frank, a native of Germany, who came to America in 1951 after a four-year apprenticeship as a firearms engraver. Henry began making knives in 1965 and has become the acknowledged leader in his specialty of making and engraving fine folders. Henry Frank does everything, even the heat-treating of the blades, and his knives are truly works of art. His skill with the engraver's tool enables him to do the most minute designs with animal heads and scroll work. Even the nail nick is delicately done. There are seven knives offered, even a tiny two-bladed pen knife with liners of solid gold, mother-of-pearl covers, and gold rivets. The price of this beauty is $465 and it will probably never be used even to trim a quill pen. Fine folders from a master like Henry Frank will undoubtedly be a smart investment for the future and the owner will never tire of admiring it in the meanwhile.

Frequently an expert (and that means anyone who has written more than one article on knives) is asked to name the best knifemakers. Making "best" lists is akin to parachute jumping sans chute and is just as dangerous. But since the newcomer does require some guidance, here is a short list of those highly regarded by their peers. In no particular order it would include Buster Warenski, Lloyd Hale, Ted Dowell, Billy Mace Imel, Bill Moran, Bob Dozier, Don Zaccagnino, Bob Loveless, Rod Chappel, Jess Horn, Ron Lake, Henry Frank, Bob Hayes—and perhaps some unknown maker who may appear by the time this is published.

Remember, if you order a knife from any of these men, or from one of the dozens of other fine makers, don't hold your breath until it's delivered. All have a waiting list of from a couple of months to a few years. However, for the avid can't-wait collector, many knife shops have been opening around the country in the past few years. Knife World in Englewood, Colo., the Knife Shop at El Paso's International Airport, Gillie & Co. in Cos Cob, Conn., and the Ramrod Knife & Gun Shop in New Castle, Ind., are a few of the stores where custom knives are sold along with knife books, sharpening tools, and related items. You may not find exactly what you want, but most shops have at least a hundred knives on show, many from top makers, and the privilege of walking out the door with the knife of your choice should be worth the premium paid.

Once you've gathered a collection (meaning anywhere from a few to a few hundred), consideration should be given to the care of knives. Steel rusts and ivory and buffalo horn are famous for their propensity to crack. A true collector generally won't use a prized knife even to cut a piece of string. There are exceptions, and Alaskan Phil Lobred even takes his best blades on hunting trips, but he has buffing wheels in his garage—and he knows how to use them—and keeps his knives in top shape. Andy Russell, the Arkansas knife expert, says the safest method is to coat the blades with oil, wrap them in waxed paper, and store them in a safe place. While the advice is sound it defeats the purpose of the

Matched pair of Bowie and fighting knives with integral guards created by Ted Dowell. The engraving is by Henry Frank and grips are of coco bolo. The pair are valued at $1,250.

typical collector: to keep his treasures on display where they may be viewed and enjoyed.

Some collectors mount knives on fancy walnut display boards and hang them on the wall. Others use a glass-topped coffee table with a box inset, and place knives inside as part of the room decor. A small amount of silica-gel will help absorb moisture. The greatest danger is storing knives in their leather sheaths. The fumes of tanning acids will eventually ruin any piece of steel. The leather will also collect moisture, and it's just as dangerous as storing a fine gun in a scabbard.

Ivory and horn are fragile materials, prone to tiny hairlines and cracks. While they are beautiful to behold, most knifemakers will warn their customers when these materials are ordered.

The question is always asked, why would anyone want hundreds of knives? The answer is, of course, that beautifully crafted knives are as much works of art as any painting or statuary. They are practical, beautiful, and were one of man's first tools and weapons.

The variations of blade shape, form, and design are practically unlimited. Rare and exotic materials are being introduced that make many knives even more desirable—and expensive. D'Alton Holder, an Arizona craftsman, uses a combination of Baltic amber and elephant ivory for handles. Other makers work in fossil ivory and Alaskan jade and even inlay gold nuggets. Naturally such hard-to-get materials will boost the price—sometimes by hundreds of dollars—but for the ardent collector who seeks the unusual, price seems to be no object.

Collecting knives isn't the exclusive province of men any-

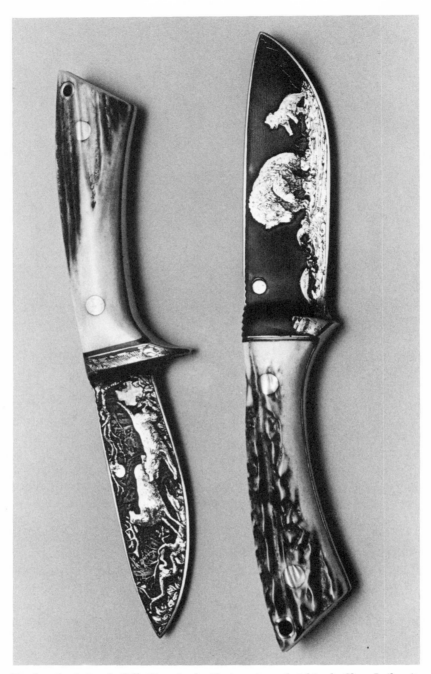

Two hunting knives by Billy Mace Imel with stag grips and etching by Shaw-Leibowitz. The etching is done in three tones and uses gold, silver, and copper. The knife at right, for example, has golden bears, silver moon, and a copper salmon. These are full-tang knives and are the work of a superb craftsman. The value is about $800 each.

more, either. One of the most noted collectors is a pretty lady named Rita Winters. Her husband began collecting in 1968 and Rita thought he was mad when he paid $45 for a Randall knife. But after George gathered about ten knives Rita began to pay attention and confesses, as the need to shine and polish took over, that she began to notice the design and character of each individual piece.

"Workmanship is the most important factor for us," Rita says, "and there are a few knives in our collection I frown on because of sloppy work. If a knifemaker doesn't care enough to clean up the little places he doesn't get my approval." Even George and Rita Winters concede there are almost too many knifemakers and feel it's impossible to get a knife from each. They have hit on a happy solution and now collect only from those who are members of the Knifemakers' Guild. Admitting it may seem snobbish, they have good reasons. Knives are becoming more expensive (they spend about $2,000 a year on their hobby), so they've had to limit themselves. Rita also feels those knifemakers serving a year's probation to enter the Guild put their work and reputations on the line. What direction are these two collectors moving in today? "We both feel the future of knife collecting is toward the more artistic knife. A hunter might acquire several knives in his search for the right blade, but the real collector will be more interested in artistry than utility."

What about faking or reproductions of the modern maker? Although many old knives—Bowies, Case and Remington Bullets—have been faked, it isn't much of a problem in the custom field. If an unknown has the ability to produce a Loveless or Dowell, then he deserves the price paid. Making a fine knife demands too many different skills and too much time for anyone to indulge in forgery; it isn't worth the worry.

Aside from the potential growth in value, the fun of collecting shouldn't be forgotten. Visiting knife shows, talking to fellow collectors, buying and swapping are all part of that fun. There are also unexpected and exciting thrills. They tell the story of a collector who saw a John Owens knife and had to have it. He kept bidding higher and higher and finally offered a Henry Bowie in trade. The fact that both men knew knives, and the Bowie was perhaps worth ten times as much as the Owens knife, made no difference. One man saw a knife he wanted and was willing to give a lot for it.

PRICES

Knives from the more famous makers, although priced high, still run a range of prices enabling most collectors to accommodate their own wallets. Nickel or sterling silver and exotic horns add to the cost.

Rod Chappel. Knives begin around $100 and move upwards for fancy daggers and bowies. Expect to pay about $300 or $400 for the finer work.

Ted Dowell. You can purchase a Dowell knife in the neighborhood of $100 and go upwards to $250 for the intregal hilt-butt knife.

Henry Frank. Around $175 to upwards of $475 for the most intricate engraving plus ivory or horn sides.

Lloyd Hale. Hale practically makes knives by cost. Send $200 and you'll get $200 worth of work. Hale doesn't limit the amount of work done so the sky's the limit. It all depends on what you want to pay.

Four folding knives by master knifemaker Henry Franks. These knives are made and engraved by Franks and all have ivory covers (sides). The small penknife at the bottom has gold bolsters and gold pins. With full engraving, plus ivory as shown, the penknife would be the most expensive, about $500 because of the amount of gold used. The others vary, but run around $400–500 each.

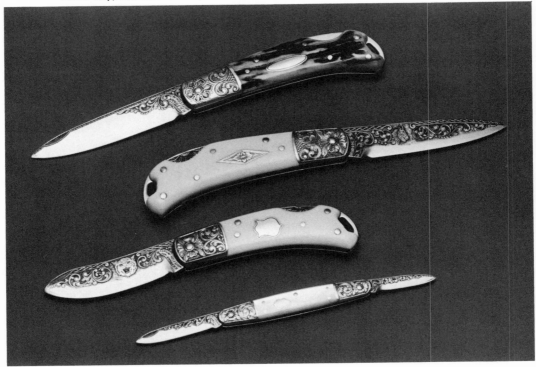

Billy Mace Imel. His prices start where others end. The least expensive knife is $185 and his prices run upward of $1,400.

R. W. Loveless. Loveless is the king and his knives start at $150. Fine-tapered tangs, superb craftsmanship, and beautiful lines. His highly prized boot knife is $275; silver guard and rare wood or ivory will add another $100 or more.

William Moran, Jr. Moran's knives have always been classics to the collector. His famed Damascus knives start at $125 *per inch of blade*. Fancy grips of rare materials plus silver or gold thread inlaid will require you to check your bank account. If you order, there is a seven-year wait.

Many lesser-known but equally superb craftsmen are doing fine work at prices considerably less than the more famous makers. Many of their pieces could well be the sought-after collectors' items of tomorrow:

Dan Dennehy. Famed for his fighting knives during the Vietnam conflict. His lowest knife is $50 and they run a comfortable easy range to upwards of $200.

Bob Dozier. A quality craftsman who does superb work. Bob's knives begin around $85 and for $125 you'll receive a truly excellent knife.

D'Holder. Knives begin at $45 and go to $160 for a Bowie. Exotic materials—amber, ivory, scrimshaw and inlaid turquoise—are his forte. Priced according to materials.

John Owens Jr. Fine well-made sporting knives that begin around $45. Owens rarely goes higher than $75 and uses 440C steel.

John T. Smith. Another excellent maker. His knives begin at $55 for an excellent hunter and run to $175 for the larger Bowies. Fine, clean work with superb bevel lines and excellent polish.

Horace Wiggins. A new maker from Louisiana. Wiggins does simply beautiful work and is the only maker I know to use (at extra cost) abalone shell slabs, sea shell slabs, and a glass-resin-impregnated cactus for handles. His prices begin at $35 and run to $80. His work is really fine and he will be a "hot" maker when his name gets around. ◄

ADDRESSES OF KNIFEMAKERS
MENTIONED

Rod Chappel
Davis Custom Knives
North 1405 Ash
Spokane, Wash. 99201

Dan Dennehy
Box 2F
Del Norte, Colo. 81132

Ted Dowell
139 St. Helens Pl.
Bend, Ore. 97701

Bob Dozier
P.O. Box 58
Palmetto, La. 71358

H. H. Frank
1 Mountain Meadow Rd.
Whitefish, Mont. 59937

Lloyd Hale
609 Henrietta St.
Springdale, Ark. 72764

Bob Hayes
Box 141
Rail Road Flat, Calif. 95248

D'Holder
6808 N. 30th Dr.
Phoenix, Ariz. 85017

Jess Horn
Box 1274
Redding, Calif. 96001

Billy Mace Imel
945 Jamison Court
New Castle, Ind. 47362

Ron Lake
38 Illini Dr.
Taylorville, Ill. 62568

R. W. Loveless
Box 7836, Arlington Sta.
Riverside, Calif. 92503

William Moran, Jr.
Rt. 5
Frederick, Md. 21701

Morseth Knives
1705 Highway 71 No.
Springdale, Ark. 72764

John Owens, Jr.
8755 S.W. 96th St.
Miami, Fla. 33156

Randall Made Knives
Box 1988
Orlando, Fla. 32802

R. H. Ruana
Box 527
Bonner, Mont. 59823

Corbet Sigman
Liberty, W.Va. 25124

John T. Smith
6048 Cedar Crest Dr.
Southhaven, Miss. 38671

Buster Warenski
Box 214
Richfield, Utah 84701

H. L. Wiggins
203 Herndon St.
Mansfield, La. 71052

Don Zaccagnino
Box Zack,
Pahokee, Fla. 33476

KNIFE ETCHERS & ENGRAVERS

Winston C. Churchill
54 High St.
Ludlow, Vt. 05149

Shaw-Leibowitz
Rt. 1, Box 421
New Cumberland, W.Va. 26047

Walter Kolouch
110 Hill St.
New Rochelle, N.Y. 10801

A. A. White Engravers
Box 68
Manchester, Conn. 06040

Lynton McKenzie
New Orleans Arms Co., Inc.
240 Rue Chartres
New Orleans, La. 70130

SELECTED BIBLIOGRAPHY

The American Blade Magazine, 13222 Saticoy Street, No. Hollywood, Calif. 91605.
The Custom Knife. Bates & Schippers.
The Gun Digest Book of Knives, Digest Pub. Co., Northfield, Ill.
Sid Latham. *Knives & Knifemakers*. Winchester Press. N.Y.
Guns & Ammo Guidebook to Knives & Edged Weapons. Petersen Publishing Co., 8490 Sunset Boulevard, Los Angeles, Calif. 90069.
The Knife Digest, A. G. Russell, 1705 Highway 71 No., Springdale, Ark. 72764.

10

ANTIQUE KNIVES

by Harold L. Peterson

Almost from the beginning men have used knives for sport as well as for work and welfare. Sports such as hunting, fishing, sailing, camping, riding, and even knife-throwing in recent years have required a knife as a necessary tool and companion. If one includes whittling and carving as a "sport," the knife is absolutely essential. For most of history, however, the problem has been to distinguish the sporting knife from the weapon or the general-purpose knife. For at least three thousand years there was really no differentiation. A good knife was a good knife, useful for any purpose its owner wished. Thus the collector has a wide-open field. He can collect almost any knife and classify it as at least a part-time sporting knife.

If one goes back to the earliest of the metal knives, he can take as an example a beautiful knife from Mycenae with gold decorations depicting a lion hunt. In the Aachen Cathedral is a scramasax, the utility knife of the northern Europeans, that is known as "Charlemagne's hunting knife." It has a clipped point and is surprisingly similar to the Bowie knife of the nineteenth century, and hunting pictures from the fifteenth century on show later hunters with just such large knives.

TYPES OF SPORTING KNIVES

Perhaps the first specialized hunting knives appeared in the hunting trousses that were especially popular in the sixteenth century. These usually consisted of a series of knives and other tools ranging from large cleavers to small eating knives plus bone saws and other tools for skinning and jointing game. Even royal hunters were supposed to take part in these activities, and there is a woodcut of Queen Elizabeth I of England being handed a knife by her huntsman so that she can take at least the first steps in dressing a stag. In Scotland there was a special series of knives

German knife of the early seventeenth century.

known as gralloch knives for hunting. They looked much like the Scottish dirk but usually had a staghorn handle, and these, with the trousse sets, are among the first precisely identifiable sporting knives, dating mainly from the late eighteenth and early nineteenth centuries.

In America, hunters of the eighteenth century carried a knife that looked much like a butcher's knife. Then, in the 1830s, came the famous Bowie knives. Again, these were all-purpose knives, useful for fighting as well as camping, digging for water, and dressing game. Some are etched with inscriptions such as "For Stags and Buffaloes" and many show hunting dogs in their decoration. After the Civil War the Bowie shape continued in a reduced size and acquired the designation "hunting knife" so that they were essentially a sporting type. Shortly after the beginning of the twentieth century appeared the smaller sheath knives, such as the Marble, with leather grips, base-metal pommel, and 4- or 5-inch blades that became popular with both hunters and Boy Scouts and are now eminently collectible as sporting knives.

Still, these were multipurpose knives. The trend toward real specialization began perhaps shortly after World War I with the work of the fabulous William Scagel. Scagel designed and handmade a whole host of knives intended for specific hunting and fishing uses. Not only were they well shaped for their purposes, they were also beautifully made, and any knife found today that bears his distinctive mark of a curved dagger is a collector's treasure indeed. It was Scagel who inspired W. D. "Bo" Randall of Orlando, Florida, to start making specialized knives, and he has carried the work of his predecessor still further with efficiently designed knives for almost every sporting purpose, including variations for type of animal, for skinning, scaling fish, etc. Since

Scottish gralloch knives of the eighteenth century.

then there have been a host of other knives by skilled craftsmen which are covered in the chapter on modern makers.

In his search for sporting knives, the collector should be certain not to overlook pocketknives. Many early hunters of the eighteenth century used jackknives—and actually a skilled hunter can dress a deer with a very small knife. As early as 1816 the *Explanation or Key to the Various Manufactories of Sheffield* by Joseph Smith illustrated four knives which it identified specifically as "Sportsmen Knives." All had two blades and a corkscrew, but some had a stone hook for removing stones from a horse's hoof, an awl, a saw blade, a fleam for bleeding, and tweezers. They were, in fact, much like the modern utility or Boy Scout knives, a pattern still carried by many sportsmen.

If one includes water sports in his category of knives, the present century has seen the appearance of a number of specialized pocket forms with fish scalers, marlinspikes for sailors, and the like. The variety is almost endless, and so the collector of sporting knives has a wide open field. He can include almost anything that appeals to him.

STARTING A COLLECTION

The beginning collector has no real problem in starting his collection. For the early types he usually must go to established dealers in arms or the major auction galleries of New York and London. There are also clubs and dealers who specialize in knives. So many knives have been made in the last century, however, that there is still the chance to pick up specimens at low prices. Winchester and Remington pocketknives, as well as Bowies and ancient types, command prices in the hundreds of dollars from a knowledgeable source. Late-nineteenth-century hunting knives, pocket utility knives, and Marble sheath knives are well within a moderate budget. And it is surprising how many of these (and some rarer types) turn up in average antique shops, flea markets, and antique shows at prices ranging from $5 to $5,000. They are definitely still available. All the collector has to do is know what he seeks and keep his eyes open. When it comes to selling a collection, however, it is usually best to seek out a

An early Bowie knife with etched blade.

Hunting knife made in the mid-eighteenth century by Will & Finck of San Francisco.

leading dealer specialist. These men have a ready clientele, know what they can get for a given piece, and can therefore afford to pay a better price than the nonspecialist. In obtaining an appraisal the same rule applies. It is the specialist dealer who can best gauge value and whose word will hold most weight. Most of these dealers belong to the American Society of Appraisers or one of the other professional appraising organizations which set standards for competence, fees, and conduct.

As with all other types of collecting, the value of sporting knives is bound to go up. There are a finite number of specimens and an expanding market of collectors. Thus the law of supply and demand is in full play. The last fifteen years have seen the price of many knives increase as much as 1,000 percent, and there is no indication that this trend will cease. If it does, it will indicate that all other prices are coming down too, and so the value increase will undoubtedly remain comparable.

PROTECTING YOUR COLLECTION

Once a collection has been started, there is always the question of how to display and protect it. This depends in large part upon the size of the collection and the space available. Some collectors install glass cases or mount large specimens on the wall. For more compact storage, however, a great majority keep the bulk of their collections in felt-lined drawers. Some cases of drawers can be purchased ready-made, or they can be made to order, usually for less than $100. There are, however, certain precautions that must be taken to protect the knives whether on the wall or in a case of drawers. The iron and steel elements should be covered with a

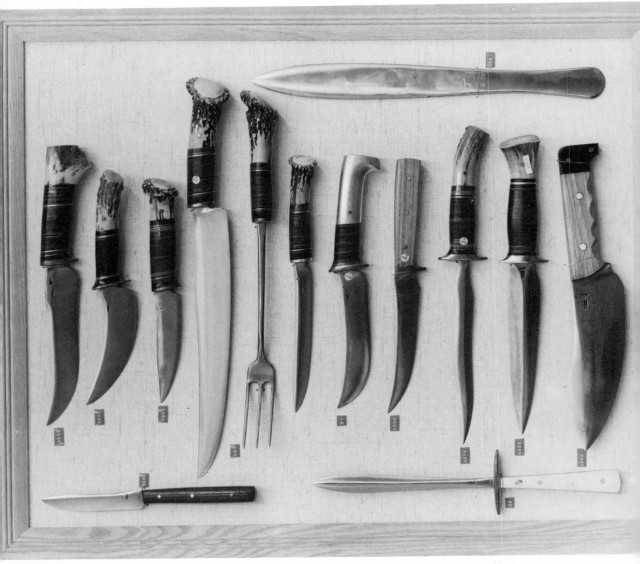

Part of the Scagel collection in the Randall Knife Museum. These specialized knives are certainly antiques, but they represent the beginning of the modern era in sporting knives.

rust preventative. Some collectors prefer a silicon. I like a hard paste wax which does not have to be renewed. From personal experience a good acid-free paste wax applied and allowed to stand twenty minutes before buffing, then followed by a second coat to eliminate skips, will prevent rust for a minimum of twenty years—the longest period I have tested—unless the blades are handled by careless visitors with sweaty hands. It is usually best to take sheath knives out of their scabbards. Some of these leather scabbards have been tanned with acid, and this is always hard on the steel. Even acid-free leather has a tendency to collect and hold moisture in humid climates and this also can be harmful.

There are also other corrosive factors that should be avoided. If you paint the inside of the drawers in which you store knives, use an oil-base or alkyd-base paint. Some of the acrylics will tarnish brass and silver rapidly in a confined atmosphere. So will some pigments such as yellow chromate. Knives with celluloid or some of the early plastic handles should also be separated from the rest of the collection and possibly stored in reasonably airtight containers. These early plastics often release corrosive gases as they decompose.

The need for security, of course, varies with the value of the collection and the area of the country. In high-crime areas, good deadbolt locks on windows and doors plus an alarm system are always advisable for a valuable collection, and publicity should be avoided. Newspaper stories are flattering to the ego, but they are also an invitation to theft. Insurance agents now even advise that specimens illustrated in books should be credited simply as from a "private collection" without giving a name. It is a sad commentary on the times, but these precautions are all becoming more and more necessary. And so is insurance. For the collector a fine-arts floater policy is usually the best. Each piece is listed and appraised with the insurance company agreeing to the values. Such policies, which offer protection against theft and fire, are relatively inexpensive and provide much comfort and peace of mind. Normally they do not protect against damage from rust or from use. They are strictly for the collector, not for the active sportsman, and virtually all of the major insurance companies offer them. ➡

SELECTED BIBLIOGRAPHY

During the last twenty-five years many books have appeared to offer guidance to the collector of sporting knives. Reprints of Sears Roebuck, Montgomery Ward, Remington, and other catalogs of the past illustrate what was offered. The *American Blade* is a current journal on edged weapons of all sorts, and the *Knife Digest* is an annual on the subject. Specific books include:

Robert Abels. *Classic Bowie Knives*. New York, 1967.

Howard L. Blackmore. *Hunting Weapons*. New York, 1971.

Albert N. Hardin, Jr., and Robert W. Heddin. *Light but Efficient: A Study of the M1880 Hunting and M1890 Intrenching Knives and Scabbards*. Pennsauken, N.J., 1973.

J. B. Himsworth. *The Story of Cutlery*. London, 1953.

Harold L. Peterson. *American Knives*. New York, 1958; paperback edition, 1975.

Harold L. Peterson. *A History of Knives*. New York, 1966. For young readers.

Harold L. Peterson. *Daggers and Fighting Knives of the Western World*. London and New York, 1968.

11

SPLIT-CANE RODS

by Len Codella with Ernest Schwiebert

In attempting to treat the subject of collecting split-cane fly rods I have qualified my approach and emphasized those rodmakers whose work is most highly regarded. Integrity of workmanship, rod design, pride of craft, quality of component materials—these are but some of the factors which set off the group of skilled artisans discussed in the following text. These qualities are not limited to the craftsmen of old, but apply equally to some of the contemporary builders.

I have chosen not to treat the split-bamboo rods of makers such as Shakespeare, South Bend, Montague, Dunton, Bristol, Landman, Devine, and Horrocks Ibbotson. Although these makers did build an occasional fine fly rod, the bulk of their work falls into the class of production rods. The techniques of mass production do not lend themselves to building quality equipment, and for the serious collector these rods are not a strong consideration. It must be pointed out, however, that these rods are a part of the overall history of split-bamboo rods and do offer the collector an opportunity to assemble an interesting yet relatively inexpensive rod collection.

All that is needed to get started in collecting rods is interest. From there your pocketbook and degree of interest will determine the direction your collecting will take. There are as many different approaches to collecting as there are rods to collect. For instance, some people collect only production rods because of their relatively low cost and easy availability. These rods can be fun to collect. Another type of collector seeks at least one rod of every maker to fill out his collection. Another might concentrate on a single maker and attempt to build an extensive collection of that maker's rods. It is a democratic process and you are left to your own devices as to how to proceed.

WHERE TO FIND RODS

Finding rods is probably half the fun of collecting. Local garage or tag sales, rummage sales, country auctions, antique shops, country sport shops, and your local sport shop are just some of the places to look for rods. The most reliable sources have proved to be reputable dealers in antique and classic fly tackle. Some rod manufacturers like Thomas & Thomas and Leonard actually publish periodic listings of used equipment for the collector and fisherman.

Len Codella of Thomas & Thomas Rodmakers, Turners Falls, Mass., and Martin Keane of Bridgewater, Conn., were two of the first national dealers in classic tackle, and both are well known for reputable dealings. Rod and tackle lists are available from both for the asking.

On occasion rods turn up through ads in local newspapers, through friends and acquaintances, and at fishing clubs. Sometimes they become available under the most unlikely circumstances. In short, if you are looking for them, you will find them.

Selling or trading rods can be done through some of the same sources as are used to acquire them. Most dealers are interested in acquiring quality rods for resale and will buy them outright, or they may be willing to sell your rods on a consignment basis, charging a nominal percentage of the sales price for this service. When dealing with another collector, you may find a reluctance on his part to pay the current market value for your rod, as all of us have a tendency to buy at bargain prices whenever possible. Often it is better to sell through a dealer, as he usually has a market for what you are selling, and if he is honest will work your deal out based on proper market prices so that you may actually realize more for your equipment than you would have on your own. There are no hard and fast rules for buying or selling used equipment, but in general it pays to know with whom you are doing business.

Consignment sales through dealers, if you are not in a rush for cash, are always a good bet, since you will realize a greater return on your equipment than by selling to the dealer outright. From his standpoint, he will be willing to accept a smaller profit on such sales since he is not required to invest his money in the rod. You get paid when the rod is sold.

PROTECTING YOUR COLLECTION

As your collection grows, you will be faced with the question of insurance against fire, theft, etc. It is wise to speak with your insurance man about a rider on your present policies to cover the value of your collection. The cost of such insurance is quite nominal in comparison to insuring coin or gun collections. A professional appraisal of your collection will be necessary for insurance purposes. Such appraisals should be performed periodically, since your collection will grow and the items in it will appreciate in value. Collection appraisals should be performed by recognized authorities on classic rods and submitted to you in writing. Such documentation, which should be kept in a safe place, is relatively inexpensive and can save you hundreds or even thousands of dollars in the event of loss.

Cane fly rods should be kept in an area where they will not be subject to extremes in temperature or to excessive moisture. A cool, dry place is best. Unless you are planning to display the rods, they should be kept in their cloth bags and aluminum tubes for best protection. The rods in their cases should not be stored horizontally, such as on the top of a closet, as gravitational force can cause them to take a permanent set. The best method I've found for storage is in an absolutely vertical position. In just a few hours, the home handyman can construct a simple storage rack of pine shelving with 2¼-inch holes bored through and spaced as desired. This permits the rod cases to be inserted vertically, and new holes can be added as the collection grows.

The best protection for the rods themselves is paste wax. Your rods should be waxed periodically, using a high-grade paste wax. It is important that there be no abrasives or solvents in the wax; I have found the Butcher brand of furniture wax to be one of the best. Waxing of both impregnated and varnished rods is suggested periodically, as this will not only enhance the appearance of the rods but help to keep the finish from drying and checking in storage.

If you desire to display the rods out of their cases, this is best done in a display cabinet such as is used for gun display. If it has locking doors, so much the better, to avoid damage from careless handling. Again the rods should be set up in a vertical position to avoid the possibility of sets or warping of the sections.

VALUES

Probably the most significant factor in determining the worth of any cane rod is its condition. Rods which are in mint (almost-new) condition are the most desirable and command the highest prices on the classic rod market. For example, there can be as much as $200 difference in the price of two identical-model Payne fly rods, if one is in almost-new condition and the other in excellent average condition. These mint rods are unbelievably scarce; most rods encountered will have been fished and will show varying degrees of wear. This wear factor, along with a number of other criteria, is what determines any cane rod's value. Rods which have tips missing, joints broken short, joints repaired,

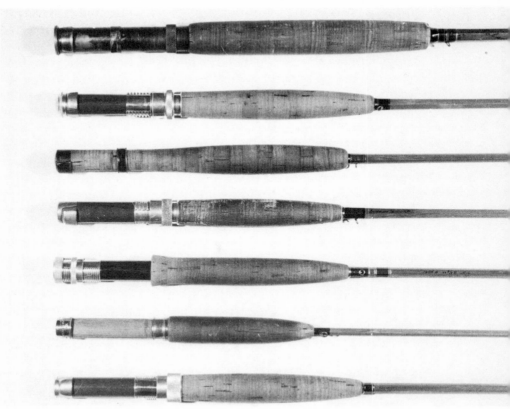

Handle styles. Top to bottom: Heddon salmon rod with blued metal seat and plug for extension; Payne down-locking reel seat with wood filler; Payne all-cork handle with blued ring and cap; Dickerson down-locking reel seat with wood filler; Howells up-locking reel seat with zebrawood filler; Leonard polished metal ring and cap over wood, and Gillum down-locker with wood filler. Photo: Matt Vinciguerra.

joints replaced by other than the original maker, checking varnish, chips or digs into the finish or, worse, into the cane itself, scoring or scratching of the metal parts, guides broken or missing, loose ferrules, etc. are not as desirable, and in some cases may be of no value whatever, depending on their degree of disrepair.

Among collectors, a cane rod that is completely original, with all original wood, wraps, fittings, and finish, is eagerly sought after. Rods that have been altered can sometimes be valueless. Restoration and repair work which does not cosmetically change the appearance of the original rod and which has been done by a recognized rodmaker is quite acceptable. After all, it is unreasonable to expect a fine fly rod not to be used for its intended purpose, and of course, through fishing, guides do wear out and varnish and metalwork does get scratched.

If care is taken to preserve the integrity of the original rod, such refinish work should not alter a quality rod's value in any way. In fact, if the quality of workmanship of the shop doing this work is high enough, this may in some cases add to the value of the rod rather than detract from it.

As interest in fly-fishing has grown, the demand by collectors and fishermen for quality fly rods has increased. As a result, availability of top-quality sticks has dwindled, driving rod prices steadily upward. While no one can predict future values, it seems likely that prices will continue to appreciate. If past increases are any indication of future value, it is interesting to note that in 1971 a sound, used Payne fly rod sold for about $225. That same rod now brings $400 on today's rod market. There is no question that quality fly rods are a sound investment, in addition to being fun to fish with.

THE GREAT AMERICAN MAKERS

Although the history of fly fishing records that Solon Phillippe, Ebeneezer Greene, Charles Murphy, and Hiram Lewis Leonard were this country's pioneers in split-cane rod construction, it is clearly Hiram Leonard who can be considered the father of the modern fly rod. This is demonstrated both in the remarkable skill and technical knowledge his work displayed and in the truly great rodmakers he trained in his shop in Bangor, Maine: men like the Hawes brothers, Edward Payne, Fred Thomas, Fred Devine, Eustis Edwards, Thomas Chubb, and George Varney.

Hiram Lewis Leonard moved his rod plant to Central Valley in 1881 to be nearer to the New York and Philadelphia rod markets and to the controlling interest of the Mills family in New York. By that time he had already developed and patented the modern split-shoulder type of suction ferrule which featured serrations on the bamboo edges and employed a waterproofing disc, silver-soldered in the ferrules to cap the cane and protect it from mold and deterioration.

By 1893 the famed Catskill Series of trout rods had evolved, firmly establishing the basic character of the modern Leonard rod. Skeletal-type reel seats with hardwood fillers, separate German silver butt caps and slide bands, cigar-shaped grips, and full reel seats of ornamentally machined German silver tubing were characteristics of the early Leonard rods and have carried down to the more modern Leonards.

The Catskill Fairy was already on the scene in a 7½-foot rod of three-piece design weighing about 2 ounces. Catskill rods were made in lengths from 7½ to 10 feet in three-piece design with light trout actions.

Under Rueben Leonard the major transition from the earlier

Leonard rod to the more modern version took place. Rueben Leonard pioneered and developed the entire Tournament Series of rods. Initially these Tournament rods were built as 9-footers weighing between 5¼ and 6 ounces. Later the series included 8- to 10½-foot rods, all of three-piece design and ranging in weight from 3¼ to 7½ ounces.

Some of the best-loved Leonard fly rods are classics that were developed under the direction of Rueben Leonard, a noted champion caster. The most popular of these was the Model 50 DF, first introduced in 1915. The rod is an 8-footer of three-piece design weighing about 4 ounces. Many of these rods were fitted with the now classic and very graceful reverse-cigar grips that tapered directly to the hooded nickel-silver butt cap with a sliding ring on the continuous cork handle.

The Leonard shop produced many truly fine classic rods from 1915 to the disastrous fire in the mid-'60s. During the period from before World War II to his retirement in 1965, George Reynolds was instrumental in refining and further honing the already sophisticated Leonard tapers into such classics as the Model 38 ACM (a delicate 7-foot, two-piece rod of 2¼ ounces), the 36L at 6 feet and 1 ounce, the modern 38H at 7 feet and 2¾ ounces, and the 37 ACM at 6 feet and 1½ ounces for #3 line. The 50 DF was well established and was joined by the famous Hunt Pattern, an 8-foot, three-piece counterpart of the 50 DF. The Hunt Pattern was designed by the late Richard Hunt, author of the classic *Salmon in Low Water*. His specifications included a slightly faster action and weight of 4⅝ ounces, and the rod was fitted with oxidized fittings and ferrules against a brown-toned cane, much darker than the traditional Leonard straw color. The wraps were dark brown to offset the medium-brown cane color.

Before the fire, Leonard also made a series of three-piece rods with particularly delicate actions suited to traditional wet-fly work. These ranged from the Model 35 at 7 feet and 2¾ ounces to the Model 46 at 9½ feet and 5½ ounces.

Some of the Leonard rods of two-piece design which became classics after midcentury included the very popular Model 65 at 7½ feet and 3½ ounces, the 8-foot Model 66, and the powerful 67 H at 9 feet and 6 ounces. Most of these rods were fitted with the standard screw-lock seat and are cherished by their owners as fine fishing tools.

Add to these some of the special tapers designed over the years—like the Knight 99, a powerful 9¾-foot rod for #9 line at 7¼ ounces designed by the late John Alden Knight for bass bugging; the Model 38½, a 7½-foot three-piece rod at 3⅝ ounces considered by some owners to be one of Leonard's best; and the countless special-built and custom rods made for exacting customers. The array of fine fishing tools to come out of the Leonard shop is mighty impressive.

For the serious rod collector or collector-fisherman, this is a blessing, as the large number of Leonard rods built over a sixty-year period puts most of the better models out of the "rare" category and into the realm of reality in market value. The current price level on today's market for used Leonard rods ranges to $235, with an occasional model worth up to $275 for such reasons as relative scarcity, fishing worthiness, exceptional condition, or a combination of these factors.

It is important to note that Leonard was one of the few shops to manufacture some fine one-piece rods over the years. Other builders made an occasional one-piece 6-foot rod, but not like the Leonard rods of 7, 8, and 8½ feet. These rods are rare and range in market value to $500 for a mint-condition specimen.

Indeed some men have spent a lifetime collecting only Leonard rods; I know of one such collection that numbers in excess of sixty rods and represents one of the finest samplings in the country of over fifty years of the Leonard tradition. While most collectors turn their efforts into acquiring representative samplings of each of the great rodmakers, it is a very easy matter to become enamored of the rods of one maker and concentrate most of one's efforts on collecting his rods.

Edward Payne and his legacy are a curious note in the history of the split-bamboo rod. Payne's beginning as only the ferrule machinist in the original Leonard shop in Bangor point up the remarkable realization that it was his E. F. Payne Rod Company that ultimately equaled and, according to many disciples, surpassed the work of his original master. There are many who believe that the Payne fly-fishing rods are the ultimate in the rodbuilder's art.

The rods designed and built by Edward Payne at the turn of the century were little different from the rods his son was making sixty years later. There were some minor cosmetic differences, but there were surprisingly few changes in the appearance of the Payne rod in the eighty-year history of the company. When Edward Payne died during World War I, his interest in the company passed to his son, James Payne, who had worked in the shop since boyhood.

The design and workmanship of these rods were so good that the demand for them was never equaled by finished rods. In fact, when Jim Payne passed away in 1970 there was a run on the remaining Payne rods in stock at Abercrombie & Fitch, which drove their prices up so dramatically that two weeks after Jim's death the last rod sold for almost $200 higher than the then market price of $225.

Edward Payne built rods of three-piece design in a limited choice of models ranging from an 8-footer at 3¼ ounces for #4 line to a 10-footer at 6 ounces for #9 line. The line included another 8-footer for #5 line at 3¾ ounces and a light 8½-footer at 4¼ ounces for #6 silk. There were two 9-foot rods—a lightweight 4¼-ounce stick for #6 line and a 4¾-ounce rod for #7 line. Two 9½-foot rods weighing 5¼ and 5¾ ounces taking #7 and #8 lines rounded out the selection. Ed Payne worked with equal relish on rods constructed of both straw-colored cane with natural-finished German-silver ferrules and fittings and in the darker brown-toned cane with oxidized ferrules and fittings.

In the early 1930s Jim Payne dropped the lighter-colored rods in favor of the brown-toned sticks which have become the Payne hallmark. Jim also added smaller rods and offered in three-piece design two 7-footers at 2⅞ and 3⅛ ounces and a pair of 7½-foot rods at 3 and 3¼ ounces in addition to his father's earlier designs. The 10-foot rod had disappeared and was succeeded by a series of rods of two-piece design. These included the rare 6-foot wand of 1½ ounces, a 7-footer of 2¼ ounces, a 7½-footer at 2⅝ ounces, and an 8-footer of 3⅞ ounces. This two-piece line was topped off by an 8½-footer of 4¼ ounces and a 9-footer at 5¼ ounces. By 1939 Payne had stopped building three-piece rods under 7½ feet and was concentrating on rods of two-piece design. The famous Payne screw-locking seat and the four Parabolic designs had now been introduced. There were now fifteen three-piece models from 7½ to 9½ feet, and the two-piece line had expanded. These included a 6-foot rod of 1⅝ ounces, a 7-foot taper of 2¾ ounces, two 7½-foot designs of 3 and 3¼ ounces, three 8-footers ranging from 3½ to 4⅛ ounces, an 8½-foot design which evolved from the butt and tip sections of a 12-foot two-handed Payne salmon rod owned by A. E. Hendrickson, and finally a 9-footer at 5½ ounces.

The Parabolic Payne rods evolved from designs developed in France by Charles Ritz, but it was actually John Alden Knight who worked with Jim Payne to develop the American versions.

These rods were of two-piece design and were fitted with graceful full-cork reel seats to reduce weight. The smallest of the four rods was 7 feet 1 inch in length, weighed 2⅞ ounces, and handled a #3 or #4 silk with equal ease. The 7½-footer weighed 3⅜ ounces and used a #5 line. The 7¾-foot taper was built in two models at 3¾ and 4⅛ ounces and handled #5 and #6 weight lines respectively.

The final Payne catalog, itself a collector's item, lists fourteen fly rods of three-piece design from 7½ to 9½ feet and

Left: Gillum stamp on aluminum band. Photo: Matt Vinciguerra.

Right: Payne pocket cap with marking. Note machining on cap. Photo: Matt Vinciguerra.

fourteen tapers of two-piece design from 6 to 9 feet. It shows a 6½-foot rod at 2¼ ounces not found in earlier catalogs and reduces the Parabolics to only two models at 7 feet 1 inch and 7¾ feet. There are seven dry-fly salmon rods with detachable extension butt. Five of these rods are of three-piece design from 9 to 10½ feet and 6⅝ to 9 ounces and two are two-piece designs at 9 feet and 6 ounces and 9½ feet and 7 ounces. Also listed are four three-piece dry-fly salmon rods with a permanent 2-inch extension butt giving the rods odd finished lengths. There is a 9-foot 2-inch rod at 7⅛ ounces; a 9-foot 5-inch stick at 7½ ounces; a 9-foot 8-inch and a 10-foot 2-inch rod at 7⅝ and 9¼ ounces respectively. Payne salmon rods, those from 9½ to 10½ feet, were made with double-built butt sections for increased strength. The series of two-handed salmon rods listed are of three-piece design and ranged from 10½ to 14 feet in length and from 10½ to 20¼ ounces in weight. These rods were double-built in both the butt and midsections and demonstrated unbelievable power. The catalog shows three bonefish rods with special noncorrosive guides and fittings as well as spinning, bait casting, and four special fly rods. These last four were a 9-foot bass bug rod at 6½ ounces, two streamer rods at 8½ and 9 feet and 5⅝ and 6 ounces, and a Canadian canoe rod at 8½ feet and 5 ounces.

No one knows for certain the total number of rods produced in the Payne shop over the eighty-year history of the company, but they have proved to be relatively scarce in comparison to rods of other makers. I am not certain whether this is due to a low number of rods produced or rather to the fact that they are such fine fishing tools that their owners are always reluctant to sell or trade them. Whatever the reason, the rods are not always easy to come by and they range to $550 on the collector's market for mint, never-fished specimens. Used rods in excellent or better condition range from $300 to $450, depending upon their length, with the shorter rods, 8 feet and under, being the most desirable and therefore higher priced.

There are countless anecdotes about Payne, many touching on his search for perfection or his stubborn honesty and integrity. Even without these reminders of his uncompromising craftsmanship, his rods tell it all.

Eustis Edwards began his rodbuilding career at the Leonard plant in Bangor. He was a cane workman of great skill and performed the bamboo functions in his brief partnership with Fred Thomas and Ed Payne which produced the Kosmic rod, a rare antique rod of considerable value.

Although Eustis Edwards built rods under his own name for a number of years, it was his sons, William and Eugene, who truly blossomed as rodmakers.

Many early Edwards rods were made in volume lots for large companies or sporting-goods stores, like Von Lengerke & Detmoldt, Abercrombie & Fitch, and Abbey & Imbrie. Later in his career he did produce some superbly modern fly rods which exerted considerable influence. He made a run of 7½-foot rods for the Winchester Repeating Arms Co. which were marketed as the Winchester rod and which created quite some stir on the Catskill rivers because of their exceptional actions—the popularity of 7½-footers on American rivers has been largely attributed to Eustis Edwards.

His best rods were a dark, deeply colored bamboo with purple wraps tipped in yellow and were built with a smooth medium action which worked almost to the grip.

I own an 8-foot three-piece rod that began life as a Eustis Edwards made of Calcutta cane. Over the years the mid and tips were replaced as a result of breakage, but always with care to protect the integrity of the original action. After a recent refinish session at Thomas & Thomas, the only part of the rod that remains original is the Edwards Calcutta butt—the mid and tips are of Tonkin cane by Edwards, Heddon, and Thomas & Thomas. The grip and reel seat are Thomas & Thomas, as are the ferrules, but the rod retains its original full working action and is one of my favorite fishing rods.

It was Billy Edwards who broke the mold and developed a unique line of four-strip rods with accompanying special ferrules, grip checks, and reel seat fittings, and his tapers were superb. These rods were built in both two-piece and three-piece designs ranging from 6 to 9½ feet. In two-piece he produced the 6-foot rod for #3 line at 1¾ ounces, a 6½-footer for #3 line at 2⅛ ounces, a 7-foot rod for #4 line at 2⅝ ounces, the 7½-foot design for #4 line at 3⅛ ounces, a 7½-foot rod for #5 at 3⅝ ounces, an 8-footer for #5 line at 4⅛ ounces, and a powerful faster-action 8-foot taper for #6 line at 4⅝ ounces. The three-piece rods included an 8½-foot rod for #4 line at 4⅛ ounces, and a 9-footer at 5¼ ounces and a 9½-footer at 5¾ ounces, both for #7 line. The biggest one he offered was a 9½-foot rod at a full 7 ounces for a #9 line.

Gene Edwards stayed with the standard six-strip rod construction and can be credited with the Special and Deluxe models. These were top-quality sticks that displayed the family resemblance to the work of Edward Payne, Eustis Edwards' colleague. The Edwards Rod Company produced less expensive models such as the Mt. Carmel and the Bristol. These too were well-constructed rods but were usually fitted with less ornate and less costly fittings.

Bill Edwards' quads range to $300 on the current market, with most selling between $150 and $250. The six-sided Deluxe and Special rods are comparably priced, while the originally less expensive rods such as the Bristol and Mt. Carmel bring $125 to $200, depending upon size and condition.

Fred Thomas was the only one of the original group at Leonard to return to Bangor. He started making rods under his name and was unquestionably one of the best who ever split cane.

His rods retained a strong resemblance to the Leonards and were similarly softer-action rods. He worked both in the straw-color cane with bright fittings and in the browntone color of rich chocolate with oxidized fittings. The Thomas grip check and check windings are unique in that the nickel-silver check ring also incorporates the fly-keeper ring. The check windings above the grip were a signature of delicate brown winds in a grouping series of three, seven, three. He used similar wraps at the top guide, which also had a unique German-silver reinforcing tongue under the silk.

His rods fully equaled the work of Hiram and Rueben Leonard and are prized by their owners. Although many of the Maine customers demanded rods to handle huge streamers and heavy tippets, he and his son, Leon, built some of the finest light-action rods that a blank check can buy.

His top-of-the-line rods were the Special and Special Browntone. The second-quality line was the Dirigo, and his least expensive model was the Bangor. The Special and Browntone rods are exquisite, with few rivals. These rods carried the best fittings and employed hardwood spacer reel seats of slide-band and screwlock design. Some of these rods were mounted with all-cork seats reminiscent of the Leonard 50 DF. The Dirigo and Bangor rods were not produced in the browntone color and employed less ornate and expensive fittings.

The Thomas shop worked in rods of three-piece design from 7½ feet to 15-foot two-handed salmon rods. The two-piece designs were built in 7 to 8½ foot lengths. The 8½-foot three-piece rod at 5¼ ounces is one of the finest tapers in its length. There was also an 8-foot three-piece at 4⅛ ounces which fishes a #5 line to perfection. Two of the best 7-foot Thomas rods I've ever seen were a two-piece Special with intermediate winds at 2⅝ ounces for a #4 line. This was a very early Thomas and is now in the collection of Dr. David Sirbasku of Houston, Texas. The other was an exquisite two-piece Browntone Special for a #3 line at 2½ ounces, now owned by actor William Conrad.

Fred Thomas and his son Leon built rods under the Thomas hallmark for over forty years, but after Fred died the company floundered and passed into receivership. Its equipment and designs were subsequently divided between Walt Carpenter and Sam Carlson, who currently own the rights to the Thomas tapers and name.

The Thomas Bangor and Dirigo rods currently range to $200 on today's market with most selling between $125 and $175. The Special rods range to $300 with most in the $200 to $250 range. The Browntone Specials command a bit higher price, ranging to $325 with most in the $250 to $300 bracket, depending upon length and condition.

Thomas & Thomas, not to be confused with the Thomas Rod Company, is a contemporary shop located in Turners Falls, Massachusetts. The name derives from the first names of the two young rodmakers, Thomas Dorsey and Thomas Maxwell, whose work has been compared to that of the bamboo arts' patron saint, Jim Payne. Both of these rodbuilders learned rodmaking in boyhood from Maxwell's grandfather. They had built their first rod at age twelve and continued their rodmaking through their college years. They both were teaching philosophy at the University of Maryland in 1973 when they decided to turn their part-time rodbuilding profession into a full-time labor of love. They bought the rodmaking equipment and a large store of thirty-year-old Tonkin cane from Sewell Dunton, combined their cumulative rodbuilding experience of over forty years, and set out to build the best rod they could.

Both men are dedicated artisans who pursue their craft with

militant fervor. They are determined to preserve the split-cane tradition as handed down by craftsmen such as Leonard, Payne, and Thomas. That kind of almost religious fanaticism has proved quite contagious, as witnessed by their ever-growing circle of converts.

The Thomas & Thomas catalog offers rods in three price ranges with the Caenis and Paradigm Series the most expensive. The Individualist grade also includes the Midge, Hendrickson, and Montana series of rods. The Thomas & Thomas Classic grade offers a less extensive selection of rod actions, lengths, and weights and is the least expensive of the line.

All rods made in the Individualist grade offer traditional swelled butt construction, are made in a large selection of sophisticated tapers, lengths and weights, and can be had in either impregnated or varnished versions. The Classic rods are straight-butt rods of medium action in some twelve models from 7 to 8½ feet. All Thomas & Thomas rods can be had in either two- or three-piece design.

Unique reel-seat designs worked in morticed walnut and cork and special grip designs complement the impressive actions these rods display.

The Thomas & Thomas shop remains as one of the last few that take seriously the custom building and special rod design aspect of rodmaking.

Although the Individualist grade offers over forty different designs in lengths from 6 to 8½ feet for line weights from 2 to 7 as well as a series of Salmon and Steelhead rods, Thomas & Thomas is always behind in back orders for special-built fly rods.

The Caenis Series for #2 lines offers three rods from 6 to 7 feet weighing from 1 to 1⅞ ounces. The #3 rods are built in five models from 6 to 8 feet at weights from 1½ ounces to 3¼ ounces. The Paradigm Series is built on special parabolic tapers designed to fish a long line if necessary and yet protect fine tippets. They are built in sizes that range from 7 to 8 feet at 2⅜ to 3¾ ounces for #4 to #6 lines.

The Midge Series is characterized by fine tip calibrations and fast line speed for tight-looped casting. There are seven models from 6½ to 8 feet at 2½ to 3¾ ounces for #4 to #6 fly lines.

The Hendrickson Series is designed to serve a versatile spectrum of needs using #3 to #6 lines. There are eight models from 6 to 8 feet from 1¾ to 3⅞ ounces.

The Montana Series incorporates a full-loading taper design with a slower casting cycle using line sizes from #4 to #8. The seven models include rods from 6½ to 8½ feet at 2⅛ to 4¾ ounces.

Dickerson signed and numbered his rods just forward of the hook keeper. "R.B." on a Dickerson means it was sold by Ray Bergman, who was a sales agent for Dickerson. Photo: Matt Vinciguerra.

On the used-rod market the Thomas & Thomas Caenis and Paradigm rods range to $325. The Midge, Hendrickson, and Montana rods range to $275 and the Classic rods to $180.

Lyle Dickerson was born and raised in Bellaire, Michigan. During his high-school years he built a few bait rods from such materials as ironwood and white cedar. He completed his degree from Hillsdale College on the eve of World War I and both his fishing and rodmaking were interrupted by service with the fledgling Air Corps in France.

Upon his return to Detroit he found work in truck and real-estate sales. He fished streams like the Mantisee, Au Sable, and Pere Marquette. The Great Depression forced him into handcrafting furniture, where he associated with highly skilled artisans with fierce pride in their work. This contact developed in him a passion for quality which undoubtedly carried over to and influenced his later work.

When he finally decided to build bamboo rods, he found no help either from books or from the craftsmen at Heddon, as their shop was closed to outsiders and the secrets of split-bamboo craftsmanship were closely guarded. He managed to purchase a few culms of cane from Heddon and by dismantling unserviceable rods was able to unravel some of the mysteries of the art. Dickerson then borrowed some fine split-cane rods and calibrated them, attempting to duplicate their tapers with homemade planing blocks and tools. Subsequent fishing on his home rivers resulted in extensive modifications of his designs and ultimately led to the unique performance associated with his rods.

Dickerson's move back to Detroit initiated his professional rodmaking career in the early '30s. Although the quality of his work rapidly became known on Michigan's rivers, there were few buyers of rods even at the modest price of $35, as few anglers could afford that cost.

It was the late Ray Bergman who really launched Dickerson and his reputation for quality. On a fishing trip to Michigan,

Bergman met Dickerson in Detroit. Bergman's favorite rod was a steep-taper tournament-type 7½-foot Leonard which Dickerson calibrated and then offered to match action for action. Bergman was immensely pleased with the new Dickerson and recounted that pleasure in print, giving Dickerson his first taste of national recognition.

I recently acquired a 7½-foot three-piece Dickerson built on the Bergman tapers. The rod is initialed R.B. after the model number above the grip and is in near-mint condition. It weighs 3¾ ounces and handles a #5 line with flawless precision. The rod's action is moderately fast, working fully toward the grip. It is the epitome of the classic dry fly rod and the craftsmanship is exquisite. The rod displays a medium-brown color and is wrapped with chocolate winds tipped black and is fitted with precision oxidized ferrules and a walnut-filled reverse-screw lock seat. Dickerson used extremely large culms of thick-walled cane and transmitted the density of the cane through his steep tapers into remarkably fast actions.

The Dickerson line included seven three-piece rods: a 7½-footer at 3¾ ounces, an 8-foot design at 4¼ ounces, an 8½-foot rod of 4¾ ounces, a pair of 9-footers at 5½ and 6 ounces, and two 9½ footers at 6 and 6½ ounces. Two-piece Dickersons were made in a 7½-footer at 3½ ounces, two 8-foot rods at 4 and 4¼ ounces, an 8½-footer at 4½ ounces, and a 9-foot design at 5½ ounces.

I recently acquired one of Ray Bergman's personal Dickersons which had been custom-built for him. It is a 10-foot, detachable-butt salmon rod at 6¼ ounces for a #7 line. It is fast, powerful, but extremely light in the hand and a valuable collector's rod.

Dickerson's rods are rare and on a par in both performance and craftsmanship with any of the finest. In the supply-demand rod market it is amazing that his rods do not command a higher price, since his total lifetime production was only slightly more than 2,000 rods. In comparison to other rodmakers, Dickerson was not as well known and I am certain that this has much to do with the relatively low prices for his rods. This will undoubtedly change as more people become aware of his work, and this factor alone sets up any Dickerson rod as an excellent investment.

The rods range currently to $350 with most bringing $200 to $300. A rod of special significance as the Bergman rod mentioned earlier would command perhaps $100 over top price. I believe these prices will climb to near double current values in the not too distant future.

The R. L. Winston Rod Company was formed in 1927 by Robert Winther and Lewis Stoner. The name was a contraction of their initials and last names. Although Winther liquidated his interest in 1933, Stoner decided to leave the company name unchanged. W. W. Loskot became a partner at the Winston shop the following year and continued for nearly twenty years until leaving in 1953. Douglas Merrick had come into the Winston Shop in 1945 to buy a new rod and never left. In 1953 Loskot sold his interest to Merrick, and the unique collaboration between Stoner and Merrick was probably the Golden Age at Winston.

Stoner died suddenly in 1957, and Gary Howells, who had been Stoner's protégé for almost ten years, came to work in the shop full-time shortly thereafter. Howells and Merrick made fine fly rods together until the early 1970s, when Gary decided to build his own rods. Merrick recently sold his controlling interest in the Winston shop to Sidney Eliason and Thomas Morgan, but remains firmly in charge of the rodmaking operations there, producing rods with a quality of workmanship that remains unchanged.

The quality of the Winston product is a reflection of the genius of Stoner and the patents for the fluted hollow-built construction he made famous. Even the ferrules on the Winston rods are uniquely Stoner, being made from an alloy of silicone copper and aluminum called duronze. They are lighter and stronger than steel, are corrosion-resistant, and are more costly than nickel silver. Winston ferrules are cut from bar-stock duronze and are individually centered, bored, drilled, reamed, and hand-lapped for a perfect fit. It is tapered to ricepaper thinness at the transition point to the cane, and the cane itself is turned to match the exact internal dimension of the ferrule. It is then driven home over a coat of cement and pinned for permanent security.

The Winston reel seats are unique too. The fillers are turned from a costly high-strength Bakelite which is almost totally free of expansion and corrosion. The fittings are jewel-polished aluminum. The smaller Winston rods are fitted with a slotted cork filler and the grips are the traditional half-Wells style.

The most popular Winston rods in the East are the Leetle Feller series. The tapers are designed for relatively short, delicate casts where accuracy is critical and carry #3 and #4 lines. There are four rods for #3 line: a 5½-footer at 1¾ ounces, a 6-footer at 2 ounces, a 6½-foot rod at 2⅛ ounces, and a delightful 7-footer at 2½ ounces. The 7-foot rod at 2⅝ ounces and 7½-footer at 3⅛ ounces, both for a DT4 line, round out the series.

The Light Trout series handle #4 and #5 lines. These rods too are delicate but demonstrate more muscle than the Leetle Fellers. There is a 5½-foot rod at 2 ounces and a 6-footer at 2¼ ounces, both for DT4 lines. The #5 rods include the 6-footer at 2½ ounces, two 6½-footers at 2½ and 2¾ ounces, two 7-foot rods at 2⅞ and 3 ounces, and a pair of 7½-foot tapers of 3¼ and 3½ ounces.

The Standard Trout rods include an 8-foot design for a #4 line at 3⅝ ounces, and two 8-footers at 3¾ and 4 ounces and an 8½-foot rod at 4⅛ ounces, all for a DT5 line. There are two 8½-foot rods at 4¼ and 4½ ounces for #6 lines and an 8½-foot stick of 4¾ ounces for a #7 line. The two 8¾-foot rods are 4⅝ and 4¾ ounces and take #7 and #8 lines. Classed as steelhead rods, the three 9-foot Winstons of 5, 5¼, and 5½ ounces take #8 and #9 lines. These rods are magnificent performers on our Western steelhead rivers as well as on salmon rivers all over the world.

Winston rods are of two-piece design and range to a high of $225 on the used-rod market for two-tip specimens. The one-tip rods range to $175. Condition is the determining factor, and average or better rods sell for $150 to $200 used with the higher price coming to rods in mint condition.

Some collectors believe that rods built by Stoner in the 1930s and early 1940s are worth a bit more in price than current rods, but I think that a good Winston is a good Winston and the nostalgia bug should be overlooked in this case.

Edwin C. Powell built his first cane rod in California about 1912. By 1922 his shop in Marysville was famous. The rods he constructed prior to 1933 were all of six-strip solid construction. That year he was granted his patent for semi-hollow construction, which launched his construction technique in a new direction. Even before embarking on a full-scale program of semi-hollow construction, the technique Powell used in building standard six-strip rods was rather unusual. Showing signs of Hardy influence, Powell would mill the inner pith from the inside of the rough-cut cane strips until there remained about ⅛ inch of dense outer power fibers. To this inner face he would glue a strip of Port Orford cedar and when the laminated strip was cured would complete the final milling cuts on a machine that he also designed and built. Quite remarkable work and an interesting concept of replacing quite useless pith material with a stronger, although not heavier, material. Powell developed the semi-hollow concept to further reduce the weight of the finished rod. This was accomplished by scalloping 6-inch hollows out of the cedar, thus leaving small solid sections for gluing strength. The result was an extremely lightweight rod of significant power with yet a delicate action for its length. Indeed many of the vintage Powell hollow-built steelhead rods are eagerly sought after by knowledgeable fishermen-collectors for their fine performance on big waters.

Powell rods were glued with animal glues, which made them a bit fragile, and the finely done intermediate winding spaced about 2 inches apart was more than ornamentation. His rods were wrapped in either brown or antique gold and the signature wrap above the grip—which also held the fly keeper—was either all black on his solid built rods or black edged in white on his semi-hollow designs. He used a reverse-screw lock seat of jewel-polished aluminum with a distinctive Bakelite filler, again a result of Hardy's influence. His grips were of full-Wells design and never varied for thirty-odd years.

Most vintage three-piece Powell rods are solid-built, while his two-piece sticks are for the most part semi-hollow-built. Powell worked mainly in longer rods suited to the northern California rivers. His 9½-foot steelhead models weighed 5½ to 6 ounces, the 9-foot rods 4¾ to 5½ ounces, the 8½-foot trout rods 4½ to 5 ounces. He built a few 8-footers at 4 to 4½ ounces and even fewer 7½-footers at 3½ ounces. These last designs are very rare.

Powell rods in mint condition range to $250 on the classic-rod market, with most rods in average condition selling in the $150 to $175 range. The rare 7½-footer would command about $300 in mint condition and about $200 to $225 in average shape.

With Tonkin cane again available, Edwin's son Walton Powell is again building the Powell rod, using his father's patents and tapers. He began as an apprentice in the Marysville shop in 1922 at age seven, and discounting one or two departures from rod-building over the years has almost a half-century of rodbuilding experience.

Gary Howells left after twelve years in the Winston shop in 1970 to build rods under his own signature. He "wanted to build rods with lightness and power of a Winston or Powell—yet with the elegance and grace of a Payne." He has certainly reached his objective. While the Winston influence shows in his work he has made subtle modifications in the tapers, which are uniquely his. The tempering process he used produces a richly toned brown cane color and his butts are hollow built giving lightness to his rods. Howell machines his own ferrules from solid bar stock duronze and hand laps each for final fit.

In all, Howells builds forty standard rod tapers ranging from 6 feet to 9 feet 3 inches and works in two-piece designs only. Gary Howells is a master craftsman who insists on performing every operation himself and is capable of producing about 100 rods a year. As his circle of devotees continues to grow, so does the wait for one of his rods, but it is well worth it.

His rods are priced new in the $250 to $300 range depending on size, style, etc. They are without question modern classics.

Paul Young was a paradox among rodbuilders. Born in 1890 in Arkansas, his background included accomplishments as a commercial fisherman, a taxidermist, tackle salesman, fly-tier, tackle-store owner and finally master rodbuilder. He possessed an intuitive knowledge of actions and rod tapers and began his rodbuilding career by modifying the wet-fly actions then in fashion. By 1927 his first experimental compound tapers had appeared, which twelve years later were labeled "parabolics" when John Alden Knight wrote about these unique actions. Paradoxically, we see Paul Young with beginnings as a set-line catfisherman on the Mississippi becoming the self-taught Stradivari of the semi-parabolic taper—a remarkable accomplishment considering the rodbuilding vacuum (with the exception of Lyle Dickerson) of the Midwest.

Young's first rods were the Special series, which included a 7½-foot taper at 3⅜ ounces, two 8-footers at 4 and 4½ ounces, an 8½-footer at 4¾ ounces, and a 9-foot Special 17 at 5¼ ounces, all of two-piece design. There was also the Special 18, a three-piece rod of 6½ ounces for a #9 line.

Young was an innovator—a creator. He cared little for how his rods looked and was constantly experimenting with new techniques, glues, and finishes. His early rods were worked in natural-color cane, and some show experiments with dark synthetic glues and resins. It was not until near midcentury that Paul more or less standardized the appearance of his rods, using a flame-tempering technique to achieve a darkened, half-carbonized finish. Even then he never stopped trying new things and sought to reduce the power-to-weight ratios in his rods. He went as far as to develop black anodized aluminum ferrules which proved surprisingly good and to employing a unique method of laminating and waterproofing the rod joints.

By midcentury, the now famous Midge rod—a 6¼-foot rod for a #4 line at 1¾ ounces—was on the market. This rod is one of the most sought-after of the Youngs, running second only to the 7½-foot Perfectionist. The Midge has the capability of protecting 5X and 6X tippets and yet delivering the fly at 60 feet with precision.

The Driggs River Special at 2⅞ ounces is a 7-foot 2-inch taper for #5 line with a fast, powerful action.

The Perfectionist is *the* Young rod and the most difficult to obtain of all the Youngs. It is a 7½-foot rod for a #4 line at 2⅝ ounces. It has the ability to cast 80 feet of line *and* protect 7X tippets—indeed a rare combination in any rod.

The Martha Marie was designed and named for Paul's wife, who maintains a cottage on and still fishes the Au Sable in Michigan. It is a strong 7½-foot dry-fly rod at 3 ounces designed for use on larger rivers. It handles a #6 line.

The Parabolic 15 is an 8-foot rod made with separate dry-fly and distance tips. The rod weighs 3¾ ounces with the dry-fly top and handles a #6 line. With the distance tips it weighs 4 ounces and takes a #7 line and larger flies. There was also the K. T. Keller version of the Para 15 with a slow-action butt and a bit more delicacy.

The Parabolic 17 is an 8½-footer at 5⅞ ounces for hair bugs and poppers. The Bobby Doerr was a 9-foot 6-ounce rod for #9 line. The Parabolic 18 at 6½ ounces and 9 feet carries a #9 line, and the Para 19 at 6½ ounces and 9 feet takes a #10. The Powerhouse rounds out the line at 9½ feet for a #11 line.

During his career Young also made a number of special rods and experimental tapers such as the Parabolic 16—a lovely 8½-footer for #7 line.

Of most interest to the collector is a series of six rods Paul built in 1958, two years before his death. He called them the Princess model at 7 feet and 2¾ ounces for a #4 line. These six experimental rods were fitted with a skeletal seat and were wrapped in black silk. They are an example of the restless nature of their maker. During the same production run Young built one 7½-foot Princess for his personal use. It was assembled with a light and heavy top characteristic of the Para 15 rods. Fitted with the light top it does well with 8X tippets and tiny flies. The heavier tip will deliver a streamer with authority at 80 feet. This very special rod is now in the collection of Ernest Schwiebert and is his most cherished fly rod.

Young's son Jack has been carrying on the family business since his father's death in 1960 and continues to manufacture the most popular of the Young rod models with the same eye for quality and workmanship demonstrated by his father.

Although new Young rods are available today at about $250, the rods built by Paul can and do command higher prices in mint condition. The Midge through the Para 15 models range to $350 among collectors, with rods that are in average condition selling at $225 to $250.

The larger models range to $225 in mint condition and about $50 less in average shape.

A mint-condition rod from current production is worth about $200 and will sell for about $160 in average or better condition.

The total lifetime production of rods by Paul Young is

relatively small and this makes the more popular models extremely difficult to acquire.

Because of their rarity, the unique Princess rods are worth about $500 in any reasonable condition and perhaps as much as $200 higher in mint condition.

Harold Steele Gillum began his rodmaking career as an apprentice in the Payne rod shop, having earlier learned how to build split-bamboo rods through his friendship with Eustis Edwards. Gillum's rods bear a strong resemblance to the designs of Jim Payne. His rods have characteristically fast tapers and are basically fast-action fly rods influenced by Edward R. Hewitt's early theories concerning rod actions. Gillum was a moody individual, and his character had a cantankerous side, often triggering quarrels with everyone, even his friends and customers. He was a friend and almost partner of George Halstead, another craftsman of split cane. Gillum's and Halstead's careers were curiously intertwined over the years and business often brought the two together. Their partnership started and failed over ferrules. Halstead had been a machinist at the Leonard shop, where he made reel seats and ferrules. The partnership centered on Halstead making the metal fittings while Gillum made the rod sections. All was go until Halstead was late in delivering the promised metalwork, and the icing on the cake for Gillum was that when they finally arrived they were not even completed. The welts, water stops, plugs, and nickel-silver tubing for the male and female ferrules were all shipped loose and mixed up in the box. Gillum was furious and ended the partnership on the spot.

"Pinky" Gillum never quite standardized his tapers or fittings, building with whatever suited his mood at the moment. His early rods were fitted with ferrules by George Halstead, and after Halstead's death he used the Super-Z ferrule and even some Payne ferrules, finally turning to making his own later on. His cane color varied from medium to dark brown, and after a bad experience with hide-glue adhesives, he turned to using a black epoxy adhesive suggested by Everett Garrison. As on the Garrison rods, the black glue lines are prominent on Gillum's work.

Gillum's total lifetime rod production never exceeded 1,000 rods, making any Gillum a scarce collector's rod. He worked mostly in two-piece design and rods from 7½ to 8½ feet surface occasionally. One of the nicest Gillums I've had in hand was a two-piece 8¼-foot rod at 4¼ ounces for a DT5 line. This rod was fast in action but extraordinarily sensitive and as fine a fishing tool as I've ever seen. It is now in the collection of my good friend Bernie Le Barre of Braintree, Mass. Gillum also made a few three-piece rods in the 8-foot length with most in lengths from 8½ to 9½ feet. Short Gillum rods in lengths to 7 feet are exceedingly rare. I have seen rods at 6 feet, 6¾ feet, and 7 feet, but only a very, very few.

Gillum rods currently range to a high of $800 for the shorter lengths in mint condition. Rods which are in average condition range from $350 to $650 on today's market.

George Halstead had a relatively short rodbuilding career. He lived at Brewster, N.Y., and built a few rods of surprisingly good parabolic action with his own ferrules and fittings. The bamboo workmanship was good; however, Halstead failed to assemble many of his rods with first-rate adhesives. Many of his rods separated along their glue facets, and very few survive today. Halstead died at a relatively young age and his skills as a rod-builder never reached their full potential.

Obviously Halstead's rods are very rare, since few were built and not many have lasted over the years. These rods can be reglued if they delaminate and restored by competent rod shops. Halstead's rods range in price to $450 for a mint-condition specimen, with rods in average condition ranging from $250 to $350.

Everett Garrison was born at Yonkers, N.Y., in 1893. In 1922 he met Dr. George Parker Holden, the famous amateur rodmaker and author of *Idyll of the Split Bamboo*. It was through Holden's influence that Garrison began his long rodbuilding career and launched the most disciplined, painstaking approach to rodmaking in the history of split bamboo. Garrison's background and education in engineering led to his scientific approach to the development of his now famous rod tapers. He also developed his own tools, precision planing forms, and other equipment. His forms used differential set-screws to control the tapers; one full turn opens or closes the forms .008 inch for absolute control.

Garrison built almost every part of each rod himself, including his fittings, rod cases, and even the poplin bags to hold the finished rod safe in the case. His attention to detail even carries over to the assembly of the planed sections. Two tips from the same rod show that the same nodes in each section were adjacent splines in the original culm, a Garrison technique to make both rod tips as identical as possible. His node placement ensures that each node is isolated, with no other nodes in the same area on the rod section. His guides are wound in opposite directions to equalize the twisting forces in the section. The finished Garrison rod has a scarlet tipping on one of the tips, green on the other, to mark it so that the angler can alternate his tips from trip to trip.

Typical Garrisons include a 7-footer at 2¾ ounces for #4

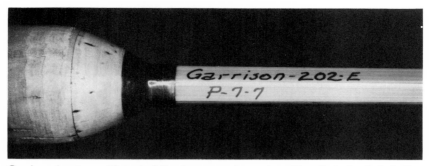

Garrison signature with typical Garrison wrapping on top of handle instead of winding check. Photo: Matt Vinciguerra.

line, a 7¼-footer at 3¼ ounces for #4 line, a 7½- and 7¾-footer at 3½ and 3¾ ounces for #5 line, and an 8-footer at 4 ounces, the last an exceptional all-around rod which helped Garrison make his reputation during the 1930s.

Everett Garrison was a genius at building split-cane rods, and his insistence on building every part himself allowed a lifetime production of only 900 or so rods. His rods were always prized as collector-fishing rods, and since his death in 1975 their price on the collector's market has continued to climb.

Currently Garrison rods are bringing $600 to $800 for rods in average condition. I know of one mint-condition rod selling recently for $1,000, probably some kind of record price for a single cane rod but a fitting tribute to one of the art's greatest builders.

Goodwin Granger developed his talents in isolation in Denver, where he began making fine hand-crafted cane rods after World War I. The Leonard influence is unmistakable in his very first rods. These were of three-piece design, done in straw-color cane with red silk winds and the unmistakable swelled butt. His early handles were copies of the Leonard cigar shape, with a nickel-silver reel seat with fixed reel hood and a sliding band. The quality of workmanship in these few early Grangers is on a par with the work of the master he copies and are highly prized by collectors.

Early on, Granger changed the cosmetic appearance to the more familiar browntoned cane fitted with a full-Wells-style handle with different colored wraps for each of the grades or models he made.

The Granger Champion was one of his first with red wraps tipped in black and was built in lengths from 8 to 9½ feet at weights of 4¼, 4¾, 5½, and 6½ ounces. Of the same design and length was the Goodwin model with jasper winds tipped in yellow. The Special had yellow silk winds and introduced the unique German-silver reverse-screwlock seat which remained a standard of the Granger line. The Special model was the first built in 7½-foot length at 3¾ ounces, and later the Aristocrat model brought in the 7-foot two-piece at 3½ ounces. Early Aristocrat models were wrapped in tan silk tipped dark brown. Later rods in this model were simply wrapped in a medium-brown color but the rod tapers were redesigned and the 7-foot model was changed to a delightful 2¾ ounces for a #4 line.

The Granger Deluxe was a top-of-the-line rod and featured jasper winds tipped yellow and included the full series of designs from 7 feet to 9½ feet.

The Deluxe Registered rods were Goodwin Granger's best and were built only to order. I recently saw one of the Registered models with two different sets of two tips. This 8½-foot classic used a #6 line with the lighter tips and a #7 with the heavier set and showed absolutely no difference in action or casting cycle when switching from one to the other.

The Granger feel is a smooth, full-working medium-fast action which seems to change very little from model to model.

The Goodwin Granger Company was acquired by Wright & McGill after World War II. The rods built under their ownership are among the finest factory production rods ever built. At mid-century their shop foreman was Bill Phillipson, who would later build fine fly rods under his own name.

The six models in production then were the Victory with orange/black variegated winds tipped in black, the Special with lime-green wraps, the Aristocrat with tan-tipped chocolate wraps, the Favorite with jasper winds tipped pale yellow, the Deluxe with black/silver variegated winds tipped yellow, and the Premier model with intricate yellow wrappings.

A small number of Granger Deluxe rods were built after Wright & McGill had abandoned cane for fiberglass. These rods were of two-piece design at 7 and 7½ feet and 3 and 3¼ ounces and used a reverse slide-band seat over a cork filler. The three-piece 8-, 8½-, and 9-footers weighed 3¾, 4½, and 5½ ounces and were fitted with walnut seats with the fixed-butt-cap slide-band arrangement. The handles on these rods were the elliptical full-Wells type later the trademark of Phillipson and were wrapped with deep scarlet winds. In spite of their Granger markings, they are unmistakably early Phillipson products.

The Goodwin Granger rods are rarer than the Wright & McGill Grangers and are considered by many to be the better rods. They range from $85 to $165 on the used-rod market. The Wright & McGill Grangers range from $75 to $140 currently.

Bill Phillipson rods included the Peerless series made with walnut screw-locking seats. There was a 7½-foot 4-ounce rod, an 8-

foot design at 4 ounces, the 8½-footer at 5¼ ounces, and the 9-foot rod at a full 6 ounces. Later these rods were made with full metal reel seats. The Peerless Specials paralleled these rods and were made to accommodate a full line size heavier in each corresponding design.

The Phillipson Pacemakers were moderately priced rods from 7½ feet and 4 ounces to 9 feet and 6 ounces and were fitted with anodized aluminum seats. The rods were wrapped with lime green winds tipped yellow.

Some of Phillipson's finest work came through the Paramount 51 series, which were made with both walnut and metal reel seats. The tapers were more delicate with the 7½-footer at 3½ ounces, the 8-foot rod at 4 ounces, the 8½-footer at 4¾ ounces, and the 9-foot rod at 5½ ounces. These rods were wrapped with jasper winds tipped with yellow and black.

The Preferred rods were of two-piece design made in 7- and 7½-foot lengths at 3¼ ounces and 3¾ ounces. Both rods handled a DT4 line.

Current market value of a sound used Phillipson runs from $75 to $135.

James Heddon & Sons in Dowagiac, Mich., produced over the years some of the finest production-made fly rods this country has seen. Their only rival in terms of quality and workmanship were the factory rods of the Goodwin Granger Company.

There were a number of models produced in a surprising range of quality. The Model 10 was the least expensive with oxidized ferrules, scarlet wraps and a cork filled reel seat. Made in a number of lengths and weights, the 7½-footer at 3½ ounces was the most popular size. As with all Heddon rods, the cane was a rich brown color and the rod displayed the customary swelled-butt construction, perhaps a throwback to the influence of earlier rodbuilders like Leonard and Murphy.

The Heddon Folsom model was a well done two-piece rod in 7- through 8-foot lengths. It was fitted with oxidized ferrules and a walnut-filled screwlock seat. Wrapped in chocolate brown tipped yellow, it looks very similar to the Payne rod. The 7½-foot model weighs 3⅛ ounces with a medium action and takes a #4 line.

The Model 17, Black Beauty, was the most popular of all the Heddon rods as it was a moderately priced rod of superb quality. Offered in lengths from 7½ to 9 feet, this three-piece design was wrapped originally in black silk with a Bakelite screwlock seat, oxidized ferrules, and a half-Wells cork grip. Later the black wraps were tipped in orange, which changed the rod's appearance somewhat. The 8-footer in this model weighs 4 ounces and takes a light DT4 line.

There were several other factory models culminating with the Model 35 Deluxe and the Model 50 Deluxe-President. These two rods were built in lengths from 8 to 9 feet ranging from 3½ to 5½ ounces. They were fitted with black ferrules, a graceful half-Wells grip, screwlock seat with burled walnut filler, and were wrapped with brown winds tipped black. They represent some of the finest factory rods ever made.

One of the finest casting Heddons I've ever seen was a Drueding Special—an 8½ footer at 4⅝ ounces for a #5 line. It was built to tapers designed by Harold Drueding, one of the guiding lights in the rod shop at Dowagiac, and is a superb fly rod.

From the skilled hands of Sam Anson, master rodbuilder at Heddon, came a very few Model 100 rods. These were called the "Rod of Rods" and were hand-worked throughout. They were fitted with gold-lacquered seats with walnut fillers, black precision ferrules, and gold-toned guides and tip-tops. They were the best Heddon had to offer. They sold in the late 1940s for almost four times the price of the Black Beauty at $35 and were made only to special order. They are rare and are exquisite casting instruments.

A mint-condition Heddon of moderate quality is worth about $125 on today's market, with rods in average condition selling for $75 to $100. The Deluxe and Deluxe-President in mint condition sell for up to $200, with most ranging to $135. The Model 100 ranges from $135 to $250 depending on condition.

The South Bend Bait Company acquired the Cross Rod Company after World War I, and for over a decade produced some excellent production rods.

The Cross rods were both single- and double-built in construction; most were double-built. The Cross action was a smooth semi-parabolic, working well down into the grip. The cane color was honey and the winds were a medium tan. The reel seats were full German silver and engraved with a Cross medallion. They were built from 7 to 9 feet in length, and the 8½-foot three-piece model at 5¼ ounces took a surprisingly light #5 line. The famous 7-foot Cross Sylph was a two-piece rod of medium-fast action weighing 3 ounces—a surprisingly light rod, considering its double-built construction.

The most unusual Cross rod I've ever seen was a one-piece 9-footer for a #7 line at 5¼ ounces. It was a rod of unbelievable power with its double-built construction and had the capability of extending a cast beyond the backing knot in the proper hands.

Wes Jordan, Orvis's master rodmaker, was a Cross protégé until Cross died in the 1930s.

After World War II, South Bend continued to make production rods under its own name and also for Shakespeare.

Cross rods on the current market will bring about $150 in mint condition, with rods in average condition ranging between $75 and $100.

Wes Jordan has been synonymous with Orvis Bamboo work for almost 33 years. Jordan was born in 1894 and joined the Cross Rod Company in 1919, forging a considerable reputation as a rodmaker. When Cross died and South Bend absorbed the Cross Company, Jordan went along to supervise the work.

In 1940 he joined the Orvis Company to supervise rodbuilding, where he remained until his retirement a year or so back. In 1941 Wes Jordan designed the screw-locking reel seat with its rich walnut filler which has distinguished the Orvis rods ever since. He and D. C. Corkran, then owner of Orvis, pioneered the techniques of impregnating the bamboo fibers with a resin compound to provide almost maintenance-free blanks. Jordan developed the entire Battenkill series of rods as well as most of Orvis's present battery of rods, including the Midge, Flea, and Nymph rods. The Orvis Deluxe and Superfine rods were built under Jordan's influence, and the Wes Jordan series of Battenkill rods are tapers personally preferred by this master craftsman.

In addition to the Battenkill-grade rods, Orvis also manufactures a less-expensive line called the Madison series. Most of these rods are built with one tip section instead of the customary two tips and are advertised as Battenkill-quality rods except for their coloration.

Used Battenkill rods sell for $125 to $150 on the current market, and used Madisons range to $100. ☙

12

ANTIQUE FISHING REELS

by Warren Shepard

Part of the fun of collecting is attempting to locate underval-
ued specimens—in the lingo of collectors, "sleepers." And
so it is with antique American fishing tackle. At this writing,
I consider antique American reels to be one of the great bargains
in sporting memorabilia. Despite the occasional high prices
quoted for some early fly reels, notably Vom Hofes and Leonards
(which may bring from $75 to $300 each), most of the good
American reels can be found by any diligent collector at exceedingly reasonable prices. Some of the finest American reels, the
Meeks and Talbots, can still be bought for under $100, and
occasionally for much less. I recently bought a collection of J. A.
Coxe billfish reels for $160. These reels were handmade by Coxe
himself at Los Angeles during the early '20s and are extremely
scarce, easily worth many times the price paid. Even the big
dealers offer bargains; during the past year I have purchased from
one of the East Coast dealers no less than three Meisselbach-
Catucci fly reels at $25 each. In 1928, the Meisselbach Reel
Company at Newark split up, most of the group going to Elyria,
Ohio, and a spin-off group, Catucci, remaining in Newark. The
Elyria Meisselbachs are moderately scarce, but the Catucci reels,
which were made only from 1928 to 1931, when Bronson bought
out the company, are really hard to come by. In the future,
Meisselbach collectors will have to pay higher and higher prices
for the Catucci variety.

THE THREE AGES OF FINE REELS

One of the first collectors of American reels was Dr. James
Henshall, author in 1881 of *Book of the Black Bass*. Dr. Henshall
started collecting probably about 1880 and was primarily interested in early Kentucky bait-casting reels. His collection included
Snyders, Milams, and Meeks, as well as most of the other early

reelsmiths along with Phillippes and other historic fly rods. His monograph on early Kentucky reelsmiths, first published in 1904 (second edition: *Book of the Black Bass*, Robert Clarke Co., Cincinnati, 1904) is the only source of this information. What happened to the Henshall collection at this writing is unknown. It was exhibited at the Columbian Exposition in Chicago in 1893, then probably removed to Bozeman, Montana, where Henshall was in charge of the U.S. Fish Hatchery. About 1909, Henshall moved to Mississippi, where he ran the U.S. hatchery for bass. In 1919 an ad appeared in the *American Angler* (Vol. IV, No. 2) offering a catalog of the Henshall collection for sale. Modern reel sleuths must locate copies of this catalog and track down the collection. The last known location of the collection was Cincinnati, Ohio, in 1919.

Another important early collector was William J. Cassard of New York City. His collection supposedly contained hundreds of fine to mint reels, both antique and contemporary. The collection, assembled from 1880 to 1900, also contained cases of flies with historical notations, rods, books, and angling photographs. The Cassard collection, if intact, would be a stupendous find today. Among the good modern collections are those of Brown University (mostly books), the Museum of American Fly Fishing, the Gladding International Sport Fishing Museum, Inc., and the Heddon plug and reel collection.

The scarcest and most desirable items in the angling fields are the very early handcrafted signed rods and reels by the American smiths from 1800 to about 1875. Most highly prized are

Orvis 1874 Patent (left) and H. L. Leonard 1877 Patent fly reels. Two of the scarcer and more sought after reels.

the brass or silver multiplying reels from the Kentucky bluegrass region by such workers as Snyder, Meek, Milam, Sage, Hardman, and Noel; the usually brass double-multiplying New York-style reels by Shipley, Andrew Clerk, Krider and Conroy; and the early split-bamboo rods by Phillippe, Murphy, Leonard, and Mitchell. These items are *very* scarce today; the collector who can find even one specimen is lucky indeed. This early handcrafted period I call the Smith Age after the rod and reelsmiths who worked then; existing specimens from the period are of museum quality.

Tackle from the last quarter of the nineteenth century is much more abundant. Most reels, by 1875, were beginning to be machine-made, and tackle factories were springing up. High quality, however, was maintained. The better reels of the period are made of German silver and usually lathe-made and hand fitted. Better makers of this period include Orvis, Leonard, Meek, Milam, Talbot, Julius Vom Hofe, Thomas Conroy, and others. It was the time of leather reel and rod cases, walnut tackle boxes,

First, second, and third model Meisselbach Expert flyreels (above) and tiny and regular Meisselbach Featherweight fly reels below. Reels date from about 1880 to 1915; "Expert" was a higher grade model.

silver trolling spoons, and hand-forged hooks. The period dates from 1875 to about 1900, and because of the high quality of workmanship I call it the Golden Age of tackle manufacture. The would-be collector of Golden Age reels should enjoy at least some success in locating collectible specimens; however, as noted earlier, prices are already fairly high.

After 1900 the American tackle industry underwent a huge expansion. Much of that growth was tied to the spreading popularity of black bass fishing and the then new method of casting the wood minnow for bass using the short Chicago-style frogging rod and a free-running Kentucky reel. American tackle giants such as Heddon, Hendryx, Horrocks Ibbotson, Pfleuger, Shakespeare, and South Bend expanded and flourished. These companies, and a score of others, made a full range of fly, plug-casting, and saltwater reels. One company, Hendryx of New Haven, boasted a factory turnout of 248 different reel sizes and models; Hendryx reportedly sold 2,000,000 reels in twelve years. Another company, Pfleuger, in 1905 had forty-six different reel models ranging from

Martin (above) and Yawman & Erbe 1889 model, automatic fly reels, shown with Loomis & Plumb ad (inventor of the automatic).

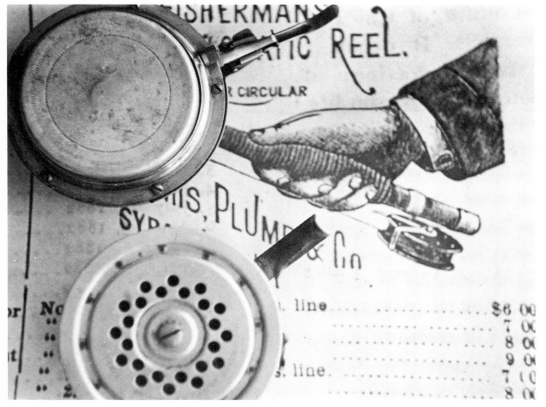

a brass fly reel at $1.47 per dozen to the top-of-the-line "Tuna" model No. 710 at $33.68. The Pfleuger line included special reels for trout fishing, plug casting, tarpon and Atlantic salmon fishing, and tuna and billfish trolling. By 1924, Pfleuger had cut back to thirty models, eliminating many of the cheaper stamped brass reels which were no longer in demand and introducing higher-quality models like the Supreme bait-casting reels at $25 and the Golden West fly reel for $6. The famous Medalist fly reel was introduced a few years later. Tackle from the Expansion Age, as I call it, 1900 to 1930, is, of course, very abundant. And just about all of it is desirable and collectible.

Representative prices for different types of reels from each *age* will be found at the end of this chapter. After 1930, with the exception of a few top-quality handmade reels like the Vom Hofe, Zwarg, Bogdan, and FinNor, reels are merely fishing tools and, as yet, not very collectible.

STARTING A COLLECTION

The best way to get into reel collecting is to make a trip to the family attic. Chances are that some of your ancestors were

Three types of American fly reel: raised-pillar Leonard (left) is Type I, protective-rim and balanced-handle Vom Hofe (center) is Type II, and British-style narrow-spool Abbey & Imbrie (right) is Type III.

fishermen. There may be an old tacklebox at Grandma's containing a few good old reels. Some twenty years ago, I started my collection this rather painless way, inheriting from a grandfather two Meek Kentucky reels; two Heddon's, including a fine Carter's Patent; a scarce and exquisite Nevada Talbot; and half a dozen assorted Meisselbachs, including a fly reel, free-spool Takapart, and a scarce Triton triple multiplier. Additionally, there were some fine rods and a copy of *Book of the Black Bass* dated 1904 wherein the author, Henshall, described the origin of the split-bamboo rod from Phillippe through Orvis, and the history of the bait-casting reel as made by the Kentucky reelsmiths Snyder, Meek, Milam, and Hardman. Handling the old inherited Meek and reading Henshall, I quickly contracted a case of "reel fever," an affliction which no prescription has yet cured. If you can find no angling ancestors hanging from your family tree, check with friends; maybe one of your fishing buddies can find you a discarded old reel or two.

Aside from "freebies" and hand-me-downs, you can always buy for cash. Reels are cheap compared to other collector items. Often $100 will purchase five to ten good specimens from the Expansion Age, or two or three Golden Age reels. But where do

Early American saltwater reels, all made by John Conroy of New York City around 1845 to 1860. Reel in center is presentation-inscribed, dated inside 1855, which is when it was made. All are double multipliers and were used mainly for casting squid for striped bass.

Wire-line trolling reels. These vary from 4 to 10 inches in diameter but all have a narrow spool of about 1 inch. They are single-action, without click. Made mostly from 1910 to 1930, they were used in trolling for salmon or lake trout. May be made of wood, bakelite, or metal. Value $5 to $15.

Variation in the size of antique fly reels, from the small Hendryx (upper left) to the giant Julius Vom Hofe single-action Atlantic-salmon reel (lower right).

you get 'em, you ask? First, there's dealers; there aren't many reel dealers yet, but here are three:

Classic Gun and Reel Co.   Martin Keane's Classic Rods
P. O. Box 1035   Mine Hill Road
Livingston, Mont. 59047   Bridgewater, Conn. 06752

Thomas & Thomas
22 Third St.
Turner's Falls, Mass. 01376

Each of these dealers publishes two or three catalogs a year containing a good listing of antique fishing reels; their prices are relatively high. However, a sample check of all three lists indicates that there are many fine values in quality Expansion Age reels for sale in the $10 to $20 range.

Another way to obtain old reels is to run a classified ad in one of the sporting periodicals or in your local newspaper. Something along the line of:

> WANTED: old fishing reels. Bait-casting, fly reels, and quality saltwater reels. Prefer brass, German-silver or silver-and-black-rubber construction. Premium for reels marked Leonard, Meek, Milam, Mills, Talbot, Heddon, and Vom Hofe. Pay cash. Or trade modern tackle.

Follets Patent, a wire-line trolling reel of rather early vintage. These are scarce, though the similar Billinghursts are scarcer.

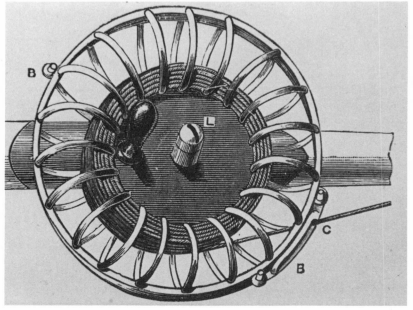

This type of ad may get absolutely no response, in which case you are running it in the wrong periodical; try another publication. Or, if you are lucky, you may get twenty or thirty replies. Of course, a lot of the material offered will be noncollectible junk. Or it may be grossly overpriced. But you can be surprised what will turn up. I got two Smith Age Kentucky reels from such an ad; I had to shuck out $100, but these are two very early J.F. & B.F. Meek reels worth many times what I paid. Another ad produced for $5 a solid-silver John Conroy double multiplier dated inside the headplate 1855 and presentation-inscribed on the outside backplate in fancy script and dated 1869. This 120-year-old fancy American striped-bass reel is one of my greatest prizes. Another ad, in a Montana newspaper, got me a Leonard 1874 patent fly reel in trade for a glass spinning rod.

The values of old reels may be estimated by examining the price guide at the end of this chapter. More precise figures may be obtained by contacting one of the national dealers mentioned earlier. All do appraisal work for estates and for tax and insurance purposes.

CARE OF REELS

Reels can be ruined by amateur reelsmiths. Some of the *don'ts* in attempting to repair old reels are:

1. Never use steel wool or other abrasive to polish an old reel. Soap and hot water works well, and lacquer thinner is permissible to remove caked grease. Brasso or Wright's Silver Cream applied with an old toothbrush or soft cloth, then washed off with warm water, is okay. But if a reel has a nice antique patina on the metal, just oil it and wipe it clean.

2. Don't attempt to straighten bent brass or German-silver parts unless you know how to anneal metal.

3. Never try to take a reel apart without having a set of jeweler's screwdrivers, with a variety of blades which will closely fit each screwhead (Radio Shack, Inc., has a nice set for $2.99).

4. If you do disassemble a reel, make a diagram as you go, and set the screws back into their original slots when you reassemble.

5. Don't spool nylon monofilament onto an antique reel that you might use for occasional fishing. The nylon mono can swell when wet and warp the reel spool or frame.

Reels can nicely be displayed on a mantle, in a shadowbox, or in a glass-faced bookcase for the larger collection. They look great in your office and immediately tell visitors that you are a sportsman and angler. Unlike rods, rifles, prints and paintings, or even antique pistols, a hundred fishing reels can tastefully be displayed in a relatively small area. And don't forget insurance.

A "Smith Age" Kentucky reel dating about 1845, turned out by J. F. & B. F. Meek of Frankfort, Kentucky. Meek later moved to Louisville, where he established a factory and made the famous Bluegrass reels, the finest casting reels that have ever been built. A closeup of the markings on the 1845 Meek shows that even the screw heads are number-matched with their corresponding slots. These early Kentuckys are considered museum-quality.

Make an inventory and file a copy with your insurance agent and another with your bank. Check your homeowner's policy for "antique limitations" and for adequate coverage. If you are not or cannot be adequately covered under your existing policy, change agents, or get special insurance. Unlike bamboo rods, rifles or paintings, though, reels can survive a fire, often without serious damage. And what burgler is going to be crazy enough to cart off a bunch of old fishing reels? ✑

SELECTED BIBLIOGRAPHY

Brooks, Lake. *The Science of Fishing*. A. R. Harding, St. Louis, 1912. Contains illustrations of early reels, pp. 38–50.

Henshall, James A. *Book of the Black Bass*. Robert Clarke Co. or Stewart Kidd Co., Cincinnati, 1904, and later editions. See chapter on reels.

Henshall, James A. *More About the Black Bass*. Robert Clarke Co., Cincinnati, 1899. Very scarce; contains excellent illustrations and descriptions of early reels.

Keene, J. Harrington. *Fishing Tackle*. Ward, Lock & Co., New York and London, 1886. See pp. 58–70.

McClane, A. J. *McClane's New Standard Fishing Encyclopedia*. Holt, Rinehart & Winston, New York, 1974. Contains a history of the Kentucky reel, mostly taken from Henshall.

McClane, A. J. *The Wise Fisherman's Encyclopedia*. Wm. H. Wise, New York, 1953. See pp. 908–16.

Waterman, Charles F. *History of Fishing in America*. Ridge Press, New York, 1975.

Wells, Henry P. *Fly-Rods and Fly Tackle*. Harper, New York, 1885. On construction; see pp. 90–99.

REPRESENTATIVE VALUES OF COLLECTORS' REELS

Maker	Type	Description	Material	Date	Value
Geo. Snyder	casting	1⅜ × 1⅞ quad. multiplying	brass	1820	$400–600
J. F. & B. F. Meek	casting	1½ × 1½ Kentucky	brass	1845	400–500
Meek & Milam	casting	1¾ × 1⁵⁄₁₆ Kentucky	brass	1855	500
J. L. Sage	fly	click fly reel, engraved	pure silver	1848	750
Conroy Makers	saltwater	3″ × 2⅜″ striped bass	brass	1845	350
B. C. Milam	casting	short handle Kentucky mkd. Frankfort	brass	1865	350–450
H. L. Leonard	fly	2½ × 1″ bronze 1877 Patent	bronze & silver	1877	400–500
C. F. Orvis	fly	3 × ¾″ 1874 Patent in script	pure silver	1874	400
C. F. Orvis	fly	3 × 1″ 1874 Patent, stamped	nickel plate	1890	150–200
Wm. Billinghurst	fly	birdcage fly or trolling reel	nickel plate	1869	150–200
Conroy, Bissett & Malleson	saltwater	3½″ saltwater double multiplier	Germ. silver	1879	200
A. B. Shipley	casting	mkd. Shipley, Phila.	brass	1885	150–200
J. Vom Hofe	fly	small size mkd. Brooklyn	nickel & rubber	1890	100–150
E. Vom Hofe	fly	small size mkd. New York	nickel & rubber	1900	85–100
Wm. Mills	fly	small size mkd. Mills Pat.	nickel & rubber	1895	85–100
Yawman & Erbe	fly	automatic, no key—1889 model	aluminum	1889	85–125
Yawman & Erbe	fly	automatic, w/key wind, 1899 model	aluminum	1899	35–60
Hendryx	fly	1½″ small click reel, var. patents	brass	1890	10
Meisselbach	fly	Expert, 2nd model, 3″ diam.	nickel plate	1889	60
Meisselbach	fly	Featherweight model, 3″	nickel plate	1895	40
Pfleuger	trolling	Captain wire line S.A. reel, 5″	Germ. silver	1890	25
Milam	casting	mkd. The Frankfort Kentucky No. 1	silver	1898	100–200
Meek	casting	mkd. Bluegrass, Louisville No. 3	silver	1900	65–100
Meek, B. F. & Son	casting	finest quality, knurled rims No. 3	silver	1895	100–150
Wm. Talbot	casting	finest quality mkd. Nevada, Mo.	silver	1895	150–250
Meek & Sons	casting	"Bluegrass" No. 3	silver	1910	65–100
Meek	casting	mkd. Horton Mfg. Co.	silver	1930	100–125
Meek	casting	mkd. Simplex & Horton, takedown	silver	1925	75–100
Talbot	casting	Kansas City, Mo.	silver	1920	65–90
Hendryx	fly	nickel-plate click reel	nickel	1910	5

Maker	Type	Description	Material	Date	Value
Meisselbach	casting	"Takapart"	nickel	1915	30–40
Meisselbach	casting	"Takapart" free spool	nickel	1920	35–50
Meisselbach-Cattuci	fly	3″ size mkd. Symploreel	bakelite	1928	75
Meisselbach	trolling	6″ size "Good Luck" wood spool	wood	1910	15–20
Meisselbach	fly	mkd. Rainbow 3″ × 1″	aluminum	1925	50
Meisselbach	S.W.	mkd. Triton triple mult.	bakelite	1920	75–100
Leonard	fly	#48M salmon reel	silver	1925	225
Heddon	casting	#3–15, Dowagiac, Mich.	silver	1925	40–65
Pfleuger	fly	"Golden West" model	black rubber	1905	75–100
Pfleuger	fly	"Four Bros—Delite" small	black rubber	1910	35–45
Pfleuger	trolling	"Taxie" 5″ × 1″ S.A. reel	brass	1915	20
Pfleuger	casting	"Supreme" early model	silver	1920	40
Pfleuger	casting	mkd. Atlas-Portage	brass	1910	15
Pfleuger	casting	"Summit" w/level wind	brass	1930	10–15
J. Vom Hofe	S.W.	"B'Ocean" billfish reel	black rubber	1918	125–200
E. Vom Hofe	fly	small, raised pillar click	black rubber	1925	75–100
E. Vom Hofe	fly	4/0 salmon reel, double mult.	black rubber	1910	150–200
Otto Zwarg	S.W.	4/0 marlin reel	black rubber	1950	150–200
Pennell	casting	Kentucky style, no level wind	nickel plate	1920	25
Union Hardware	fly	"Sunnybrook" 2½″ × 1″	nickel plate	1920	20
South Bend	fly	"Oreno" #1100A	aluminum	1940	25
Shakespeare	casting	"President" model	plastic	1940	25–35
J. A. Coxe	casting	Model 25C	aluminum	1940	75–100

13

FISHING FLIES

by Theodore A. Niemeyer

U nlike the fine collections of guns, books, rods, reels, and sporting art, the search for historic and important fishing flies has been undertaken by only a handful of collectors whose backgrounds are as diverse as anyone could imagine. They are not, as one might suspect, all fly-tiers bent on studying the styles, patterns, and techniques of others.

The finest and most extensive collections in existence today are those located in museums, private fishing clubs, and fly-tying authors' dens.

A substantial amount of material is available if one has the intensity and persistence to plan a simple approach to collecting and is willing to invest a small amount of money and a lot of time in achieving his goal.

Unless you are blessed with a substantial bank account I would direct your search for old and historic flies to those of North American origin. That is not to say that the beautiful flies of Halford, Lunn, Baigent, Pryce-Tannant, etc. do not exist. They do exist; however, they are in the possession of collectors who guard them well, and it would take a lot of money to obtain them. For these and other reasons I place particular attention on the North American market. The history and intrigue of fly patterns tied by the likes of Gordon, Hewitt, Cross, Martinez, etc. can be a challenge of sufficient proportions to test the most ambitious collectors.

Before you attempt to put together a collection, I suggest you consult some of the excellent reference books dealing with fly-tiers and their fly patterns. You will find that only a small number of good-quality colored photographs are available in these books. To guide you in your search, it is best to study the fly-tiers' work firsthand. This means locating a collection and spending a substantial amount of time studying.

The collector has a great variety of types and styles of flies to choose from. I suggest you start out by concentrating your efforts on the types of flies you know best. The advantages of this approach are many. If you have a limited budget, collecting one or two styles of flies will keep your expenditure within its limits. Remember that the cost of framing and preserving your collection is considerable. Some may prefer the "scattershot" approach to collecting, but I would discourage that, since one ends up with little of value and a great quantity of garbage. If you concentrate on the very best work of a handful of tiers, a collection of considerably more substance and greater resale value will result. Many collections I know of contain only those flies available in quantity from retailers coast to coast. This approach is fine if your intent is to have a fine collection of "standard" flies to pass on to your son's son. It would be of little value for at least another twenty to fifty years. There are some exceptions, but it follows that most good contemporary fly-tiers will not be given proper credit for their abilities until their tying days are over. Fly-tiers are much like artists in this respect.

STYLES OF FLIES

In the early days of trout and bass fishing on the North American continent, flies were generally European patterns purchased from the excellent tackle stores of London and the fly-tiers of Scotland and Ireland.

That has changed dramatically, and today we find the North American fly-fisherman using patterns designed specifically for our waters by local tiers.

The following list of styles could well form the basis for a fine collection utilizing only one or two from the total.

Trout flies. These include traditional flies of European origin but tied for North American trout waters; hackled flies, representing aquatic insects during the (subaquatic) larval and pupal stages; winged wet flies, probably the most prevalent style of fly fished today; nymph flies, more popular today than ever before, and the least known in number of patterns among trout flies; streamer flies, traditional, hackled and hair-winged to represent the small fish that trout devour in great quantities; and dry flies, used and touted by the "purist."

Salmon flies. These include traditional flies, copied from the many pattern books of English, Scottish, and Irish authors; and hair-winged flies, conceded to be of North American origin and now a favorite style of many fly-fishermen.

Bass flies. These include traditional flies, usually a large solid-winged fly in vogue during the early 1900s; and deerhair flies, very popular among today's better bass fly-fishermen.

Above: A finely tied Red Quill by Art Flick. Photo: Matt Vinciguerra.
Below: Innovative pattern for *Isonychia bicolor* by Matt Vinciguerra. Photo: Matt Vinciguerra.

Saltwater flies. These include shad flies—few patterns exist since the number of fly-fishermen seeking the shad are small when compared to trout, bass, or salmon fly-fishermen—and other patterns for stripers, coho, tarpon, bonefish, and many other saltwater species; such flies are limited in number but gaining in popularity each year.

CATEGORIES FOR COLLECTING

I tend to get better results in searching for flies by following various categories and placing relative values on each category. In that way expenditures can be controlled much better. Here are those that I have attempted to follow.

Fly-tying authors, deceased. This can be subdivided into North American authors and foreign authors. Obviously the amateur category among deceased authors is a difficult one to fill. They tied primarily for themselves and a few friends, and there is little chance of locating more than a handful. The professional is another matter. Those who wrote books found considerable demand for their flies after publication and sold a great quantity as a result. Many old-timers still have good quantities of flies purchased from now-deceased pros.

Commercial fly-tiers, deceased. Most of our "standard" patterns, although developed by nonprofessional tiers, were best tied by early professionals. Since the use of flies for fishing in North America is relatively new when compared to Europe, this category is rather small. It is one of the most important categories nonetheless. Availability of these flies on the market is surprisingly good.

Fly-pattern originators. The most pleasing of all flies to obtain is a popular pattern tied by its originator. I can think of no greater success in collecting flies than to obtain a pattern directly from its originator along with a note signed by him, or her as the case may be. No question of authenticity here.

Contemporary fly-tying authors. Obtaining flies from the gentlemen in this category can be both easy and difficult. It depends of course upon your approach and the attitude of the author. A sincere approach and good price are consistent with success.

Contemporary tiers. These can be either professional or amateur. It is relatively easy to obtain the work of the contemporary professional fly-tier. He is actively tying all year, and although he may only tie for a retail outlet he will willingly advise you where his flies can be purchased.

The amateur in this category is another matter. Do not be discouraged, however, by the seemingly unavailability of a certain tier's work. The amateur is very proud of his work, and my experience in collecting from these people indicates an eagerness on their part to display their talent. More often than not they refuse to accept compensation. A trade is often the best offer you can make. Fly for fly, a book for a dozen flies, or a box of hooks, etc. is good trade bait.

The futures. I use the term "futures" for lack of a better term describing the many excellent young (some not so young) tiers who are developing new patterns, sometimes crude but nevertheless effective. I willingly accept all such patterns offered to me as gifts or in exchange for my patterns. The fly-tier-collector has an advantage here. I learn a great deal as a tier and am also confident that some of what I receive will become important in the future.

STARTING YOUR COLLECTION

Whether you choose to start a small or a large collection, it is wise to set some expenditure limits in advance. Consider not only the cost of the flies you are seeking but the additional expense of preserving and displaying them. Space must be set aside to accommodate large collections, and care must be taken to provide the best physical location in your home or club.

Upon choosing a style or category, next list the fly-tiers you feel best represent the tying skill you want displayed. Choose the patterns you want from each tier selected and locate a source for purchase. With your most persuasive approach in person or by letter, you have made a good start.

Fly-tiers are notorious for seldom answering mail and are even slower in filling a request. As any good collector will tell you, persistence pays rich dividends.

I have found it advantageous to appear in person when seeking a purchase of important flies. The seller of flies generally wants to know that his item is being sold to someone who will assure him of its contined safe keeping and proper display. The intent of the purchaser is easily recognizable to the fly-tier. He is proud of his work and of necessity has come to judge the quality of the person seeking his flies.

MARKET VALUES

I was surprised recently when one of my contemporaries offered me a set of his flies at what I considered to be about four times the fair market value. When I paid the amount specified to avoid offending my friend, he told me, without being asked, that flies being sought by collectors are becoming quite scarce and that if a collector wanted a tier's very best work he had best be prepared to pay for them. I found this to be a bit coarse on the part of my friend but it is true that tiers more and more are realizing that a new and distinct market of collectors is emerging. The old standard agreement that called for 50 cents or "a buck a fly" is a thing of the past.

Referring to the categories previously listed, I offer a broad-based price guide. There are exceptions to each category and it is expected that all categories will go up from year to year.

Fly-tying authors, deceased. Complete set of flies by the author as described in the text: no limit. Individual flies by the author as described in the text: $6 to $10. Individual flies by the author not described in the text: $4 to $10.

Commercial fly-tiers, deceased. Individual flies originated and tied by the tier: $4 to $10. Standard individual flies tied by the tier: $2 to $8.

Fly-pattern originators. Individual flies tied by the origina-tor: $4 to $10. Individual flies not originated by him but tied by him: $2 to $6.

Contemporary fly-tying authors. Individual flies tied by the author: $2 to $10.

Contemporary tiers. Individual flies: $1 to $4.

The future—no minimum

FINDING FLIES

I have frequently been asked by persons observing my personal collection of flies and art: "Where do you find all this material to display?" The answer is not an easy one. I previously mentioned that if you are beginning a collection, seek the fly-tiers who will best represent the category of flies you have selected. Visit them in person if at all possible, and don't forget to show a sincere interest in their total work. The slightest indication that the intent is to turn a quick profit from your collection will send you home with an empty bag.

One factor continues to stand out when I am seeking flies of a particular tier, and it is that for every accomplished fly-tier there must be at least 100 fly-fishermen who do not tie their own flies. Flies tied by some of those aforementioned tiers have a habit of ending up in the fly boxes of the non-tier. The stuffed fly boxes of some of these fellows would astound you. Surprisingly this tends to be my best source of valuable flies.

Be alert to any auction where fishing equipment is listed in estate contents. Some extremely valuable items have found their way into my collection as a result of my activities at auctions.

Contacting other collectors in person suggesting an agree-ment to trade or purchase is becoming commonplace. None of the collectors I know today is actively engaged in selling valu-able flies. I suppose this will change as the market value rises and the collecting activities of fly-fishermen and others increase. For now we must be content to seek our prizes from other sources.

As more persons enter the field of fly collecting, undoubtedly there will emerge a broker of sorts.

A seldom-used approach is advertising in the various sporting magazines and club and organization publications. Dealing via the mails can be a risky business at best, and I strongly suggest a "no deal" basis if what you receive cannot be authenticated during an agreed-upon inspection period.

AUTHENTICATING AND APPRAISING FLIES

For many years now we have been blessed with excellent books listing many of the fly patterns both old and new. How many of these books can you name that show the author's or originator's flies in quality color reproduction? Without top-quality photographs or authentic originals in his possession, the average collector cannot determine whether the purchase he is contemplating is an authentic one. The purchaser must then honor the statement of the seller as to its authenticity.

Losses from unauthentic purchases can be minimized by a thorough study of originals in another person's collection or visits to museums to study collections held there. You will be in a

An all-black streamer tied early in the fabled career of Mrs. Carrie Stevens. Its value is enhanced because it is attached to its original identifying card. Photo: Matt Vinciguerra.

position to determine authenticity "on sight" if some attention is paid to study.

There are many persons capable of verifying the authenticity of certain patterns tied by a limited number of selected fly-tiers. But there are only a handful capable of determining the authenticity of the work of more than three or four tiers.

Fly-tiers can be identified much the same as artists. There will always be a signature of sorts built into each fly, and this is the key to knowing the real thing. It is virtually impossible to duplicate another tier and dupe the well-trained collector or appraiser.

I suspect that almost every active fly tier today has in his possession the beginnings of a small collection of important and historical flies. There is a natural inclination to simply trade flies with other fly-tiers, and I believe most of us accumulate many flies in this manner. We placed little value on them at first and were more interested in the technique of tying than starting any type of collection. But the value is there and should not be overlooked. If your collection of flies has now reached the point where you are interested in selling all or parts of it, I can only suggest that you solicit the appraisal of the handful of acknowledged experts in this field. You will find most of them associated with museums and they will surely charge a fee for their services.

As with any art form, the collector of old fishing flies wonders what value might be placed upon his prized possession some years from now. I personally think such collections will increase in value and if properly preserved and displayed will bring a considerable return on one's investment.

I can assure anyone who is hesitant about starting a collection that he can escalate the value of his collection dramatically if he will cleverly, but in good taste, complement his flies with suitable art work. The art need not be expensive, but the viewer should be able to observe some correlation between the flies and the print.

PRESERVING YOUR COLLECTION

The most handsome of fly displays I have seen were those framed with the artist's original paintings complemented with flies created at his own tying vise. That is a very unusual combination, but nonetheless exists as a sample of what can be created. To be certain that these flies would not be lost to insects devouring them or the ravages of rust causing the fly body to discolor and disintegrate, special precautions must be taken before sealing them permanently in glass frames.

Fishing flies are tied directly to some form of metal hook, probably made of steel or steel alloy with a protective coating. Given the proper combination of moisture and exposed metal surface, rust will appear and eventually harm your display. To avoid such problems it is suggested that a light coat of machine oil be applied to all of the exposed hook surface, taking great care not to touch any parts of the materials bound to it. Some of the newer silicone sprays may be used but caution must be taken not to spray this substance on any of the feathers, fur, or hair.

When mounting the fly do not allow any materials such as metal mounts, wire, or moisture-bearing substances to rest against the hook.

Those materials containing natural animal oils seem to last indefinitely. Those materials that appear to be drying out and look brittle should not be steamed or brushed. The results could be devastating. In cases where you must repair, feathers can be salvaged by application of feather glazing purchased from fly-tying supply houses. Glazing in this manner tends to darken a dried-out feather, but this is better than losing a valuable fly.

Should you obtain flies that appear to have lost some of their material to the ravages of insects, it is suggested that you place them for a period of two weeks or more in a sealed glass jar containing a liberal quantity of paradychlorobenzene crystals. This will kill any insect that may have infested the fly but may not destroy insect eggs. Remove the flies from the bottle and carefully brush all fur feathers and hair with a fine camel-hair brush, taking care to remove all loose material.

Everyone has heard of steaming flies to restore the original shape, but you can totally destroy flies with this method. Consider if you will that steam is water and if you hold the fly in steam you will saturate it. The shank of the hook, which is buried under body materials of fur, floss, or tinsel, will probably rust as a result of the steaming. A method better designed to restore the appearance of your flies and minimize rusting is to apply a small quantity of hot air with a hand-held portable hair dryer.

DISPLAYING YOUR FLIES

All fishing flies have a good side and a bad side, and it is to your advantage to display only the good side. This may not always be possible because of the design of your frame and the layout of the flies. It may be necessary to sacrifice the good side in favor of maintaining a good color balance.

The materials used in most fishing flies will eventually become bleached if exposed to direct sunlight or bright lights. Avoid placing your collection where such damage might occur.

Discourage insects from ruining your collection by sealing each frame as airtight as possible. Check each frame periodically, and at the slightest indication of trouble open the frame and correct the problem.

FLY-TIERS IMPORTANT TO THE COLLECTOR

The following list is by no means a complete one. However, it will provide a good start for anyone beginning a collection. The tiers are in alphabetical order.

John Atherton. Author of the classic book *The Fly and the Fish*.

John Auco n. A Canadian tier of superb Atlantic-salmon flies.

Dan Bailey. Proprietor of one of the finest tackle stores in the world.

Ray Bergman. One of the all-time greats of Catskill fame and author of the great book *Trout*.

William Blades. Fly-tying author and superb innovator.

Edgar Burke, M.D. Author and superb tier.

William Charles. Trained in the "Bill Blades" school and master of nymph patterns.

Herman Christian. Known primarily among Eastern trout fishermen; schooled in the "Catskill" theory.

Rube Cross. "Eloquent dry flies" best describes this Catskill great.

This Mottled Stone Fly Creeper unmistakably shows the tying artistry of George Grant. Photo: Matt Vinciguerra.

Elsie Darbee. Flies tied with her "home-grown duns" are sought by all Eastern trout fly-fishermen.

Harry Darbee. Superb fly-fisherman, fly-tier, conservationist, and a real gentleman.

Charles DeFeo. Dean of all salmon fly-tiers. No finer man ever set foot in the crystal waters of North America.

James Deren. Owner of the Angler's Roost, where all the great North American tiers eventually pass through.

Walter Dette. Considered by many to be the finest tier of dry flies in North America.

Winnie Dette. Superb tier of those great Catskill patterns.

Wallace Doak. Supplier of fine Atlantic salmon patterns.

Art Flick. His book *Streamside Guide* tells it all. Demanding and particular in his tying.

Keith Fulsher. A unique talent as an innovator and a top-rated salmon tier.

Don Gapen. Father to the great "muddler."

Syd Glasso. An excellent West Coast tier.

Cock Robin by the dean of American salmon-fly tiers, Charles DeFeo. Photo: Matt Vinciguerra.

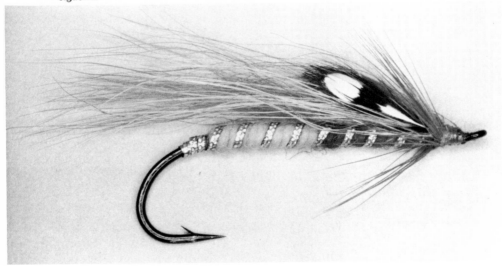

Theodore Gordon. A fly by Mr. Gordon could "make" your collection. They won't come easily.

George Grant. Great, great innovator of Western nymph patterns.

Elizabeth Greig. Her ability to tie the wet fly has gone unmatched with the possible exception of one other tier.

Ira Gruber. Self-styled tier of primarily Atlantic-salmon patterns.

Don Harger. Tier of superb Western fly patterns.

Edward Hewitt. Catskill fly-tier supreme.

Herb Howard. Close ties to Ray Bergman style are evident in his fine work.

Preston Jennings. Unique tying talent covered in his *A Book of Trout Flies*.

Walter Johnson. Superb tier of Western steelhead patterns.

Poul Jorgensen. Author of two fine books, he is top-rated as an innovator specializing in salmon flies.

Lefty Kreh. You have to like this guy! His saltwater flies are super.

Charles Krom. Wet flies and nymphs tied by Krom are among the finest ever tied in North America.

Jim Leisenring. Copied but never equaled in his talent to tie hackled wet flies.

Edson Leonard. Author and good tier.

Chauncey Lively. Excellent tying talent—dry fly oriented.

Mary Marbury. Author and tier of many of the early North American patterns.

Vincent Marinaro. Selective fly-tier and author of *A Modern Dry Fly Code*.

Don Martinez. A leader in the development of Western patterns.

Joe Messinger. Performed matchless work with spun deer hair.

Hook, ribbing, and wing are all that remain of this unique mayfly pattern attributed to Alex Rogan. Photo: Matt Vinciguerra.

John Mickievicz. Excellent nymph designer and tier.

Bill Nation. Originator of many splendid British Columbia patterns.

Ted Niemeyer. Nymph design-oriented tier.

Lew Oatman. The dean of hackle-wing streamer patterns.

Jim Pray. West Coast "great" and developer of many unique steelhead patterns.

Louis Rhead. A wonderful imagination and deft hands produced a multitude of questionable patterns.

Mike Roche. A proponent of the exact-imitation school.

Alex Rogan. Superb designer of the "old world" style.

Polly Rosborough. Great fisherman, author and super tier.

Richard Salmon. Author and expert on the Catskill fraternity of tiers.

Peter Schwab. Accomplished tier of Western steelhead patterns.

Ernest Schwiebert. Superbly gifted tier and fly-fisherman.

Ed Sens. Creator of many excellent nymph patterns.

Helen Shaw. Extremely talented tier and author.

Ernie St. Clair. Uncanny ability to create exact copies of nymphs.

Roy Steenrod. Catskill tier supreme.

Carrie Stevens. Creator of many great streamer patterns for Maine waters.

William Sturgis. Author and talented tier.

Al Troth. Superb Western nymph tier.

Ted Trueblood. Superior fly-fisherman and tier of superior fish-taking patterns.

Harry Van Luven. Designer of unique Western steelhead patterns.

Matthew Vinciguerra. A student and photographer of entomology whose unique fly designs have influenced many Eastern tiers.

Ralph Wahl. Another of the good West Coast steelhead tiers.

Leonard West. Author and pattern historian.

Charles Wetzel. Designer of many patterns and author of considerable fly-tying literature.

Dave Whitlock. Artist, author, and superb "big fly" designer.

Lee Wulff. Superb fly-fisherman, conservationist, and tier.

Yas Yamashita. Incredible, exact imitation work on nymphs. ➤

SELECTED BIBLIOGRAPHY

A study of the following books will enlighten the collector of fishing flies sufficiently to begin to recognize significant differences and unique traits of the many tiers.

Bates, Joseph D., Jr. *Atlantic Salmon Flies and Fishing*. Stackpole Books, Harrisburg, Penn., 1970.

Bates, Joseph D., Jr. *Streamer Fly Tying and Fishing*. Stackpole Books, Harrisburg, Penn., 1966.

Blades, William F. *Fishing Flies and Fly Tying*. Stackpole and Heck, Inc., Harrisburg, Penn., 1951.

Combs, Trey. *The Steelhead Trout*. Northwest Salmon-Trout-Steelheader Co., Portland, Ore., 1971.

Flick, Art. *A Master Fly-Tying Guide*. Crown Publishers, Inc., New York, 1972.

Smedley, Harold Hinsdill. *Fly Patterns and Their Origins*. Westshore Publications, Muskegon, Mich., 1943.

14

FISHING LURES

by Seth R. Rosenbaum

I t appears that an era is ending. The days of buying fishing
tackle, for the sole purpose of pleasurably catching fish, are
gone. At last, fishing tackle has joined other memorabilia and
true antiques as items to be collected as well as used. The first
pieces of fish-catching equipment to become collectible were
reels, especially precision-made casting reels. Next, fine bamboo
rods were bought for display, rather than for fishing. Other
traditional, old equipment, related to fly fishing, followed. The
latest type of fishing equipment to become collectible is lures.

What are lures? They are any nonedible (by fish) device, with
hooks, that deceives fish. This deceitfulness causes the fish to
take the lure in its mouth and become hooked. Lures, especially
flies, go back to the 1600s, when Izaak Walton described an
artificial caterpillar made of chenille. George Herter, president of
the large Minnesota company that bears his name, produces a
lure he attributes originally to Dame Juliana Berners. As the good
Dame wrote her angling treatise while Columbus was mucking
around Cuba (1496), this lure would certainly be the ancestor of
all. This oldest type of lure, not a fly, was a metal fish. The metal
was so shaped that water resistance made the lure move and flash
in an eccentric fashion. These pieces of metal evolved into
English Devons, present-day spinners and spoons.

Nothing much happened in the next three hundred years.
Kings fell; governments were formed; wars started; forks were
invented; but if you disdained live bait, you were limited to using
flies, spoons, or spinners. In 1810 something new emerged. This
was a fishlike device, consisting of a finned metal head and a
painted body made of a soft material, either silk, canvas, or
porpoise hide. This device, called a False or Phantom Minnow,
incorporated two new hook techniques. The barbed hook and the

treble hook made their appearances. As with many fish lures to follow, as many as six trebles, netting eighteen hooks, were put on a 4-inch lure! No further major type of lure innovations appeared until 1890.

The lures described so far were developed for freshwater fishing. For collection purposes, note must be made of lures developed for sea fishing. The use of artificial saltwater lures goes back to the earliest Polynesians and the Eskimo and American Indians. They all used lures made of bone and shell, usually as part of a fish hook of the same materials. These carried over to the 1800s, when American fishermen used similar lures, called jigs, to catch fish. These lures were trolled on tar lines from sailing ketches and heaved out and hauled in the surf, also without rod or reel. In 1911, N. A. Dickson invented a wooden jig for tuna trolling. A characteristic of all jigs of this era is the use of a black hand-forged blacksmith's hook.

In 1897 appeared the first recorded lure, now defined as a plug. A plug, also called an artificial minnow, differs from other lures as it basically imitates a minnow and is usually made of wood. In the beginning, there were a few made of hollow aluminum, and by 1910, they were made to look like frogs, crawfish, and mice, but, basically, a plug is still minnowlike in appearance. Granted, some look more like Salvador Dali's idea of a minnow, but they do have a recognizable head and body and most have painted or glass eyes. In later years, rubber and plastic have been used in place of wood.

IDENTIFYING LURES

Plug collecting is just starting. I do not believe there are now 500 plug collectors in the world. This compares with an estimated 5,000 fishing-reel collectors. There are great advantages to collecting something at the beginning. Obviously, there is not much competition and prices are low. Indeed, plugs are still often considered throwaway junk. How many reel collectors wish they had made acquisitions twenty-five years ago when reels also had little secondhand value? There is, however, a disadvantage to early collecting. This disadvantage is the problem of identification. As plug collection is new, the collector will have to make his own appraisals. The person who has plugs for sale will almost always be someone who doesn't know if the plug is new or old, rare or common, original or imitation. Therefore, the collector will have to look for certain identification on a plug.

The first and most helpful is writing of some sort. This is present about a third of the time. Some manufacturers, such as Heddon, Creek Chub, and South Bend, have identification on 80 percent of their plugs. Others, mostly manufacturers of single plugs, do not. The two places to find writing are on the metal (engraved) as the mouthpiece or spinner, or on the body (stenciled), usually the back. Also, if the plug is in the original box, the box will have identification on it. Most plugs made before 1950 were individually boxed. Some of these earlier boxes are also collectible, especially the metal and wooden ones.

In addition to the writing on a plug, other points of identification can be looked for. These are helpful but not infallible. Look for wood bodies and glass eyes. In later years, fewer and fewer plugs were made this expensive way. Look for patent dates on the metal. This, at least, will tell you the oldest a plug could be. Look at the hook hangers. Many plug manufacturers had their own specific style of hook hangers. Some always used grommets of a specific size. Heddon, in particular, changed its hook style many times (at least five) over its seventy-five-year history. Like other companies, it also changed, in small detail, individual plugs. A similar example of this detail change is the Jitterbug, a popular surface lure, made by the Fred Arborgast Co., which, during World War II, could not get metal for the face lip. A colored plastic front plate clearly dates this lure.

Depending on your age, you may or may not have fished with the items you are collecting. In any case, a serious collector today will have to also collect reference plug pictures. The best sources for these are fishing catalogs and fishing magazines.

REFERENCE MATERIALS

There are three types of fishing catalogs. All can have excellent reference material and pictures. The oldest of these for plug information are from 1903, and those for spoons and spinners are from 1860 on. The first type is the catalog put out by the manufacturer. This, of course, shows only his own product but shows the complete line available, as of the catalog year. It also most

Herter's "Dame Juliana Berner" lure—essentially a metal fish. Photo: Stuart Fink.

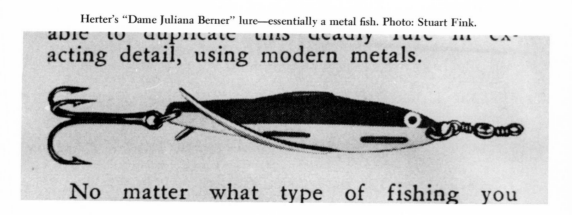

able to duplicate this deadly lure in exacting detail, using modern metals.

No matter what type of fishing you

fully, of all catalogs, describes the lure as to size, color, and special characteristics. Some companies were mostly lure manufacturers. Others had all types of tackle, with plenty of lures included. All companies issued new catalogs every year. These catalogs always had the company's basic lures plus a few new ones. Also, tackle companies published a wholesale, as well as a retail, catalog. For lure-identification purposes, the only small difference between these is that the wholesale catalog usually has additional descriptive detail.

Secondly, there is the sporting-goods catalog. These were published for mail-order businesses. They never covered just lures, like the manufacturers' catalogs; they advertised either mixed fishing tackle or mixed sporting goods or mixed everything. An example of the last group would be Sears Roebuck and Montgomery Ward. The advantage of all these catalogs is that they carry lures of all major and popular companies at that time. From them, you can get a broad collection of plug pictures for that year. These also were published and slightly updated and added to each year for plug identification. They do not always give full information. In many cases, the plug is named but the lure maker's name is not given. Sometimes, large mail-order houses, such as Abbey and Imbrie (New York City, 1860–1940), had companies such as Heddon put "Abbey and Imbrie" on a Heddon plug.

The third type of fishing catalog is the pocket catalog. These little gems were packed with the plug and contained many pictures. Many of the smaller plug makers only put out pocket catalogs. The same catalog was usually used year after year. Also, pocket catalogs, unlike larger catalogs, rarely had dates, so the year of manufacture cannot be told from them.

Most readers are familiar with hunting and fishing magazines. They go back to the 1890s. Before that, they existed in

The "Devon Minnow," another metal lure. Photo: Stuart Fink.

tabloid form. Many libraries have excellent magazine collections, together with copying machines. A day spent riffling through a library's files will result in the start of an excellent reference file. Note that the page-numbering system used in early years was quite different than today's system. The early magazines started the year (January issue) with page 1. If there were 80 pages in January, the February issue started with 81. That means that if you pick up a middle-of-the-year issue, it would start with something like page 416. A further point to look out for, in looking something up, is the advertising pages which were in the beginning and end of the magazines. These were normally numbered with an "A" added. A typical August 1915 issue of *Field & Stream* would start with page 1A; run to 8A; start again with page 333 to 440; and close with 9A to 38A. These magazines, however, usually had advertisers' indexes either in front or in back. These indexes were broken down by type of advertiser, so you can look up the index, look under Fishing Tackle, and check out these ads for plug pictures.

A few fishing books published between 1900 and 1940 have plug pictures. Unfortunately, for many years, tradition, if not logic, frowned on using company or trade names. As a result, many authors drew a picture of a "typical" plug, which, of course, is useless to a collector.

STARTING A COLLECTION

The three "F's" of plug collecting are: fathers, fishing tackle stores, and flea markets. Start with your fishing relatives, the older the better. If your father, or your friend's father, or grandfather, fished (did anyone ever have a fishing mother?), see if you can locate a fishing cache. Fishermen rarely throw tackle out. Don't assume that a veteran trout or bait fisherman wouldn't have plugs. These are just the people who receive incongruous, nonusable gifts such as plugs, and store them away, unused, for

The "Phantom Minnow" had a silk body. Photo: Stuart Fink.

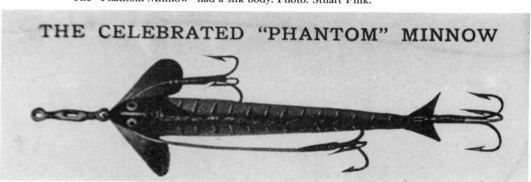

THE CELEBRATED "PHANTOM" MINNOW

years. It doesn't hurt to ask any boy you meet, with a tackle box, if he has any old plugs to sell. Fathers give them their old worn-out tackle to start them fishing. Some of this old stuff is highly collectible and can be had for small change. If you feel that this is taking advantage of small children, offer them a new plug for their old one.

Until 1950, you could walk into a tackle store and have hopes of turning up a few plugs that were twenty or thirty years old. Many stores had trading boards where, for a quarter, you could take a plug you wanted from the board and leave your own. If a store didn't sell a plug, it stayed on the shelf for many dusty years. After the 1950s, with new merchandising methods and the advent of blister packages, goods no longer gathered dust. However, if you pass a tackle store that doesn't look too modern, stop by.

Flea markets, tag or garage sales, and auctions are all a prime source of collectible fishing tackle. Unfortunately, you will have to spend lots of time to find a small amount of tackle. Of this, plugs will be in the minority. Dick Miller, a reel collector from Hudson, Mass., attends flea markets carrying a tied bunch of very long fishing rods. He says this lets the dealers spot him as someone who wants fishing tackle, and if they have any tackle to sell, he gets called.

From 1900 to 1950, a new name-brand plug cost 75 cents to $1.25. Spinners and spoons cost less. Even today, with the excep-

The earliest spoons: the Buel, patented in 1893, and the Skinner, patented in 1874. Photo: Stuart Fink.

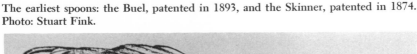

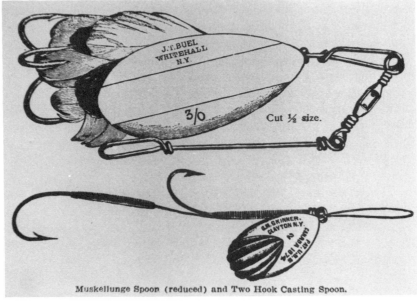

Muskellunge Spoon (reduced) and Two Hook Casting Spoon.

Heddon Patent Hook Fastening

THE new Heddon Double Screw Hook Fastening, now used on all "Dowagiac" Minnows, is the last word in successful hook suspension. Each gang of hooks can be almost instantly detached for sharpening or replacing, by turning out the small screw with the point of a knife blade. One or two turns of the double screw hook then releases the gang.

This new double screw hook cannot be turned by the fish. It is always in a fixed position, presenting the gang in such a way that effective hooking of the fish is nearly certain and preventing the hooks from striking the body of the bait or interlocking.

Three of Heddon's hook changes, with advertisement of their 1917 hook hanger. Photo: Stuart Fink.

tion of oversized muskellunge or saltwater plugs, the cost of a new plug rarely exceeds $2.50. This means you can still find collectible plugs selling for small amounts of money. Undoubtedly, when plug collecting becomes more advanced, prices will increase.

CARE AND DISPLAY OF LURES

All wood and metal lures are very durable. Even plugs that have received heavy use and spent lots of years in use maintain their good looks. The same cannot be said for plugs wholly or partially made of rubber or animal dressing (feathers and bucktail). Rubber wears worst of all. Many rubber lures, especially frogs, were made fifty years ago. Most will be in poor shape today. Creek Chub's Fintail Shiner was made with rubber fins. It rarely can be found with the fins still intact. Also, early attempts (1930) at painted plastic lures were unsuccessful. The paint never dried. Some of these, forty years later, are still tacky. Heddon's first Spooks were this way. But with those exceptions, delicate handling is not needed with old lures.

There are many ways lures can be nicely displayed. They look quite well in small shadowboxes. Their small size lends them to mounting in old printers' type-slug boxes. If space is available, they can be hung on fish or hammock netting. For this last, bear in mind that plugs have hooks. Don't hang the net where people traffic.

Plug and lure collectors collect differently and classify differently. While most lure collectors specialize in plugs, others only collect spoons, others spinners, others saltwater lures, and still others only West Coast salmon plugs. Within plugs, some collectors specialize in just one or only a few of the many lure manufacturers. As far as classifying, plug collectors are individualists. You can break down your collection classification by color, size, or special characteristics such as number of hooks and jointed or not jointed. No matter how you arrange your collection, you will find it advantageous to keep a file index. Simply write on an index card the name of the plug and the name of the manufacturer. You can write a small story on the back of the card saying where and when you got it, how much it cost, and where to find an identification picture. You should have only one card for each plug name. When you get more than one of a plug, put all this information on the back of the card. If you collect on a broad spectrum, you will find that about a third of your plugs cannot be identified, or only partially identified. In these cases, an exchange of information with fellow collectors is most helpful. A lure collectors'

The 1930 Heddon "Meadow Mouse" was relabeled "Mermouse" for Abbey & Imbrie, a well-known catalog house. Many major lure companies followed this practice. Photos: Stuart Fink.

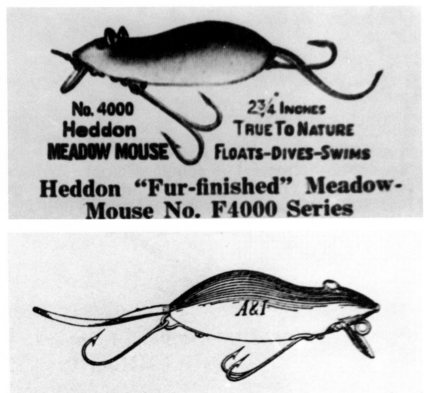

club could formalize this exchange or serve as a valuable affiliation. An excellent example of such a small club is the National Fishing Lure Collectors Club (NFLCC), 4727 South Kelly, Springfield, Mo. 65804.

SOME PLUG MANUFACTURERS AND PLUGS 1900–1950

Company	Best-known plugs	Company	Best-known plugs
Arbogast	Hawaiian Wiggler	Moonlite	Moonlite Bait
	Jitterbug	P&K	Wirlaway
	Tin Liz	Paw Paw	Wata Frog
Bunyan	Dodger	Pflueger	
Creek Chub	Darter	Enterprise	Globe
	Ding Bat		Mustang Minnow
	Fintail Shiner		Neverfail
	Gar Minnow		Pal O' Mine
	Injured Minnow		Pop Rite
	Pikie		Surprise
	Tiny Tim	Rush	Tango
	Wiggler	Shakespeare	Dopey
Decker	Decker Bait		Glo Lite Pup
Donnaly	Jersey Wow		Grumpy
Heddon	Crab Wiggler		Kazoo
	Crazy Crawler		Mouse
	Dowagiac		Paddler
	Flaptail		Revolution
	Gamefisher	South Bend	Rhodes Frog
	Luny Frog		Bass Oreno
	River Runt		Dive Oreno
	Super Surface		Fish Obite
	Tadpolly		Surf Oreno
	Vamp	True Temper.	Vacuum Bait
	Zaragosa		Crippled Shad
Jamison-Shannon	Coaxer	Wilson-Hasting	Speed Shad
	Wig L Twin		Wobbler
Millsite	Beetle		
	Paddle Plug		

A NEW BAIT

BING'S WEEDLESS NEMAHBIN MINNOW

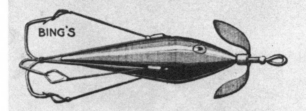

This is a new underwater bait about four and one-quarter inches over all. This bait possesses perfect casting and hooking qualities and cannot be surpassed as a lure for either bass or pickerel. The Nemahbin has been thoroughly tried and pronounced a crackerjack by all who have used it, and is fitted with weed guards which makes it a perfect bait for use in weedy water.

No. B N W 1 Silver, Each - 75c

No. B N W 3 White Enamel, Each 75c

Old pocket catalogs are a good source of information and are also collectible in themselves. Photo: Stuart Fink.

Another picture from an old pocket catalog of fishing gear. Photo: Stuart Fink.

SELECTED BIBLIOGRAPHY

One of the best ways to track down a lure is through the outdoor magazines, using the advertisers' indexes as I have described above. The magazines to check are *Field & Stream*, *Forest and Stream*, *Fur Fish and Game*, *Hardings*, *Hunting and Fishing*, *National Sportsman*, *Outers*, *Outing*, *Outdoor Life*, *Rod and Gun*, *Sports Afield*, and *Sporting Good Journal*. Try to find a library that has bound copies of these magazines.

Books that have illustrations of plugs include:

Bergman, Ray. *Fresh Water Bass*. Knopf, 1942.

Bergman, Ray. *Just Fishing*. Penn/Outdoor Life, 1932.

Carroll, Dixie. *Fishing Tackle and Kits*. Stewart & Kidd, 1919.

Fox, Charles K. *The Book of Lures*. Freshet, 1975.

Major, Harlan. *Salt Water Fishing Tackle*. Funk & Wagnall, 1939.

Melner, Sam *et al*. *Great American Fishing Tackle Catalogs*. Crown, 1972.

Outdoorsman's Handbook. Field & Stream Pub., 1910.

Outers Book. Outer Pub., 1911.

Rhead, Louis. *Fishermen's Lures and Game Fish Food*. Scribner's, 1920.

15

FISH DECOYS

by Robin Starr

Fish decoys seem destined to become one of the last nation-
ally recognized forms of American folk art to be discovered
by collectors. Whereas other collectible items such as
patchwork quilts, baskets, duck decoys, and weathervanes were
made and used in every corner of the country, fish decoys have
derived a large measure of anonymity from their very localized
use. It was only on the large and frozen freshwater lakes of
Minnesota, Wisconsin, Michigan, New York, and New England
that hardy sportsmen could enjoy the sport of spearfishing
through the ice. The only remaining bastion of spearfishing is
Minnesota, where it is still legal to spear northern pike. In all
other states, and for all other species of game fish, spearing is now
illegal.

As the name implies, a fish decoy's purpose was to attract
certain game fish to a point close enough to the surface to be
within range of a deadly wrought-iron spear. This was done by
cutting a hole in the ice, lowering the decoy on a line to the
bottom, and slowly raising it to the surface in a circular motion.
Covering the hole in the ice was a shanty, darkened for better
vision into the murky depths. Stories are told of upwards of
10,000 shanties on one lake stretching as far as the eye could see.
The most prized targets for the spearfisherman were the pickerel,
muskie, northern pike, and sturgeon, but many other species
found their way via the spear to the frying pan.

Although found in numerous shapes and sizes, there are
certain characteristics which are common to all authentic fish
decoys. First, and most important, is that unlike most other forms
of fish lures, a fish decoy has no hooks. Occasionally an illegal
spearing decoy was used carrying one or more hooks, but this
practice was frowned upon by both the law and the sportsmen.
Second, in order to force the decoy to sink to the bottom, some

Part of the author's collection, demonstrating one way to display fish. Here the fish are wired on to a 4-foot-high burlap-covered pegboard. The muskie carving on the top is not a decoy but was once a decoration on the wall of a Minnesota sporting-goods shop.

sort of weight had to be attached. In the majority of cases this was done by filling a cavity in the underside of the decoy with molten lead. Finally, all fish have some number of fins attached to a wooden body. These were usually made of copper or tin, and were designed for both realism and stabilization in the water.

Collecting fish decoys is naturally easier if you are fortunate enough to live near the areas where they were used. Here one can still chat with the old carvers and occasionally locate an old spearfisherman with a cigar box full of his hand-carved fish decoys tucked away in a dusty corner of the cellar. Getting him to part with these prizes is, of course, the dream of any collector and one of the factors which makes collecting so rewarding. However, the rest of us who live in other parts of the country must rely on friends, antique dealers, or other fish-decoy collectors. Quite often duck-decoy collectors also collect fish decoys, or at least have a couple in their collection. For this reason more and more fish decoys are becoming available for sale or trade at decoy shows around the country as well as at antique shows and flea markets where knowledgeable dealers are beginning to recognize the market for this relatively little-known form of folk art.

Once you have located one or more fish decoys, the question arises as to their worth. To date, since there is such a limited national market for this commodity, it is suggested that each decoy be judged on its own merits and valued accordingly. Needless to say, there are innumerable attributes to be considered. If, however, there was such a thing as an "average" fish decoy it would probably be painted red and white, be about 6 inches long with metal fins, and command a price of anywhere from $8 to $22. An extra work or show of ingenuity by the carver such as carved gills, leather fins, glass eyes, or a carved wooden tail would be rewarded with an increase of value. Once a collector has seen many fish decoys it becomes easier to compare the relative merits of each piece, but until then he must rely on the integrity of the person

Identifiable by their shape as sunfish, these examples from 3 to 4½ inches in length are representative of decoys currently available in the $10-20 range.

A 10-inch blue-black carp decoy from Michigan with glass eyes, carved scales and a curved carved tail. This fine example of American folk art, made about 1930, is valued at $75.

Two extremely scarce frog decoys, 2 inches and 6 inches long and valued at $20 and $35 respectively. Attached to the larger frog is an old jigging stick used to lower the decoy into the water.

Two manufactured fish decoys, each 6 inches long. On the left is a nearly perfect replica, made of molded plastic, of a pickerel. The other, made of wood with metal fins, is more stylized in shape and paint pattern.

with whom he is dealing. Certain unusual items, such as a well-carved 40-inch sturgeon decoy, could command a price in the hundreds of dollars for its folk-art qualities alone. But pieces of this quality are extremely scarce. Sturgeon decoys were used and are found almost exclusively in Wisconsin, and it is interesting to note that they were often carved to be the exact length as the then-current legal minimum-size sturgeon under the law. Then, as the sturgeon swam over the decoy, it was easy to see if the fish was a "keeper" or not. In the early days the limit was 24 inches but later was increased to 40 inches.

The men who carved fish decoys had two main considerations which influenced their work. The first was to produce a functional piece which would attract fish. The second factor which guided their hands was the desire to express themselves as artists and craftsmen, for these men were proud of their efforts. Realizing that everyone who carved had varying degrees of talent in this direction, we can understand the individualism found in fish decoys and why there are so many different variations. Although it appears that the majority of fish decoys were carved by spearfishermen for their own use, there were also several professional carvers in the early 1900s, especially in Minnesota and Michigan. These artisans spent the spring and summer months carving a large inventory of decoys, and then as the winter freeze approached they would travel around the countryside to such places as barbershops, bars, service stations, and sporting-goods stores selling their wares for as little as 50 cents each. The work by these makers tends to be quite stylized and streamlined, varying only in size and paint pattern, but is nevertheless avidly sought after by discerning collectors.

It should also be recorded that several attempts by manufacturing companies to make fish decoys were made. These compa-

These three 5-inch fish, which are valued at between $15 and $30, illustrate the varied styles and decorating techniques of different carvers.

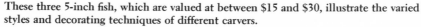

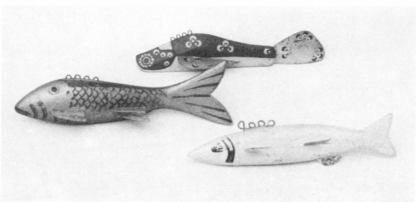

An extremely realistic 7-inch bluegill from Buffalo, Minn., made about 1970. Although not very old, this piece was actually used and exhibits superb craftsmanship. It is valued at $40.

nies, although often small, produced some very interesting and collectible items. Patents were obtained and some ingenious creations, such as a fish with a light inside of it, were made. For the most part, however, manufactured fish tended to be made of some type of plastic material or composition, were boldly colored, and were extremely lifelike in appearance. They hold a definite spot in the history and story of fish decoys. Indeed, a collection of all the types of manufactured fish would be a formidable and extremely varied one.

It is recommended that anyone who decides to collect fish decoys should weigh the attributes of a generalized versus a specialized approach. On the one hand a collector could try to accumulate a well-rounded representation of all the styles and grades of fish available. This approach is advised for the collector without easy access to a source of fish decoys or one who wants a very large collection. There are several varied possibilities when one considers specializing, such as only fish carved in New England, the work of a particular carver, or perhaps a collection of sunfish decoys only. One of the most difficult specialized collections would be one of frog decoys. Authentic old frog decoys, which were used in the same manner as fish, are extremely difficult to locate and are a prized addition to any collection.

As is the case with other types of collections, there are related items which when displayed with the fish enhance the understanding of how the fish were used. For example, a collection might contain at least one handmade spear. These spears, which are themselves very collectible items and are becoming quite scarce, usually were forged of wrought iron and have anywhere from three to six tines. Other related items, such as the Currier and Ives ice-fishing print or old fish boxes which were made to carry fish decoys, are also a welcome addition. The scope and range of a good collection is limited only by the imagination and the ingenuity of the collector.

I believe that there is no better time than now for someone to acquire a fine collection of fish decoys at a reasonable price, and that the value of fish decoys will grow rapidly. ➤

SELECTED BIBLIOGRAPHY

Bishop, Robert. *American Folk Sculpture*. E. P. Dutton & Co., Inc., New York, 1974.

Colio, Quintina. *American Decoys*. Science Press, Ephrata, Pa., 1972.

Pennington, Wil. "Fish Story," *North American Decoys*, Fall 1973.

16

DERRYDALE BOOKS AND PRINTS

by F. Phillips Williamson

Who can say what motivated Eugene Connett to found The Derrydale Press? Certainly any interest he had in the late 1920s was aided and abetted by Ernest R. Gee. Regardless of just how Derrydale began, it was the beginning of the finest publishing house of sporting books and prints that has ever appeared on the face of the earth.

In *The Colophon 1938, The Annual of Bookmaking*, Connett wrote: "This press specializes solely in issuing limited editions of sporting books—chiefly American sporting books. If one examines a collection of the sporting books published in this country, he will be struck with the very low average of quality exhibited, and when the American books are compared to those published in England there is little cause for wonder as to why so many of the old English sporting books are avidly collected, and fairly plentiful, while the American books are sought after by only a few, and are relatively scarce.

"It was to remedy this situation that I established The Derrydale Press in 1927. I believed that if someone would publish a group of American sporting books in sufficiently attractive formats, these books would not be carelessly thrown away during spring house cleaning fifty years from now, but would survive in reasonable numbers through the years, just as the finer British ones have. And if these books were preserved, there would be a record of the greatest period of sport the world has yet seen—even greater than in England after the Napoleonic wars.

"It may be of some interest to note what we consider proper subjects for sporting books. With very few exceptions the so-called 'field sports,' such as foxhunting, fishing, riding, horse racing, yachting and breeding horses and dogs, constitute the subjects of our sporting books. Games and pastimes, such as football, boxing, tennis, swimming, and so on, rarely are included. There are exceptions, of course, such as our new book on skiing.

"The problem was not to design books in the modern manner, nor to seek formats which through their striking originality would call attention to themselves; but to find sound and worthwhile texts and to issue them in easy-to-read and dignified volumes which would appeal to conservative people. For sportsmen are very conservative, as a rule.

"They have worn pink in the hunting field for a good many generations—excellent proof that it is the best thing to wear when foxhunting; they carry on wing shooting just as they did in 1727 when the first book on the subject in English was published, except for the minor changes made necessary by the invention of the breech-loading shotgun; and, with the exception of similar improvements in fishing tackle, angling is done exactly as it was in 1654 when the first edition of Izaak Walton's *Compleat Angler* appeared. They have kept the pedigrees of their race horses since before 1700 when the Darley Arabian and the Byerly Turk were imported into England, to found the present breed of thoroughbreds. Yes, sportsmen are conservative, and their books should be so designed.

"An extended consideration of the matter convinced me that Caslon type in sizes twelve and fourteen, on pages measuring overall 6¼ x 9½, 7½ x 10 and 9½ x 12¼, provided, with generous margins, the most comfortable and easily read books. Almost all of our book pages conform to these specifications. Not very exciting, but after ten years of experience I have had no cause to change my mind as to the soundness of my choice.

"As my books were made for people who would really read them, I felt that any decoration which attracted attention away from the text itself was unsound. So there is a total lack of exotic running heads and misplaced (I almost said misbegotten) folios in our books. Once in a while we have permitted ourselves the luxury of doing a book that has been pronounced fairly good looking by those whose business it is to know such things—just to keep our hand in. But as a rule we are content to stick to our very simple and easy-to-read pages. . . . if you were to ask me to state my bookmaking creed briefly, I would answer thus: first make a book that is easy to read; second make a book that is dignified and somewhat conservative in style; third make a book in tune with the finest tradition in that class of book; fourth—and this almost sums up the others—make an honest book; fifth—and most important of all—make a book for the great-grandchildren of your present customers."

The first publication Connett produced did not bear the imprint of The Derrydale Press and came out in 1926 (*American*

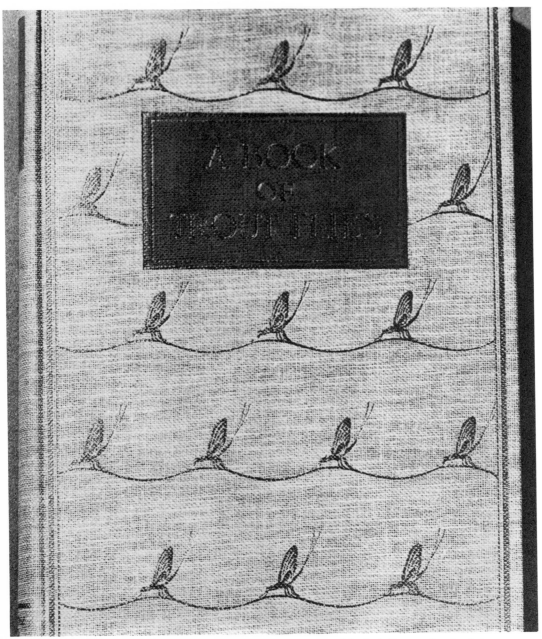

A typical first-class binding and cover design by Derrydale. It is Preston Jennings' *A Book of Trout Flies*, with hand-colored plates of flies. Photo: Matt Vinciguerra.

Trout Streams by Henry A. Ingraham, in two editions). The first publication ever to appear under the name of The Derrydale Press was a small book, cheaply bound (and said to be set on a hand press by the author), entitled *Magic Hours* by Eugene Connett. This appeared in 1927 and was the beginning of a fourteen-year span in which a series of sporting books and prints encompassed the hunting, shooting, fishing, yachting, skiing, and coaching fields as well as works on dogs, odd subjects, and horses. A smattering of privately printed works complemented this labor of love. A total of 221 volumes were produced by Eugene Connett.

Compared to the sporting authors that Connett had in his stable, nearly all of the so-called sporting authors of today fall way short. The various works by Sheldon, Buckingham, Clark, Newman, Pickering, and Edmund Ware Smith have no equal in today's sporting publications. The books all had limited runs (total runs were set down in each work) and the deluxe bindings of a few were works of art.

In the Depression of the 1930s, many of the deluxe editions were "sold out" prior to publication. In the early 1940s, ads appeared offering $100 for a copy of Nash Buckingham's most famous work, *De Shootinest Gent'man*. This was for a regular edition that was published at $7.50; a deluxe edition did not exist.

Connett's selection of both subject and author show the fine hand of a publishing genius. The paper, the bindings (with the exception of a few early works), the type, and the illustrations are praiseworthy.

Most prints published today are almost calendar in quality compared to Derrydale Prints. Connett brought to America, in the print line, a process that had been seldom used in the United States: aquatint, or prints watercolored by hand. The artist would do an oil painting or a watercolor, the press would print, on good-quality paper, the outline and lettering, and then the artist would watercolor what is called an artist's proof. These proofs were given to commercial artists, who would watercolor the prints by hand and return them to the publisher. The publisher or the artist would approve the coloring, then the print would be signed and/or numbered. It is evident that in a number of instances where the author was deceased, Connett most likely gave the final approval.

The set of four polo prints by Paul Brown, the set of three foxhunting prints by Voss (the fourth print of the set, "Tally-Ho," was published by Frank Lowe after the Derrydale Press ceased to exist), the set of four A. B. Frost prints, Schaldack's "Woodcock," Clark's "The Alarm" and "Mallards Rising," Boyer's two fishing prints, and Megargee's "Staunch" and "Steady" are truly the pick of the crop. The color of the leaves in the A. B. Frost's "October Woodcock Shooting" is one of the best examples of a perfect aquatint print.

The prints never exceeded 250 in total run, and since they were often colored by contract tied with sales, many were never colored and finished. A few of these uncolored prints have come on the auction market in recent years as warehouses and storerooms have closed out.

A large number of the prints retailed at $25. Some of these prints, today, will bring $750 to $1,000. With the print-collecting craze sweeping the United States today, lithographed signed prints bring $45 and up with runs from 450 to 2,000. Derrydale prints are the real sleepers in today's art world, and the fickle public will awake one day to realize that the present craze (and prices) for lithographed long-run prints will pass. All collectors, of anything, would do well to find the time to read a book by Mackoy written in 1845 titled *The Extraordinary Popular Delusions of the Madness of Crowds*.

Some of the uncolored Derrydale Press prints that have surfaced have landed into the hands of some stupid sharp operators. The best examples are some of Megargee's "American Shooting Scenes" (along in the same issue by Lynn Bogue Hunt), where all the woods are deep green (browns were the base of the originals) and the bird shooters' jackets are red. No bird shooter worth his salt ever wore anything prior to 1941 but dark-brown duck (or some of the softer fabrics—but all *brown*). In fact, red bird-shooting coats were not even made then. (Woolrich did make a red-and-black-plaid heavy wool deer hunter's jacket.) A few other prints have been colored with colors whose bases were not made until after 1955.

If you are a serious print collector, try to buy from a reliable dealer (or owner) who will certify the past ten-year history of the print. One unlettered artist proof is known to have had reproduction letters printed since 1945. One thing is fairly certain, however: Derrydale prints will never be totally reproduced again as they first were.

Any print or book collector should be aware of two major hazards—light and dampness. A good library should be in a room where the humidity is controlled and all lighting indirect. This is even more important for prints. Dampness will cause foxing, and light (sunlight and fluorescent, which is just as deadly as sunlight) will cause fading and color change. Prints should be framed in full size, uncut, and never matted. Unframed prints are best stored flat in a Hamilton-type wooden plat or drawing file with tissue paper between.

There are a limited number of dealers who specialize in

sporting books, and far fewer who specialize in sporting prints. A quick review of *Bookman's Weekly* will bring forth a list of dealers specializing in sporting books, but it's every dog for himself to find the prints. There are a few—The Old Print Collector in New York, Sesslers in Philadelphia, Purnells Art Gallery in Baltimore, and so on.

Pick the subject you are interested in and start looking for the Derrydale Press books and/or prints. There are still excellent bargains to be found! ⟁

PRICES OF DERRYDALE BOOKS

Note: Prices are for copies in excellent condition. Deduct up to 40 percent for other conditions. All 221 volumes are listed.

1926

	Price
American Trout Streams, Henry A. Ingraham, 350 numbered copies	$ 125
Deluxe Edition, 150 numbered copies	750

1927

Magic Hours, Eugene V. Connett, 89 numbered copies	1,700
Memories of the Gloucester Fox Hunting Club, 375 numbered copies	30
The Sporting Works of Somerville and Ross (7 volumes), 500 numbered and signed sets	220
1, *Some Experiences of an Irish RM*; 2, *Further Experiences of an Irish RM*; 3, *In Mr. Knox's Country*; 4, *Dan Russell, the Fox*; 5, *All on the Irish Shore*; 6, *Wheel Tracks*; 7, *Irish Memories*	
Trouting Along the Catasauqua, Frank Forester, 423 numbered copies	130
The Dalmation, Franklin J. Willock, 200 numbered copies	220
Roads and Harbours, Arthur Ketchum, 150 numbered copies	100

1928

The American Shooter's Manual (printed for Ernest Gee), 375 numbered copies	60
Some Early American Hunters, 375 numbered copies	75
The Spicklefisherman and Others, Frederick White, 740 copies	55

Deluxe Edition, 35 autographed copies	650
Hell for Leather, 375 numbered copies	35
Early American Sporting Books, Ernest R. Gee, 500 copies	60
Deluxe Edition, 50 copies	600
Hounds and Hunting Through the Ages, Joseph B. Thomas, 750 copies, 1st edition	400
Deluxe Edition, 50 copies	1,400
Memories of Manhattan, Charles Townsend Harris, 1,000 copies	50
Cooking in Old Creole Days, Celestine Eustis, 500 copies	200
Pydie's Poems, Mary Cole Wallner, 100 copies	100
Antiques and Amber, Anne Lloyd, 250 copies	25
150 copies signed & numbered	155
War Without Fighting, L. Rodman Page, Jr., 100 numbered copies	225
Gee's Hunting Diary, Ernest R. Gee	180

1929

Feathered Game from a Sporting Journal, Eugene V. Connett, 500 numbered copies	180
50 Deluxe autographed and numbered copies	1,350
Trout and Angling, Jerome V. C. Smith, 325 copies	90
Deluxe Edition, 50 copies	600
The Travel Diary of an Angler, Henry van Dyke, 750 copies	55
Let's Ride to Hounds, Anole Hunter, 850 copies	50
Deluxe Edition, 50 numbered copies	400
Hounds and Hunting Through the Ages, Joseph B. Thomas, 2nd Edition, 250 copies	350
Between the Flags, H. S. Page, 850 copies	40
The Horse of the Desert, Wm. Robinson Brown, 750 copies	90
Deluxe Edition, 75 numbered copies	600
The Sporting Works of David Gray, 3 vols. boxed, 750 sets numbered	80
Gallops I; Gallops II; Mr. Carteret	
Certaine Experiments Concerning Fish and Fruit, John Taverner, 100 copies	600
Charles Cotton and His River, G. G. P. Heywood, 50 copies	600
The Westminster Kennel Club, 100 copies	500
El Grecco, Frank Gray Griswold, 100 copies	200
Why, Jean Dwight Franklin, 900 copies	50
100 copies on special Dutch Charcoal paper, signed	200
Poems, Mary Riley Smith, 200 copies	60
The Sportsman's Portfolio of American Field Sports (Printed for Ernest R. Gee), 400 copies	75
Cherished Portraits of Thoroughbred Horses, W. S. Vosburgh, 279 copies	600
Deluxe Edition with colored plates, 21 copies	800

1930

Marguerite Kirmse's Dogs, Marguerite Kirmse, 750 copies	100
Upland Game Bird Shooting in America, Eugene V. Connett, Regular Edition, 850 copies	200
Deluxe Edition, 75 copies	800
The Epping Hunt, Thomas Hood, 490 numbered copies	50
Foxhunting Formalities, J. Stanley Reeve, 990 copies	30
Deluxe Edition, 99 copies numbered and autographed	350
Gentlemen Up, William B. Strett, 850 copies	85
Deluxe Edition, 75 copies numbered and autographed	200
Aintree—Grand National Past and Present, Paul Brown, 850 copies	50
Deluxe Edition, 50 copies	450
The Sporting Novels of Frank Forester (4 vols.), 750 sets boxed and numbered	200
I, *The Warwick Woodlands*; II, *My Shooting Box*; III, *The Quorndon Hounds*; IV, *The Deer Stalkers*	
Records of the Town of Brookhaven, Book A, 200 copies	150
Abdul, An Allegory, Aimstead Keith Baylor, 500 copies	25
In Memoriam, Mary Boyd McCormick, Henry B. McCormick	300
The Sportsman's Companion (Printed for Ernest R. Gee), 200 copies	110
The Deerstalkers, Frank Forester, 750 copies	35

1931

The Practical Dog Book, Edward C. Ash, 500 copies	50
In the Shadow of Mount McKinley, Wm. N. Brach, 750 copies	75
Colonel Hawkee's Shooting Diaries,	60
Pteryplegia, on the Art of Shooting Flying, Mr. Markland, 300 numbered	50
Deluxe Edition, 200 numbered, signed, and colored	125
Stray Shots, Roland Clark, 500 copies	300
Deluxe Edition, 35 copies	1,500
Hunting Pie, Frederick Watson, 750 copies	30
The Book of the Fox, Richard Clapham, 750 copies	40
Famous Horses of the American Turf, Neil Newman, Vol. 1, 750 copies	75
Jumping the Horse, Capt. Vladimir S. Littauer, 950 copies	60
Four Centuries of Sport in America, Hubert Manchester, 850 copies	100
American Dry Flies and How to Tie Them, Dr. Edgar Burke, 500 copies	220
Trout Fishing in Secret, H. G. Pickering, 99 copies, signed	500
Records of the Town of Brookhaven, Book C, 200 copies	150
Selected Poems of Louis B. Rolston, copies unknown	100
Gallant Fox, William Woodward, full leather, folding case	100

1932

The English Springer Spaniel in America, Henry Lee Ferguson, 850 copies	85
Records of North American Big Game, P. N. Gray, Editor, 500 copies	180
John Peel, John Woodcock Graves, 990 copies	45
Famous Horses of the American Turf, Neil Newman, Vol. II, 750 copies	75
Riding Reflections, Capt. Piero Santini, 850 copies	45
Tennis Origins and Mysteries, Malcolm D. Whitman, 450 copies	90
The Silver Horn, Gordon Grand, 950 copies	300
Records of the Town of Brookhaven, Book B, 200 copies	200
The Hunting If, Angela Shortt, 100 copies	200

1933

Yacht Racing Log, Harvey Stone	100
Famous Horses of the American Turf, Neil Newman, Vol. III, 750 copies	75
Polo Ponies, Their Training and Schooling, Lt. Paul G. Kendall, 850 copies	45
A. B. Frost, Henry W. Lanier, 950 copies	245
The Thunderer, "M.B.," 950 copies	40
Colonel Weatherford and His Friends, Gordon Grand, 1,450 copies	55
Dog Days on Trout Waters, H. G. Pickering, 199 copies	500
The Gibbs Family of Rhodes Island, George Gibbs, 150 copies	150
A Bigelow Background, Ashley Bigelow, 25 numbered copies	400
Hunting Trails on Three Continents, Boone & Crockett Club, 250 copies	60

1934

Millions for Defense, Loomis & Stone, 950 numbered copies	50
Fishing a Trout Stream, Eugene V. Connett III, 950 copies	75
Riding and Schooling Horses, Lt. Col. Harry D. Chamberlain, 950 numbered copies	40
Old Man and Other Colonel Weatherford Stories, Gordon Grand, 1,150 copies	60
De Shootinest Gent'man, Nash Buckingham, 950 numbered copies	300
Wild Fowl Decoys, Joel Barber, 55 numbered and signed copies with miniature decoy	700
The Warwick Woodlands, Frank Forester, 250 numbered copies	160

Paul Bunyon and Resinous Rhymes of the North Woods,
Thomas G. Alvard, Jr., 166 numbered copies (blue bind-
ing)   35
332 numbered copies and signed on title page (green bind-
ing)   18
North American Big Game, compiled by Prentiss N. Gray,
published by Remington Arms Co. by The Derrydale
Press   600
Thoughts Upon Hunting Kit, Eugene S. Reynal, 500 copies   200
Deluxe Edition (quantity unknown)   300

1935

American Big Game Fishing, Connett, Editor, 950 copies   160
Deluxe Edition, 56 copies   750
The Belviedere Hounds, D. T. Carlisle, 1,250 copies   35
Hits and Misses—A Polo Sketch Book, Paul Brown, 950
numbered and signed copies   45
Life and Sport in Aiken, Harry Worcester Smith, 950 copies   35
Sporting Stables and Kennels, Gambrill & Mackenzie, 950
numbered copies   60
A Book of Trout Flies, Preston Jennings, 850 numbered
copies   200
Vol I & Vol. II (Vol. II—*Flies*) Deluxe Edition, 25 num-
bered and autographed copies   4,500
Colonel Weatherford's Young Entry, Gordon Grand, 1,350
copies   45
Dogs in the Field, Marguerite Kirmse, 685 numbered cop-
ies   140
Grouse Feathers, Burton L. Spiller, 950 numbered copies   100
Messenger, John Hervey, 500 numbered copies   30
The Coaching Club, Reginald W. Rives, 300 numbered
copies   350
Deluxe Edition, 30 copies   1,000

1936

An Artist's Game Bag, Lynn Bogue Hunt, 1,250 numbered
copies   300
Deluxe Edition, 25 copies   1,000
Thoroughbred, Burton L. Spiller, 950 numbered copies   75
New Lines for Flyfishers, Wm. Bayard Sturgis, 950 copies   55
Mark Right, Nash Buckingham, 1,250 numbered copies   90
Angling of the Test, H. G. Pickering, 297 numbered copies   70
197 numbered and signed   300
Wing Shots, Albert Dixon Simmons, 950 numbered copies   60
Jing, John Taintor Foote, 950 numbered copies   50
The Horse—Its Action and Anatomy, Lowes D. Luard, 150
numbered copies   200
Tranquillity, Col. Harold P. Sheldon, 950 numbered copies   100
Riding, Benjamin Lewis, 1,250 copies   60

Will You Walk Into My Garden, Clara C. Lenroot, 200
   copies   100
Temples and Topees, William Hale Harkness, 200 num-
   bered copies   200
Lady Suffolk, John Hervey, 500 numbered copies   175

1937

Falling Leaves, Philip H. Barcock, 950 numbered copies   60
Before the Mast in Clippers, Lt. Com. H. Allen Gosnell, 950
   numbered copies   65
Men Against the Rule, Charles Lane Poor, 950 numbered
   copies   65
Tigers of the Sea, Col. Hugh D. Wise, 950 numbered copies   40
Firelight, Burton L. Spiller, 950 numbered copies   80
Bolinvar (2 volumes), Marguerite F. Bayliss, 950 numbered
   copies   75
The Derrydale Cook Book of Fish & Game, 2 vols. boxed, L.
   P. DeGouy, 1,250 numbered sets   160
A *Decade of American Sporting Books & Prints*, Eugene V.
   Connett III, 950 numbered copies   50
Atlantic Salmon Fishing, Charles Phair, 950 copies   200
   Deluxe Edition, 2 vols. (one w/flies), 40 copies   4,000
Neighbors Have My Ducks, H. G. Pickering, 227 numbered
   copies   350
Out of Halifax, Wallace R. MacAskill, boxed, 950 num-
   bered copies   55
   450 copies for Canada   50
Training Hunters, Jumpers and Hacks, Lt. Col. H. D.
   Chamberlain, 1,250 numbered copies   40
Ole Miss, Nash Buckingham, 1,250 numbered copies   90
Skiing—The International Sport, Roland Palmedo, 950
   copies   75
   Deluxe Edition, 60 copies   300
John Tobias, Sportsman, Charles E. Cox, Jr., 950 num-
   bered copies   70
A *Tomato Can Chronicle*, Edmund Ware Smith, 950 num-
   bered copies   90
Gunner's Dawn, Roland Clark, 950 numbered copies   110
   Deluxe Edition, 50 copies   800

1938

Not Their Breed & The Forgotten Man, Clarence Budding-
   ton Kelland   70
A *Memoir of Andrew Jackson Africanus*, William Woodward, boxed, 150 numbered copies   350
Tales of a Big Game Guide, Russell Annabel, 950 numbered copies   70

Full Tilt, Keene & Hatch, 950 numbered copies	30
Upstream and Down, Howard T. Walden II, 950 numbered copies	65
More Grouse Feathers, Burton L. Spiller, 950 numbered copies	100
The Medchester Club, Kenneth Brown, 950 numbered copies	20
Martha Doyle, Richard E. Danielson, 120 numbered copies	25
Roland Clark's Etchings, Roland Clark, 800 copies	450
Deluxe Edition, 50 copies	1,600
Sportsmen All, Capt. Paul Curtis, 950 numbered copies	55
Pack and Paddock, Ted Sheppard, boxed, 950 numbered copies	60
High Country, Rutherford Montgomery, 950 numbered copies	40
Foxhunting Is Different, Samuel J. Henry, 950 numbered copies	35
Tall Tales and Short, Edmund Ware Smith, 950 numbered copies	85
Bloodiness, Nash Buckingham, 1,250 numbered copies	125
A Collection of Verse, Stella Sharpe Waterstone, 500 copies	75

1939

The Happy End, Ben Ames Williams, 1,250 numbered copies	50
Random Casts, Eugene V. Connett III, 950 numbered copies	100
The Moon Is Waning, Scott Hart, 950 numbered copies	20
Game in the Desert, Jack O'Connor, boxed, 950 numbered copies	80
'Long Shore, Joel Barber, 750 numbered copies	75
The Southborough Fox, Gordon Grand, 1,450 copies	55
Breeding Your Own, Clarence E. Bosworth, 120 numbered copies	25
The Western Angler, Roderick Haig-Brown, 2 vols., 950 numbered copies	200
Gunnerman, Horatio Bigelow, 950 numbered copies	55
Veiled Horizons, Ralph Bandini, 950 numbered copies	65
The Gentlemen's Companion, Charles H. Baker, Jr., 2 vols., 1,250 numbered copies	165
British and American Game Birds, Pollard, Barclay, Smith & Connett, 125 numbered, signed, and remarqued copies	350
Special Edition, 10 copies	800
Ho Hum, the Fisherman, William Hale Harkness, 100 numbered copies	550

1940

Tranquillity Revisted, Col. H. P. Sheldon, 485 numbered
copies   100
Big Stoney, Howard T. Walden II, 550 numbered copies   70
The Story of American Foxhunting, Vol. I, 1650–1861, J.
Blan Van Urk, 950 copies   100
Red Coats in Chester County, J. Stanley Reeve, 560 num-
bered copies   85
Bull Terriers, the Biography of a Breed, L. Cabot Briggs, 500
numbered copies   150
Hobby Horses, Amy Freeman Lee, 200 numbered and
signed copies   70
Merry Xmas Mr. Williams 20 Pine St., N.Y., H. G. Picker-
ing, 267 numbered copies   220
Paperback edition, 267 numbered copies   70
A Private Affair, Col. H. P. Sheldon (for Colonel Woods
King)   300

1941

Point, J. Horace Lytle, 950 numbered copies   55
Be a Better Horseman, Capt. V. S. Littauer and Bert Clarke
Thayer, 1,500 copies   50
The Story of American Foxhunting, Vol. II, 1865–1906, J.
Blan Van Urk, 950 copies   100
The One-Eyed Poacher of Privilege, Edmund Ware Smith,
750 numbered copies   90
My Shooting Box, Frank Forester, 250 numbered copies   150
Summer on the Test, John Wallace Hills, 300 copies   300

1942

The Happy End, Ben Ames Williams, printed for the Clove
Valley Rod & Gun Club, November 19, 1942, 1,250
numbered copies   85

PRICES OF DERRYDALE PRINTS

Price

1928

Saratoga Racing Acquatints (set of 4: "Morning Exercise,"
"In the Paddock," "At the Barrier," "Over the Liver-
pool"), Edward King, 80 sets, signed $800

1929

Somerville & Ross Prints (I, "A Conspiracy of Silence"; II, "Occasional Licenses"; III, "Put Down One and Carry Two"; IV, "The Compte De Pralines"), E. E. Somerville, 50 numbered and signed sets   1,500

"The Aiken Drag," Edward King, 80 numbered and signed   100

Two Angling Dry Points:

   "The Lips of the Pool," Ralph L. Boyer, 60 signed and numbered proofs   200

   "At the Riffle," Ralph L. Boyer, 60 numbered and signed proofs   200

Hunt Race Lithographs (set of 4), Edward King (IV, "Full Cry," printed 1930)

   American Hunting Scenes:

    I, "The First Flight," Edward King, 250 signed   250

    II, "Well Away," Edward King, 250 signed   250

    III, "The Check," Edward King, 250 signed   250

Belmont Terminal Lithographs (set of 2: "The Paddock," "The Finish"), Edward King   100

American Shooting Scenes: "Quail Shooting," Edward King   300

Hunting Lithographs (set of 2: "The Chicken Coop," "Blood Will Tell"), Edward King, 250, signed   450

1930

Woodcock Shooting: "In the Birches," Edward King, 350 signed   100

Quail Shooting: "The Briar Patch," Edward King, 350 signed   100

Diana Goes Hunting (set of 4: "Her First Meet," "Alone with the Hounds," "In and Out," "Her First Brush"), Edward King, 250 signed   300

American Polo Scenes (set of 4: "Down the Field," "On the Boards," "The Save," "The Goal"), Paul Brown, 175 signed   3,500

"Pheasant Shooting," Edwin Megargee, signed only   300

American Hunting Scene, IV: "Full Cry," Edward King, 250 signed   250

1931

"The Fox," Marguerite Kirmse, 250 signed   600

Fathers of American Sport (set of 6: "William Henry Herbert," "Thaddeus Norris," "George Washington," "Commodore John Cox Stevens," "Samuel Morris," "Col. William Ransom Johnson"), Ralph L. Boyer, 250 signed   250

"Woodcock," William J. Schaldach, 250 signed   750

"Woodcock Shooting," Edwin Megargee, 250 signed only 300
"Grouse Shooting," Edwin Megargee, 250, signed 300
American Steeplechasing Scenes: "The Meadowbrook
    Cup," Paul Brown, 250 signed 150

1932

American Cock Fighting Scenes (set of 4: "Challenge,"
    "Striking," "Struck," "Victory"), Edwin Megargee, 250
    signed 1,200
American Horse Show Scenes:
    "Rochester," Edward King, 250 signed 100
    "A Glorious Burst," Edward King, 250, signed 250

1933

"The Hounds," Marguerite Kirmse, 250 signed 600
"October Woodcock Shooting," A. B. Frost, 200 numbered 1,500
"A Chance Shot," A. B. Frost, 200 numbered 1,200

1934

"Grouse Shooting in the Rhododendrons," A. B. Frost, 200
    numbered 800
"Coming Ashore," A. B. Frost, 200 numbered 1,200

1936

"After a Big One," Ralph L. Boyer, 200 numbered and signed 300
"Maryland Marsh," John Frost, 150 signed and numbered 275

1937

"An Anxious Moment," Ralph L. Boyer, 250 numbered and
    signed 300
"The Alarm," Roland Clark, 250 numbered & signed 1,200
"Down Wind (Pintail)," Roland Clark, 250 numbered &
    signed 450
"Hoick! Hoick! Hoick!" Paul Brown, 250 numbered &
    signed 250
"Pressing Him," Paul Brown, 250 numbered & signed 250

OTHER PRIVATELY PRINTED PRINTS 1927–1937

"Gallant Fox" by T. Ivester Lloyd for William Woodward 100
"Faireno" by Martin Stainforth for William Woodward 100
"Omaha" by Martin Stainforth for William Woodward 100
"A Tight Line" by Samuel Hawitt for Ernest R. Gee 100

"Great Dane Head," Maud Earl   25
Bookplate for Viola T. Winmill   25
Copperplate for Lester Karow   25

1938

Large plate w/watermark for "Upstream and Down" num-
   bered and signed by Walden and Weiler, 60 copies   200
"Sanctuary (Green Wing Teal)," Roland Clark, 250 num-
   bered & signed   450
"Staunch," Edwin Megargee, 250 numbered & signed   250
"Steady," Edwin Megargee, 250 numbered & signed   250
"The Scout (Mallard Drake)," Roland Clark, 250 numbered
   & signed   450

1939

"Winter Marsh (Can)," Roland Clark, 250 numbered &
   signed   750
"Dawn (Widgeon)," Roland Clark, 250 numbered & signed   350
"Closing In," Edwin Megargee, 250 numbered & signed   125
Foxhunting in America:
   "Over the Open," F. B. Voss, 250 numbered & signed   750
   "On a Fresh Line," F. B. Voss, 250 numbered & signed   750
"The Rose Tree Fox Hunting Club," Joseph P. Sims, 150
   numbered & signed   1,500

1940

"A Straggler (Broadbill)," Roland Clark, 250 numbered &
   signed   600
"Calm Weather (Redhead)," Roland Clark, 250 numbered
   & signed   750

1941

"Off Soundings," Gordon Grant, 250 numbered & signed   150
"The Weather Mark," Gordon Grant, 250 numbered &
   signed   150
"Taking Off (Blue Wing Teal)," Roland Clark, 250 num-
   bered & signed   750
"Canada Geese," Edgar Burke, 250 numbered & signed   225
Foxhunting in America: "Working It Out," F. B. Voss, 250
   numbered & signed   750
"Music Ahead," Paul Brown, 250 numbered & signed   250
"Kennel Bound," Paul Brown, 250 numbered & signed   250
"Dropping In (Canada Geese)," Roland Clark, 250 num-
   bered & signed   550

1942

"Mallards Rising," Roland Clark, 250 numbered & signed   1,200

PRICES OF RELATED PUBLICATIONS

A Portfolio of Circulars Describing Sporting Books & Prints
   (published by Derrydale) $500
A Decade of American Sporting Books and Prints—Paper
 Wrappers (catalog)   25
Derrydale Sporting Books #6 1931–32 (catalog)   100
Derrydale Press & Winward House Sporting Books #7 1935
   (catalog)   100
Derrydale Sporting Prints #7 1931–32 (catalog)   120
Mrs. Randolph Catlin. *The Derrydale Press.* 1957.   20
W. C. Thompson. *Publications of The Derrydale Press*
   1927–1941. 1953.   20

17

ANGLING BOOKS

by Arnold Gingrich and Ernest S. Hickok

If one considers the number of books that have been written by fishermen, the inevitable conclusion is that here is a breed of man that is always questing, always optimistic, extremely inventive, and completely uninhibited concerning his own opinions. This combination of traits has resulted in some outstanding angling works, as well as a steady market for them.

Advice about book collecting in general is given in the chapter on hunting books, and there is no point in repeating it here. The purpose of this chapter is to draw attention to a representative list that, for one reason or another, has attracted the interest of anglers and to indicate a price range where a collector can have a reasonable expectation of acquiring them to satisfy his thirst for knowledge and/or his pride of acquisition. Within the price range, the buyer will have to decide for himself the relative importance of condition, rarity, subject matter, provenance, and the intensity of his personal desire to own.

Obviously, no such list can have any pretensions to completeness, as there are more than five thousand angling books in English alone, and since English angling literature had a head-start of some three hundred years over American, the majority of the titles of interest to collectors have always been those of English origin. In this century, however, the balance has begun to be redressed, and in this selected list, intended to reflect the most active interest of present-day collectors, American books outnumber the English by around four to one—reversing the actual numerical ratio of the two literatures.

The price groupings are broad, and in general the older the book the nearer it will approach the top end of the indicated price range. The exceptions to this usually reflect the scarcity value imparted to a volume by an extremely limited edition.

Bargains are increasingly difficult to come by, as the last

decade's explosion of interest in fly-fishing has driven prices up enormously, and the listings in rare bookdealers' catalogs average three times higher now than they did in the early to middle sixties. But diligent search through the secondhand book bins, particularly away from metropolitan centers, may still turn up a collector's item at a junkyard pricetag. Still the reward, per man-hour of time invested in such quests, is apt to work out to somewhat less than coolie wages.

Walton is a special case, since there are well over three hundred editions of that unique all-time angling classic. Your chances of stumbling upon one of the first five, from the seventeenth century, are less than nil of course, but copies of the last century's editions are likely to turn up almost anywhere, as the *Compleat Angler* has always enjoyed much wider literary currency than any other fishing book.

The beginning collector, like the beginning fisherman, is usually interested only in quantity, as he indulges his desire to read about his favorite sport. Then, as with anglers, an inclination to specialize soon manifests itself, and what was begun as a mere grabbag of wanted reading matter begins to refine itself into a collection, as the fisher-reader begins to become aware of differences in editions and questions of condition. He soon feels the need for some books about fishing books such as Hills, Robb, Wetzel, or Goodspeed (or if he has become hooked on Walton, such as Oliver, Horne, Marston, or Wood), and he finds that these books about rare books are rare books themselves. He learns, if he acquires some of them, that first editions are not always the most desired editions (it's the *third* 1851 edition of Pulman, for instance, that contains the first mention of the dry fly as such) and that a badly battered or incomplete copy of even a prized angling book is valueless as a collector's item. By this time he has either given up collecting and gone back to fishing or if he hasn't, he has acquired sufficient expertise that he has started to specialize—collecting Derrydale Press items, for instance, where the minimum per title is from $40 to $50 and on up to $1,000—and has no further need of such general guidance as could be offered here.

By the same token, we have limited the scope of our listing to items under $300. Above that there are "rarities of a rarity," to echo Walton's "recreation of a recreation," such as the original 1888 Douglas edition of Dean Sage, which today commands some seven or eight times our top figure (and the only reprint itself costs $500), and on up, even from there, to the rarefied fiscal stratosphere where the original editions of Walton fetch, or at least demand, a king's ransom. In a book of general circulation, it seems pointless to probe such arcane areas of a hobby that, unless pursued to a degree of mania, should be and remain an innocent pastime.

Of course, unless the prices of all fishing books soon stop mounting as they have in recent years, angling may become an endangered sport, too expensive even to read about.

And the following list, if inflation continues its inexorable and unabated spiral, may become almost quaintly antiquated before it even achieves print. ➤

$5–$25

Beebe, Wm. *The Arcturus Adventure*. New York, 1926.

Bergman, Ray. *Just Fishing*, 1932

Berners, Dame Juliana. Modern Translation. 1933.

Blake, W. H. *Brown Waters*. Toronto, 1915.

Brooks, Joe. *The Complete Book of Fly Fishing*, 1958; *Trout Fishing*, 1972.

Carroll, Dixie (Cook, C. B.). *Fishing Tackle & Kits*. 1919.

Cleveland, Grover. *Fishing & Shooting Sketches*. 1906.

Cross, Rube. *The Complete Fly-Tyer*.

Crowe, John. *The Book of Trout Lore*. 1947.

Farrington, S. Kip, Jr. *A Book of Fishes*. 1946; *Atlantic Game Fishing*, 1937; *Pacific Game Fishing*, 1942.

Farson, Negley. *Going Fishing*. 1943.

Flick, Art, ed. *Art Flick's Master Fly-Tying Guide*. Current.

Foote, John T. *Anglers All*, 1947; *Broadway Angler*, 1937.

Gabrielson and Lamonte. *The Fisherman's Encyclopedia*. 1950.

Grey, Sir Edward. *The Fallodon Papers*. 1926.

Grey, Sir Edward. *Fly Fishing*. 1899.

Grey, Zane. *Tales of Fishes*. 1919.

Haig-Brown, R. L. *Pool & Rapid*. 1932.

Hallock, Chas. *The Fishing Tourist*. 1873.

Hampton, John F. *Modern Angling Bibliography*. 1947.

Henshall, J. A. *Bass, Pike, Perch & Other Game Fish of America*. 1903.

Holder, C. F. *Big Game Fishes of the U.S.* 1903.

Humphrey, Wm. *The Spawning Run*. 1970 (current).

Knight, John Alden. *Black Bass*.

Kreider, Claude M. *Steelhead*. 1948.

La Branche, George M. L. *The Dry Fly and Fast Water and the Salmon and the Dry Fly*. 1951.

Lampman, Ben Hur. *A Leaf from French Eddy*. 1965.

Leisenring, James. *The Art of Tying the Wet Fly*. 1943. (First edition very rare; worth more.)

Lucas, Jason. *Lucas on Bass Fishing*. 1947.

Marston, R. B. *Walton & The Earlier Fishing Writers*. 1894.

McDonald, John. *The Complete Fly Fisherman*. 1970. (First edition of 1947 worth more.)

National Geographic Society. *The Book of Fishes*.

Ritz, Charles. *A Fly Fisher's Life*. 1960.

Schwiebert, Ernest. *Matching the Hatch*. 1955. (First edition worth more.)

Shaw, Helen. *Fly Tying*. 1963.

Sosin, Mark, and Clark, John. *Through the Fish's Eye*. 1973 (current).

Swisher, D. and Richards, C. *Selective Trout*. 1971 (current).

Taverner, Eric. *Trout Fishing from All Angles*. 1929.

Traver, Robert. *Trout Madness*. 1960.

Van Dyke, Henry. *Fisherman's Luck*. 1899.

Wells, Henry P. *Fly-Rods & Fly Tackle*. 1885.

Westwood & Satchell. *Bibliotheca Piscatoria*. 1966.

$25–$100

Allerton, R. G. *Brook Trout Fishing*. New York, 1869.

Bates, Jos. D., Jr. *Streamer Fly Fishing*, 1950; *Trout Waters & How to Fish Them*, 1949.

Beecher, Henry Ward. *Star Papers*. New York, 1855.

Bergman, Ray. *Fresh Water Bass*, 1942; *Trout*, 1939.

Best, Thomas. *A Concise Treaty on the Art of Angling*. 1787.

Blakey, Robert. *Angling Literature*. London, 1856.

Bowlker, Richard and Charles. *The Art of Angling*.

Bradford, Chas. B. *The Brook Trout and the Determined Angler*. New York, 1900.

Brooks, Joe. *Salt Water Fly Fishing*. 1950.

Chambers, E. T. D. *The Ouananiche and Its Canadian Environment*. 1896.

Cross, Rueben R. (Rube). *Tying American Trout Lures*. 1936.

Curtis, Brian. *The Life Story of the Fish*. 1949.

Davy, Sir Humphry. *Salmonia or Days of Fly Fishing*. 1832. (First edition of 1828 worth more)

Dawson, George. *The Pleasures of Angling*. 1876.

Dunne, J. W. *Sunshine & The Dry Fly*. 1924.

Everett, Fred. *Fun with Trout*. 1952.

Farrar, C. A. J. *Farrar's Illustrated Guide Book to the Androscoggin Lakes*.

Farrington, S. K., Jr. *Atlantic Game Fishing*, 1939; *Pacific Game Fishing*. 1942.

Flick, Art. *Streamside Guide*. 1947.

Forester, Frank. *Frank Forester's Fish & Fishing of the United States & British Provinces*. 1849.

Fox, Charles K. *Rising Trout*, ltd. ed., signed, 1967; *The Wonderful World of Trout*, ltd. ed., signed, 1963.

Francis, Francis. *A Book of Angling*. 1867.

Gill, Emlyn M. *Practical Dry Fly Fishing*. 1912.

Goodspeed, Chas. E. *Angling in America*, ltd. ed., 795 signed copies. 1939.

Gordon, Sid. *How to Fish from Top to Bottom*. 1955.

Grimble, A. *The Salmon Rivers of Scotland*. 1902.

Griswold, F. G. *Observations on a Salmon River*. 1921.

Grove, Alvin R., Jr. *The Lure & Lore of Trout Fishing*. 1951.

Halford, F. M. *Dry-fly Fishing in Theory & Practice*, 1 of 100, 1973 reprint; *Modern Development of the Dry Fly*, 1910.

Hammond, S. H. *Hills, Lakes & Forest Streams*. 1854.

Harding, E. W. *The Flyfisher & The Trouts Point of View*. 1931.

Henshall, J. A. *Book of the Black Bass*. 1881.

Hewitt, E. R. *A Trout & Salmon Fisherman for Seventy-Five Years*. 1948.

Hewitt, E. R. *Secrets of the Salmon*. One of 780. 1922.

Hills, John W. *A History of Fly-Fishing for Trout*. 1921.

Hoover, Herbert C. *A Remedy for Disappearing Game Fishes*. Ltd. edn., 990 copies. 1930.

Horne, Bernard S. *Compleat Angler—1653–1967—A New Bibliography*. 1970.

Hunt, Richard C. *Salmon in Low Water*. ed. of 500. Anglers Club.

Jordan, D. S., and Evermann, B. W. *American Food and Game Fishes*. New York, 1902.

Koller, Larry R. *Taking Larger Trout*. 1950.

La Branche, George M. L. *The Dry Fly & Fast Water*. 1914.

Lamb, Dana S. *Bright Salmon & Brown Trout*. Ltd. edn., 350 copies. 1964.

Marinaro, Vincent C. *A Modern Dry Fly Code*. 1950.

McClane, A. J. *McClane's New Standard Fishing Encyclopedia*, current. Revised (earlier editions worth less).

McDonald, John. *The Complete Fly Fisherman*. 1947.

Mottram, J. C. *Fly Fishing—Some New Arts & Mysteries*. 1915.

Needham, Paul R. *Trout Streams*. 1938.

Norris, Thad. *The American Angler's Book*. 1864.

Oliver, Peter. *A New Chronicle of the Compleat Angler—1653–1936*. 1936.

Orvis, C. F., and Cheney, A. N. *Fishing with the Fly*. 1883.

Prime, W. C. *I Go A-Fishing*. 1873.

Prouty, Leonard. *Fish—Their Habits & Haunts*. 1883.

Radcliffe, Wm. *Fishing from the Earliest Times*. 2nd edn., 1926.

Rhead, Louis. *American Trout Stream Insects*, 1916; *The Speckled Trout*, 1902.

Robb, James. *Notable Angling Literature*. 1947.

Roosevelt, Robt. B. *Game Fish of the Northern States of America & British Provinces*. 1862.

Roosevelt, Robt. B. *Superior Fishing*. 1865.

Salmorr, Richard. *Fly Fishing for Trout*. 1952.

Schaldach, Wm. *The Wind on Your Cheek*, edn. of 200, 1972; *Currents & Eddies*, 1944.

Scott, Genio. *Fishing in American Waters*. 1869.

Shepard, Odell. *Thy Rod & Thy Creel*. 1930.

Sheringham & Moore. *The Book of the Fly Rod*. London, 1931.

Smedley, Harold H. *Fly Patterns and Their Origins*. 1943.

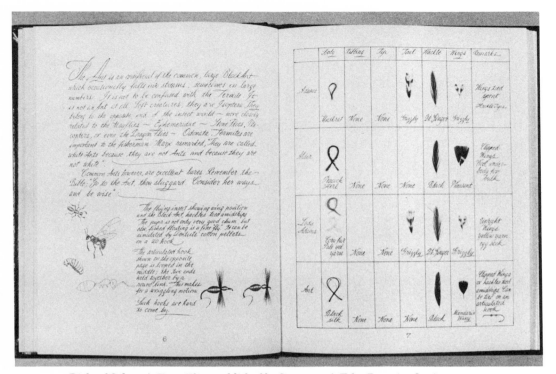

Richard Salmon's *Trout Flies*, published by Sportsman's Edge Press, is a fine investment for either the advanced or the beginning collector. It was published in an autographed and numbered edition of 589 copies at $95; each copy contained, tipped in, the actual materials for almost 50 flies. Photo: Matt Vinciguerra.

Smith, Jerome V. C. *Natural History of the Fishes of Massachusetts.* 1833.

Southard, Chas. Z. *The Evolution of Trout & Trout Fishing in America.* 1928.

Sparrow, W. S. *Angling in British Art.*

Taverner, Eric. *Salmon Fishing.* 1931.

Turrell, W. J. *Ancient Angling Authors.* 1910.

Walton, Izaak. *The Compleat Angler.* (See text.)

Wertheim, Maurice. *Salmon on the Dry Fly.* Edn. of 500, 1948.

Wetzel, Charles M. *Trout Flies.* 1955.

Wilson, Eugene. A *Pilgrimage of Anglers.* Edn. of 500, 1968.

$100–$300

Aldam, W. H. A *Quaint Treatise on "Flees and the Art of Artyfichall Flee Making."* London, 1876.

American Angler's Guide. (John T. Brown.) New York, 1845.

Atherton, John. *The Fly and the Fish.* 1951.

Bergman, Ray. *With Fly, Plug & Bait.* Edn. of 249, signed, 1947.

Burke, Edgar. *American Dry Flies and How to Tie Them*. Edn. of 500, Anglers Club, 1931.

Chetham, James. *The Anglers Vade Mecum*. 1700.

Comeau, N. A. *Life & Sport on the North Shore of the Lower St. Lawrence & Gulf*. 1909.

Connett, Eugene. *American Big Game Fishing*, 1935; *Fishing a Trout Stream*, 1934; *Random Casts*, 1939.

Coxe, Nicholas. *The Gentleman's Recreation*.

Crawhall, Joseph. *The Complete Angling Book*. Edn. of 100.

Grey, Sir Edward. *Fly Fishing*. Edn. of 150, vellum, 1930.

Hackle, Sparse Grey (A. Miller). *Fishless Days*. Edn. of 591, Anglers Club.

Ingraham, Henry A. *American Trout Streams*. Edn. of 350, Anglers Club, 1926.

Jennings, Preston J. *A Book of Trout Flies*. Derrydale, 1935.

Johnson, F. M. *Forest, Lake & River*. 2 vols. Edn. of 350, 1902.

McClane, A. J. *The Practical Fly Fisherman*. 1953.

Marbury, Mary Orvis. *Favorite Flies and Their Histories*. 1892.

Phair, Charles. *Atlantic Salmon Fishing*. Derrydale, 1937.

Schaldach, Wm. *Fish*. Edn. of 1,560.

Schwiebert, Ernest G., Jr. *Salmon of the World*. Edn. of 750, 1970.

Scrope, Wm. *Days & Nights of Salmon Fishing in the Tweed*. 1843.

Wetzel, Chas. M. *American Fishing Books*. Edn. of 300.

Wood, Arnold. *A Bibliography of "The Complete Angler."* Edn. of 102, 1900.

Wulff, Lee. *The Atlantic Salmon*. Edn. of 200, 1958.

18

❦

HUNTING BOOKS

by Angus Cameron

Many of the items discussed in this book are of relatively recent interest to collectors. The sportsman who elects to assemble a collection of, say, all the nineteenth-century wooden fishing lures he can find is something of a collecting pioneer, and only time will tell whether he is merely enjoying a pleasant hobby or enriching his heirs.

Book collecting, however, is one of the most venerable of civilized activities. Like coin and stamp collecting, it attracts tens of thousands of investors and hobbyists, it supports hundreds of dealers, and it has developed its own rules and media. Anyone who wants to take up book collecting seriously—hunting books or any other kind of book—would be well advised to learn the rules of the game. Although later in this chapter I will try to explain a few of the rules and will list some current values of individual titles, be warned that the true rare-book market is not for the incautious or the ingenuous, and this brief chapter can do no more than sketch in the bare outlines.

However, book collecting does not have to be approached as a way of making money, like playing the stock market. I, frankly, collect books on hunting and shooting primarily because I am a hunter and shooter and I want to read the books, and most likely reread them. And good books, whether they be "how-to" books like Jack O'Connor's *The Shotgun Book* or hunting-adventure books like Hornaday's *Campfires in the Rockies*, do increase in value. Few of the books in the field of hunting are enormously valuable (of course, a first edition of the Emperor Frederick's book on falconry would be in the big leagues), but many have prices now in the hundreds—books that could have been bought by the carton for a few dollars at country auctions of bygone decades.

Sometimes such great appreciations in value are the result simply of rarity. Sometimes there are unique or freakish considerations—an upside-down title page, an inscription of significance on the flyleaf, marginal annotations by someone famous. But it is my contention that, especially for the beginning collector, the best values are the best books. If you collect the good books, in many instances time will turn them into collector's items, and you can relax in the knowledge that the books you have enjoyed reading are never going to be worth less than when you bought them, and they may be worth a good deal more.

WHAT TO COLLECT

The essence of a good book collection, as distinguished from a mere accumulation, is not a sprinkling of titles that are expensive individually, but an overall organization or focus of some kind that gives the collection shape. In a well-rounded collection, each item's value is enhanced by its companions.

My collection, though a modest one, does include all the books written by the inimitable Frederick Selous. Selous, who was killed in his sixties in the World War I skirmishes in his beloved Africa, was one of the most notable European hunters in those fabulous decades when a man could live the hunting life as his forebears lived during the last Ice Age, in a world of game unmatched in variety and numbers. He was a fine naturalist and a fine writer. I enjoyed reading him, bought his books whenever I could find them, and ended up with all of them—the most obvious, and certainly one of the most satisfying, ways of collecting: by author. If you enjoy reading Jack O'Connor, you might try to find all his books—from his earliest, which were novels, to his most recent, on sheep hunting. Some are in print and some are not, but there is no doubt that an O'Connor collection, not too difficult to assemble now, will increase in value. Another hunting writer well worth collecting is Elmer Keith, the doughty old mountain man and ballistics expert whose autobiography recently appeared.

Many authors are not thought of primarily as hunters or hunting writers, yet a collection of their books would grace any hunting collection. For example, books on exploration, particularly Artic exploration, are often filled with hunting lore. Jackson's *A Thousand Days in the Artic* included all sorts of polar-bear lore and even ballistics information. Nansen's *In the Artic* and *Farthest North* also include much hunting material. Teddy Roosevelt is an overwhelming example (and his fine books are surprisingly inexpensive, because they were printed in very large quantities to start with). Fiction writers who deal with hunting are another category. The star is certainly Hemingway, but there are many others you can discover for yourself and whose works you can track down. Books written by or about pioneers of one type or another are bound to be of interest to the hunter—for example, Alaskan hunter-bushpilot-guide Harmon Helmericks has never written a book specifically on hunting, but all his books are rich sources of hunting lore.

Another obvious and satisfying tack to take is to collect by topic. Whatever your favorite hunting quarry—big game, upland birds, waterfowl, small game—you can build a collection around it. If deer are your main interest, you may start with a few current and recent books, probably mostly "how-to" books. Then you may try an older book you hear of, such as Larry Koller's *Shots at Whitetails*, or a still older classic such as Theodore S. Van Dyke's *The Still-Hunter*, first published in 1886. And then you may discover that there is scarcely an account of deer hunting in English more thrilling than Charles St. John's *The Muckle Hart of Ben More*, about a seven-day hunt for a huge stag in the wild reaches of Scotland's Highlands. And this kind of bookish exploration may widen your horizons further; after all, St. John wrote other books too, and before you know it you may find yourself with a library not just of deer books but of eighteenth- and nineteenth-century books on all kinds of hunting in Scotland. Starting with an interest in a topic, you will have acquired an interest in an author who wrote on it, an interest in a special and colorful hunting locale, and an interest in a historical period; the books you have acquired chart the course of your literary voyage, and so they form a true collection with a coherence and significance unique to you as a sportsman-collector.

Another approach, and quite a popular one, is to collect books illustrated by certain artists. I buy every book I can find that was illustrated by Carl Rungius. There are many contemporary sporting and wildlife artists—Bob Kuhn is a favorite of mine—whose illustrations will certainly enhance the future value of the books they illustrate regardless of their authors, and of course in many cases the authors are collectible in themselves.

Some specialists collect not just books but sporting catalogs. Really old ones are valuable; if you run across the first Winchester catalog to list the Model 94, you've got something. Don't throw your catalogs away as the years pass; today's catalog is tomorrow's collectible item, and even if you aren't interested in collecting them yourself, if you give them storage space you'll eventually end up with a series that can be traded or sold to other collectors.

There are numerous other ways to focus a collection, of course. Perhaps what I would emphasize most, at least for collectors like myself who are motivated more by the pleasures of reading than by the excitement of speculation in rare books, is to follow your interests wherever they take you and thus allow the focus to be your own personality.

BUYING NEW BOOKS

It is easy enough to keep abreast of current publishing. Although not too many hunting books are reviewed in the general media, many newspapers, large and small, publish outdoorsman's columns and articles that frequently contain reviews. As a hunter, you probably subscribe to specialized hunting publications that review books regularly. If you are a member of one of the outdoor book clubs, you'll be offered not only the current selection each month, but also a number of alternates.

I should say a word about the current state of hunting-book publishing. Few hunting books are printed in large numbers. First printings are apt to be around 5,000 or even less, and generally there is no subsequent printing; American hunters have never been avid book buyers. The major selections of the outdoor book clubs are an exception: they can be printed in quantities of 10,000 up to 100,000. But by and large, hunting books are printed in small quantities, and pass out of print within a few years because their long-term sale, though it may be steady, is too small to encourage publishers to reprint.

This situation is a perennial grief to me, because I am a book editor and would dearly love to publish many more hunting books than my company could sell, and if I could I would keep the best ones in print forever. But it works to the collector's advantage in several ways.

In the first place, it means that a book you buy simply for its merit when you hear about it or see it advertised as a new book will fairly soon become a truly collectible item—an out-of-print book available only through the rare- and used-book markets that may increase in value.

In the second place, it means that publishers frequently remainder relatively new hunting books. That is, they sell their entire stock to remainder houses at a very low price, at or even below the cost of manufacture. The remainder houses, such as Marboro Books, pass these low prices on to their customers; you can get last year's $20 book for a few dollars. Thus if you take the trouble to get on a few remainder-house mailing lists and study their periodic listings closely, you can build a library of brand-new and barely out-of-print books at a quarter of the cost. In fact, this is really the only way to acquire modern hunting books at modest cost, because very few such books ever appear in paperback editions.

Limited editions of new books are in a special category. As with numbered prints and etchings, a limited edition of a book is intended to be an instant collector's item. Once the publisher's stock is sold out at his list price, no more can be printed regardless of demand, and the price on the rare-book market is free to rise. Sometimes limited editions are published simultaneously with an ordinary trade edition, and the only difference is a somewhat more expensive binding, a slipcase, and usually the author's signature. The sportsman who buys books only to read will see little point in paying several times more for the limited edition. However, there are some—serious collectors, those with a special feeling for the author, simply those with a craving for fine bindings and other details—who appreciate them; a market for them does exist, and they can be a sound investment.

BUYING OUT-OF-PRINT BOOKS

Why do books go out of print? Because there is insufficient demand for them.

Why do some out-of-print books increase in value, sometimes to hundreds of times their original cost? Because there is great demand for them.

That may seem contradictory. Many an author whose book has gone out of print has upbraided his publisher when he discovered that the book is fetching $25 on the rare-book market. But there is no contradiction, just cause and effect. There are a few dozen people in the world who want the book badly enough to pay $25. Most of those few dozen would be delighted if the publisher reprinted the book and made it available again at its original price—say, $10. A couple of them would still want the original printing anyway; they specialize in first printings. Meanwhile, the publisher has had to print a minimum of several hundred—actually, usually 1,000 copies is the least it is possible to reprint at a reasonable manufacturing cost—and must try to sell them. If he doesn't think he has a good chance, he is certainly not going to reprint the book, and it almost certainly is going to cost the few who really want it more and more in the rare-book market. Thus the *absence* of sufficient demand in the new-book market *creates* a demand in the used-book market.

The price of an out-of-print book fluctuates according to supply and demand. The supply of a just-remaindered book far exceeds the demand, and the price is very low. A long-out-of-print book may be unknown to sportsmen and collectors (deservedly or not) and hence not in demand, and again the price is very low—regardless of the supply, in this case. Or a long-out-of-print book such as Roosevelt's *African Game Trails* may be in considerable demand, but also widely available because of large past printings, and hence only moderately priced.

Rare-book prices are also affected by the edition number, the condition of the binding, and other details, and thus two copies of the same book can vary considerably in price.

Since this is a supply-demand, buyer-seller situation, obviously the only way to know what the "fair" price of a book should be is to keep in touch with the action. The easiest way to do this is to get on the dealers' mailing lists and to subscribe to the rare-book periodicals (some of these are listed at the end of the chapter). If you are buying or selling, you can advertise in these periodicals yourself—though you cannot expect many big bargains this way; most of the collectors you'll be dealing with are apt to know a good deal more than you do.

The simple way to get a book you want is to go to a dealer. Say you're looking for a copy of Charles Sheldon's *Wilderness of the Denali* to complete your collection of the works of the famous hunter-naturalist-writer. You can wait till you see it listed in the dealers' catalogs at a price you're willing to pay, or you can let a dealer or two know you're looking for it. Having the dealer act as your agent in this way will drive the price up a little, perhaps, but that is fair enough, and it may be well worth it to you to complete your collection.

One of the great pleasures of any kind of collecting, of course, is satisfying the larcenous urge most of us try to repress in other areas of life. "I got it for a song"—the collector's cry of triumph, even though he may be a millionaire able to afford the going price many times over. Go ahead—look for bargains, not just on the tables of secondhand-book stores but in dark corners in the sheds and barns of antique dealers while your wife looks for pressed glass or footed salt cellars. The prices are usually so low that you can buy anything that appeals to you; even if it turns out to be worth nothing on the rare-book market, you'll have a few hours of reading and another item for your library. ✒

REPRESENTATIVE BOOK PRICES

There are thousands of titles that could be of interest to a collector of sporting books. The brief listing here is given merely as an introductory glimpse of the market.

$5–$25

Babcock, Havilah. *My Health Is Better in November*. 1970.
Buckingham, Nash. *De Shootinest Gent'man*. 1941.
Clark, Roland. *Pot Luck*. 1945.
Elman, Robert. *The Atlantic Flyway*. 1972.
Fitz, G. *North American Head Hunting*. 1957.

Franck, Harry A. *The Lure of Alaska*. 1939.
Free, James L. *Training Your Retriever*. 1949.
Freeman, Edw. A. *How to Hunt Deer*. 1956.
Hagie, C. E. *How to Hunt North American Big Game*. 1946.
Haig-Brown, R. L. *Panther*. 1946.
Harbour, Lt. Col. Dave. *Modern ABC's of Bird Hunting*. 1966.
Hightower, John. *Pheasant Hunting*. 1946.
Hornaday, Wm. T. *Campfires in the Canadian Rockies*. 1906.
Hornaday, Wm. T. *Campfires on Desert & Lava*. Various dates.
Johnson, Peter H. *Parker—America's Finest Shotgun*. 1961.
Koller, Larry R. *Shots at Whitetails*. 1948.
Lytle, Horace. *Gun Dogs Afield*. 1942.
Murray, Wm. H. H. *Adventures in the Wilderness*. 1869.
National Geographic Society. *The Wild Animals of North America*. 1963.
O'Connor, Jack. *The Complete Book of Rifles & Shotguns*. 1961.
O'Connor, Jack. *The Rifle Book*. 1949.
O'Connor, Jack. *The Shotgun Book*. 1965.
Ormond, Clyde. *Complete Book of Hunting*. 1962.
Peper, E., and Rikhoff, J., eds. *Hunting Moments of Truth*. 1973.
Phillips and Hill. *Classics of the American Shooting Field*. 1930.
Phillips and Lincoln. *American Waterfowl*. 1935.
Robinson, Jimmy. *Forty Years of Hunting*. 1947.
Roosevelt, Theodore. *Good Hunting*. 1907.
Roosevelt, Theodore. *The Wilderness Hunter*. 1902.
Ruark, Robert. *The Old Man and the Boy*. 1962.
St. John, C. *The Muckle Hart of Ben More*.
Salisbury, Howard M. *Duck Guns, Shooting & Decoys*. 1947.
Scharff, Robert. *Complete Duck Shooter's Handbook*. 1957.
Sell, Francis E. *The Deer Hunter's Guide*. 1964.
Seton, Ernest Thompson. *Wild Animals I Have Known*. Various dates.
Shields, G. O. *Hunting in the Great West*. 1884.
Van Dyke, Theo. S. *The Still-Hunter*. Various dates.
Ward, Roland. *Records of Big Game*. 1964.
Waterman, Chas. F. *The Hunter's World*.

$25–$100

Annabel, Russell. *Tales of a Big Game Guide*. 1938.
Babcock, Philip H. *Falling Leaves*. 1937.
Barker, Capt. F. C., and Danforth, J. S. *Hunting & Trapping*. 1882.
Boone & Crockett Club. *Hunting Trails on Three Continents*. 1933.
Burrard, Maj. Sir Gerald, and others. *Big Game Hunting in the Himalayas & Tibet*. 1925.
Camp, Raymond R. *Duck Boats: Blinds: Decoys*. 1952.
Connett, Eugene V., ed. *Duck Shooting Along the Atlantic Tidewater*. 1947.
Forester, Frank (H. W. Herbert). *American Game in Its Season*. 1853.
Forester, Frank. *Field Sports of the United States and British Provinces*. 1860.

Grinnell, Geo. B. *American Game-Bird Shooting*. 1910.
Heilner, Van Campen. *A Book on Duck Shooting*. Various dates.
Leffingwell, William B. *The Art of Wing Shooting*. 1894.
Nansen, Fridtjof, Dr. *Farthest North*. 1897.
O'Connor, Jack. *Game in the Desert*. 1939.
Roosevelt, Theodore. *African Game Trails*. 1910.
Roosevelt, Theodore. *Hunting Trips of a Ranchman*. 1885.
Schaldach, Wm. J. *Upland Gunning*. 1946.
Sheldon, Charles. *Wilderness of the Denali*. 1960.
Ward, Rowland. *The Sportsman's Handbook to Practical Collecting & Preserving Trophies*. 1891.

$100–$300

Clark, R. *Gunner's Dawn*. 1937.
Hoffman, C. F. *Wild Scenes in the Forest & Prairie*. 1839.
Phillips, John C. *George Washington—Sportsman, from His Own Journals*. 1928.
Queeny, Edgar M. *Prairie Wings*. 1946.
Sheldon, Charles. *Wilderness of the Upper Yukon*. 1911.

DEALERS IN HUNTING BOOKS

Any good book dealer—and there are many hundreds—will know something about sporting books. Those listed here make a specialty of them.

Angler's and Shooter's Bookshelf
Goshen, Conn. 06756

The Charles Daly Collection
36 Golf Lane
Ridgefield, Conn. 06877

Morris Heller
Swan Lake, N.Y. 12783

Ernest Hickok
382 Springfield Ave.
Summit, N.J. 07901

The Sporting Collector
Box 1042
Laurence Harbor, N.J. 08879

19

CATALOGS AND PERIODICALS

*by F. Phillips Williamson
and Allan J. Liu*

Austin Hogan, curator of the American Museum of Fly Fishing, once stated: "Catalogs and periodicals are where you separate the men from the boys. Anyone with the money can get the books. It takes hard work to get the catalogs and periodicals." Austin is not far from wrong, but it's still fun to find a $100 book for $1 in a garage sale.

Catalogs have been long overlooked, but they recently have started catching collectors' interest. How can one collect guns, rods, reels, decoys, shells, or waterfowl calls without eventually desiring to document them with catalogs? Designs change over the years, and a catalog is the best evidence to date an item *if* you can acquire a run of catalogs so the date can be established when the "collectible" was first introduced and when it last appeared.

While catalogs and periodicals are great reading, you get something more important: a feel and mood of the time. You sense the pride of workmanship and the feeling of quality—and sometimes the despair when the market failed to appreciate the product. Like the man who reportedly made a fantastic goose call—it is said to have really worked but it failed to sell because the call could not be heard by the human ear; only a goose could hear it.

Today, if Madison Avenue does not tell you something is good, you just know it isn't! In the old days the best ad was a satisfied customer. Testimonials were an important section of any catalog (Weatherby still carries them from the world's best hunters). If a buyer was satisfied he would tell his friend. The friend would seek out a catalog to find out what models were available and the price range.

Currently there are few real markets (or dealers) specializing in catalogs or periodicals. Occasionally a book dealer will list one or two. The only way to really find them is to work. Look. Tell

The 1939 World's Fair issue of Stoeger's catalog has sold for more than $200. Photo: Matt Vinciguerra.

your friends, the rubbish man, the bulk paper collector. Send out want lists. And above all, keep at it. Our want lists have had some items on them for thirty years (some of them have been bought and sold in that time, but either the word came too late or a dollar problem prevailed). Get there first, as most folks clean out Grandpa's house after it's sold and catalogs and periodicals are the first thing in the trash.

It is really hard to hang a dollar sign on a catalog or periodical now, but things are looking up. A 1951 Payne Rod Company catalog has sold for $50. The World's Fair edition of Stoeger's Gun Catalog has sold for $300. Recently, at auction, a group of Derrydale flyers and catalogs brought $600. Prewar Abercrombie & Fitch catalogs are a treasure. For war buffs, try some of the early Bannerman catalogs.

About 1914, the famous story "De Shootinest Gent'men" by Nash Buckingham appeared in a periodical entitled *Recreation*. A Nash Buckingham collector might just have to have a copy.

Some authors never wrote books. Theodore Gordon, considered to be the founding father of fly-fishing in America, was a prolific periodical contributor. His notes were never found, and Gordon never wrote a book. Magazines with his work are certainly collectible. As a sidelight, Gordon also wrote articles on upland gunning—rare items if you can find one.

If you are a gun buff, look for issues of *The Rifleman* when Thomas G. Samworth was editor. Samworth is one of the greatest gun book/magazine editors.

Other periodicals to look for include *Forest & Stream* (weekly), *Recreation*, *Anglers Club Bulletins*, and many more.

There is no hard and fast rule in collecting periodicals. Look! You have to find something that will interest you. Get the periodical intact—especially with front and rear covers.

It is somewhat easier to suggest what catalogs to collect. Any with a legendary name is worthwhile. Winchester, Parker, L.C. Smith, Stoeger, and Stevens had fine gun catalogs.

Fishing catalogs have gained attention with the publication of *Great American Fishing Catalogs*, by Samuel Melner and Hermann Kessler. Use this as a starter, but look for catalogs of rodmakers (instead of dealers); they will have the greatest future demand.

Keep your eye peeled for anything by Derrydale, Frank Lowe, Abercrombie & Fitch, Herter's, L. L. Bean, or David Abercrombie, prior to 1945. It may be only a paper flier, but it may be collectible to someone. When you have what is a real treasure and of great interest to you, protect your investment. Either bind it or have a slipcase made. The reason some of the publications are so scarce and sought after (like *Forest & Stream*'s little paper book *Shore Birds* that came out at 15 cents) is that they failed to survive the years. ✒

The 1951 Payne Rod Co. catalog. Photo: Matt Vinciguerra.

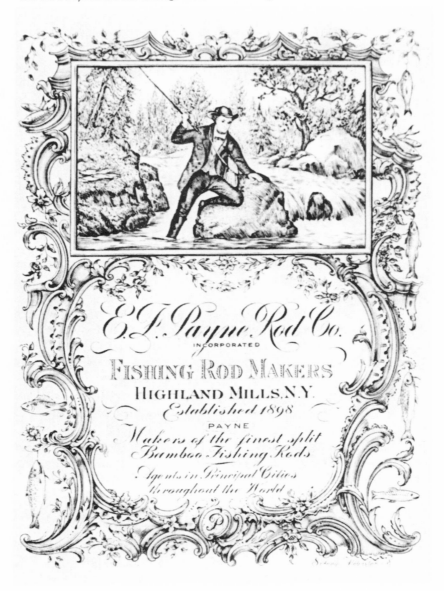

ABOUT THE
CONTRIBUTORS
by Allan J. Liu

One of the most enjoyable tasks in compiling this book was contacting and working with the various contributors. Each of them is an expert in the particular field I asked him to discuss—which means that each of them has an intense interest in some facet of collecting or in several. A true collector is never bored, and, at least to another collector, never boring; his enthusiasm is infectious and carries over to many areas of his life. The *American Sporting Collector's Handbook* crew are a fascinating bunch, and I want to say a few words about each of them. They are in alphabetical order.

Angus Cameron (Hunting Books) has been collecting books on hunting, fishing, and other outdoor subjects for a great many years, and he has also been making them: since 1935 he has been in publishing, first at Little, Brown and Company and since 1959 at Alfred A. Knopf. His own book on owls, *The Nightwatchers*, illustrated by Peter Parnell, is a classic, and, of course, he has assisted at the birth of the many of the distinguished sporting books that have come from Knopf.

Len Codella (Split-Cane Rods) is the proprietor of the Angler's Den, a tackle shop specializing in fly-fishing. In the fall of 1975 he merged with the Thomas & Thomas Rod Company, and he now operates out of Turners Falls, Mass. He is a member of the Henryville Conservation Club and is active in Trout Unlimited.

Norm Flayderman (Sporting Firearms) is one of the best-known authorities and dealers in collector's arms; his regularly issued catalogs are the most often cited in the business. He is Staff Arms Consultant to the U.S. Springfield Armory Museum, Arms Consultant to the U.S. Marine Corps Museum, Arms Consultant to the state of Connecticut for its Colt collection, and an appraiser for both the Winchester Gun Museum and the Gettysburg National Museum. He has written many articles on gun collecting and is currently compiling a book that will undoubtedly become the American gun collector's bible. Flayderman is also well known in the fields of American art and whaling history, and is the author of a classic work on the folk art of scrimshaw.

Jene C. Gilmore *(Federal Duck Stamp Prints)* has been National Art Chairman for Ducks Unlimited since 1972, and for eight years he was DU's New York Area Chairman. While he lived in New York he was with Ralph Terrell's Crossroads of Sport; in 1972 he moved to the West Coast and is now Executive Director of Petersen Galleries, the country's leading gallery for Americana, Western art, and sporting art. Gilmore's *Art for Conservation* (1971) is the first complete book on duck stamps.

Arnold Gingrich *(Angling Books)* has written several classic books on fishing—*The Joys of Trout, The Well-Tempered Angler, The Fishing in Print* (the last an excursion through five centuries of angling literature)—and is best known to general readers for his monthly page in *Esquire,* the magazine he founded over forty years ago. He has many other interests, from music to motor cars, but perhaps none so keen as fishing and books on fishing.

Ernest S. Hickok *(Angling Books)* is a leading collector and dealer in books, prints, and paintings and a well-known expert in the field of hunting and fishing artifacts. He is a member of the New Jersey State Council of the Arts and the Advisory Council of the New Jersey State Museum, and is one of the directors of the Summit Art Center.

Drew Holl *(Original Art)* left the advertising business when the opportunity arose to purchase The Crossroads of Sport, Inc. His lifelong interest in field sports and the collecting of its art now became his vocation. Besides being an active partner in Crossroads, Drew belongs to Safari Club, Ducks Unlimited, and Anglers Club of New York.

Alfred F. King III *(State Duck Stamp Prints)* sold his seat on the New York Stock Exchange in 1973 and decided to make his longtime hobby of collecting a career. He is the owner of Sportsman's Edge, Ltd., which has become one of the finest sporting and wildlife galleries in the country.

Sid Latham (*Modern Handmade Knives*) has worn a knife from the Arctic to the Amazon and from North Africa to New Guinea. He is a New York-based photographer specializing in outdoor subjects, and a few years ago he was commissioned to photograph some knives for a magazine—and was bitten by the knife bug. Characteristically, he went after the craftsmen to find out all he could, and in 1973 published *Knives & Knifemakers*, now an essential guide and reference for knife collectors.

Theodore A. Niemeyer (*Fishing Flies*) is one of the few experts who can identify almost any fly tied by past and present masters, and he is a master tier himself; his nymph patterns are considered among the finest. He is a member of the Federation of Fly Fishermen and United Fly Tyers, Inc. With William Cushner and Charles DeFeo, he has assembled a collection of flies unmatched anywhere.

Harold L. Peterson (*Antique Knives*) is Chief Curator of the National Park Service and has been in the museum field for more than thirty years. He is the author of twenty-four books and hundreds of articles on arms and antiques in general. He has served as Honorary Curator of Edged Weapons at the West Point Museum, Consultant to Colonial Williamsburg, Plymoth Plantation, and the Henry Ford Museum, and Associate Curator of the Field Artillery Museum at Fort Sill. He is also Founder and Past President of the Company of Military Historians, a member of the Executive Council of the International Association of Museums of Arms and Military History, and a member of the Board of Advisors of the National Historical Society.

Seth R. Rosenbaum (*Fishing Lures*) has a collection of more than 3,000 plugs. A computer consultant by trade, he tried not to let business interfere with fishing. His New York apartment features mounts of both a record Icelandic salmon and a 12-foot broadbill swordfish, and also a number of sergeant majors, which he captured himself in the Dry Tortugas.

Leo Scarlet (*Federal Duck Stamps and Postage Stamps*) has been in the stamp business since 1929, and is known as an authority on the stamps of the United States and Canada. He is a member of all major stamp societies. He was president of the American Stamp Dealers' Association for four years.

Ernest Schwiebert (*Split-Cane Rods*) published his first book, *Matching the Hatch*, in 1955, and since then his name has become a byword among fly-fishermen. His other books include

Remembrances of Rivers Past and *Nymphs*, and the massive *Trout*—perhaps the first book to come along worthy of borrowing Bergman's title—is scheduled for publication in 1976. Schwiebert is an architect and urban planner by profession.

Warren Shepard (*Antique Fishing Reels*) began collecting tackle in 1955 as a hobby; he is a geologist, currently active as an oil explorationist in the Rockies. He has been an outdoor writer and photographer for ten years, and his pictures and articles have appeared in all the major outdoor magazines. He is the owner of the Classic Gun and Reel Company, a Director of the American Museum of Fly Fishing, and Founding President of the Joe Brooks Chapter of Trout Unlimited.

George Ross Starr, Jr. M.D. (*Wildfowl Decoys*) began collecting decoys in 1948 and has currently accumulated more than 1,500. He is the author of *Decoys of the Atlantic Flyway*, and has written on both decoys and decoy making for magazines and books. He is active in Ducks Unlimited, the New England Woodcarver's Association, the Long Island Decoy Collectors, the Midwest Decoy Collectors, and the Wildfowlers Association of Great Britain and Ireland. Dr. Starr is in general practice in Duxbury, Mass.

Robin Starr (*Fish Decoys*) got the collecting bug from his father, Dr. Starr. He has been collecting fish decoys since 1972; his other fields of interest include duck decoys and Derrydale and other sporting books.

Charles R. Suydam (*Cartridges, Shotshells, and Accessories*) is the author of *The American Cartridge* (1960) and the soon-to-be-released *American Pistol and Revolver Cartridges 1790–1975*, as well as numerous articles in magazines. He is currently on the editorial staffs of *The Gun Report*, *The American Rifleman*, *Arms Gazette*, and *The International Cartridge Collector*.

F. Phillips Williamson *Derrydale Books and Prints, Catalogs and Periodicals*) began his sporting library in the late 1930s; it now covers the entire range of hunting throughout the world and includes books in many languages. He has a nearly complete collection of both the Derrydale books and the Derrydale prints; the list of Derrydale publications he supplied for his chapter had never been compiled before. He has hunted throughout the world—but says his best trophy is the memory of a thousand campfires. ➤

INDEX